NBC 2180   19.50-25/-14.63   Y-79

W9-AQQ-875

NBC 2180   19.50-25/-14.63

LOST TORONTO

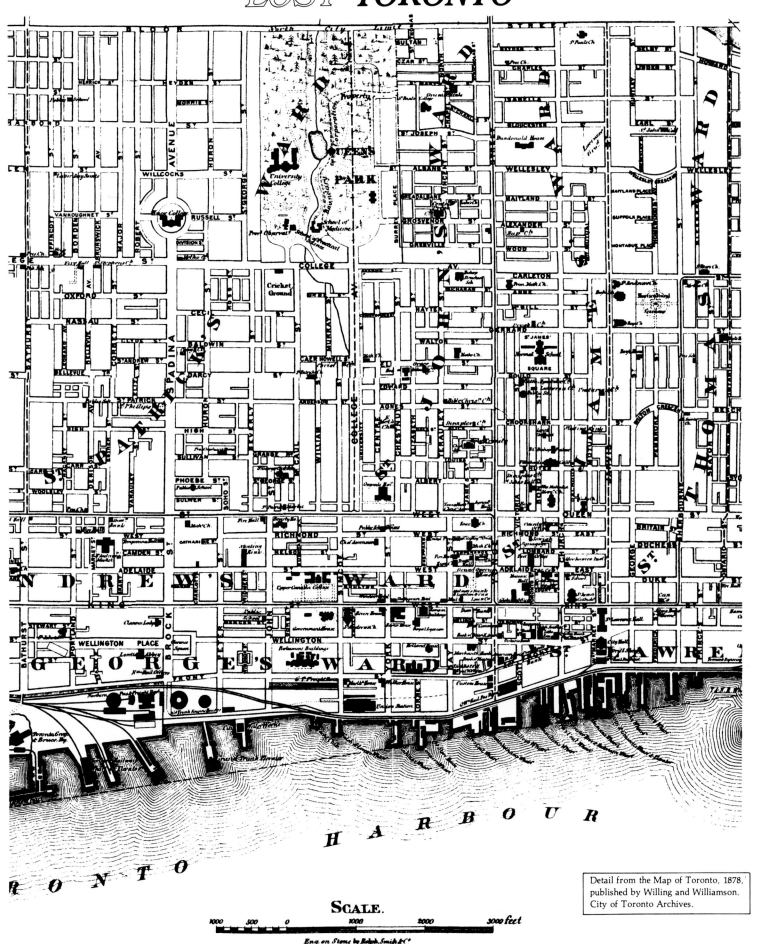

SCALE.

1000   500   0   1000   2000   3000 feet

Eng. on Stone by Ralph Smith & Co.

1 THE CUSTOMS HOUSE, *c.*1876

LOST TORONTO

William Dendy

Toronto · Oxford · New York
Oxford University Press
1978

Canadian Cataloguing in Publication Data

Dendy, William, 1942-
Lost Toronto

Includes index.
ISBN 0-19-540294-4

1. Historic buildings — Ontario — Toronto.
2. Toronto, Ont. — Buildings. I. Title.

FC3097.7.D45   971.3'541   C78-001526-6
F1059.5.T688A233

ISBN 0-19-540294-4
1 2 3 - 0 9 8
Printed in Canada by
THE BRYANT PRESS LIMITED

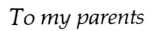

To my parents

Contents

CONTENTS

CONTENTS

CONTENTS

CONTENTS

ALL MODERN PHOTOGRAPHS WERE TAKEN BY WILLIAM DENDY

Preface

Toronto is not yet 200 years old. Compared with the great cities of Europe, and many in North America, it is a traditionless upstart. But in the period since its founding in 1793 Toronto accumulated a rich treasury of domestic, public, and commercial buildings, to satisfy the needs of its citizens, that extended far beyond the purely functional. This book presents one part of the history of Toronto as told through its architecture: the history that pertains to buildings that are no longer standing. For these buildings—most of which were demolished between 1900 and 1965 for new construction or, more commonly, for parking lots—the book constitutes a kind of family history. The houses, banks, railway stations, churches, shops, and public buildings illustrated and discussed here were built between 1807 and 1930. Covering almost the entire range of use and purpose, they were constructed of marble, stucco, wood, brick, and steel. Some were palatial, some thoroughly working-class in character. What draws them together—like the men and women who marry into, or are born into, a family—is that they are all part of the heritage of Toronto, and were once part of its image to the outside world and to visitors.

Unlike most books that have studied the demolished buildings of a single city, *Lost Toronto* is not organized according to the basic type or use of the buildings presented, but according to their location. Beginning with the Customs House and Bank of Montreal at the intersection of Front and Yonge, the entries have been arranged much as a visitor might have come across the buildings on some imagined day between 1900 and 1930. It is hoped that the reader—with reference to the map at the front of the book and to the bird's-eye view that is the last plate—will obtain a sense of what the city really looked like to the people who lived in Toronto and who visited it, and the relationship of buildings to their neighbours (and to those that still survive).

The picture of Toronto that emerges from this treatment is not complete (quite apart from the omissions imposed by limitations of space), for much of the perishable and intangible 'character' with which the buildings were endowed by those who used them is inevitably missing. Still, the architecture itself adds a dimension to our understanding of the people of Toronto. For example, such buildings as the McMaster Warehouse, Government House, the 1911-13 Bank of Toronto, Metropolitan Methodist Church, and Long Garth amply demonstrate the knowledge, self-confidence, and sophisticated taste of people, or groups of people, who in standard history books are often little more than money-making or political ciphers. And nowhere does the architecture speak more clearly of the city than in two uncompleted projects that are included here: Eaton's College Street and the Federal Avenue/Vimy Circle/Cambrai Avenue planning schemes. Both were proud statements, in consciously international terms, of the confidence and wealth of the city; both were designed to give Toronto an important and dignified image (one that would firmly remove the obnoxious label of 'Hog Town'). In their very incompleteness they tell more about the crisis of confidence and economics that overtook the city and its leaders in 1920-30 than could ever be explained in simple facts and figures.

Not every building in this book has been demolished. Six buildings are still standing but more-or-less lost under later additions, or so endangered by decay or creeping neglect that their entries might be regarded as presumptive obituary notices. (The 1830 Bank of Upper Canada on Adelaide Street East—the oldest purpose-built bank in the country—was seriously damaged by fire while this book was being written.) But all the buildings inevitably raise the question of preservation in Toronto. For an architectural historian the demolition of so many fine buildings is an irreparable loss. However, it must be admitted that a few of them—like the houses on Caer Howell and some of those on Albert Street—were not built of the most permanent materials: they disappeared, or would eventually have disappeared, from simple deterioration and decay. But most of the other buildings were more soundly built of stone and brick, often with the finest possible craftsmanship. William Cawthra's house and A.R. McMaster's warehouse were both consciously intended as lasting personal or corporate symbols. This is also true of the banks and churches illustrated here. No one envisaged, when each one was being built, the ultimate fate of the building, or charted—as often happens today with new high-rise office buildings—the date on which it would be considered obsolete and consigned to the wrecker.

Another mitigating factor is that some of these buildings were demolished in favour of other designs that are equally fine. Thus one regrets the loss of Kivas Tully's Bank of Montreal and C.S. Cobb's Registry Office but glories in the Darling & Curry bank, which replaced the first, and in Viljo Revell's City Hall, which followed the second. Not so easily accepted, however, are the demolitions of the second Union Station and the Customs House at Front and Yonge. But at least an unavoidable problem of functional obsolescence condemned the first; and the destruction of the second came at a time when few even among connoisseurs had any appreciation for the richly detailed forms of mid- and Late Victorian architecture, especially when their original splendours were concealed under decades of soot and general deterioration. (Changes in taste have led to the disappearance of more of the buildings illustrated here than functional obsolescence—the usual and almost always specious argument put forward to justify demolition—or even fire.)

In the case of most of the lost buildings in this book, however, it is impossible to accept demolition with equanimity. This is particularly true of buildings like William Kauffman's Masonic Hall or C.A. Walton's Arcade, which were replaced by buildings that—whatever their functional or profitmaking superiority—are unredeemably dull clichés of contemporary architecture. It is even more true of a large number of buildings like the Ontario Bank, the Mechanics' Institute, the Toronto Exchange, and the McMaster Warehouse, whose sites stand empty as parking lots.

Most discouraging of all are the more recent demolitions of the 1911-13 head office of the Bank of Toronto and the 1846 Provincial Lunatic Asylum—both distinguished examples of their periods. Renovation to serve new functions was possible in both cases, and there can be little doubt that a great injustice was done to the city by their demolition—all the greater in the second instance because it was sponsored by the Government of Ontario.

The preservation of most of the buildings in this book as living, cared for, respected elements in the ongoing life of Toronto would have provided a touchstone of stability for the development of the twentieth-century city. (In cities as diverse as London, Paris, and Leningrad, this is exactly how the preserved and renovated monuments of earlier periods are used and appreciated.) With the disappearance of so many historically important and potentially useful buildings from the Toronto streetscape, many of the city's links with its past and its cultural heritage were broken. The pessimist might say that, as so much of value has gone, further efforts at preservation are useless and irrelevant. This is most emphatically not the case. The state of most of the buildings in this book that still stand points up the need for continued work on preservation, as do the numerous other existing buildings that are equal in importance to those illustrated here: the Don Jail, which is just as important as Howard's Asylum; Lennox's Bond Street Congregational Church, which is very much the equal of his Broadway Tabernacle, though in a different style. The same is true of the row of shops on the west side of Yonge, south of Wellington, when compared with Victoria Row. Henry Langley's Bank of British North America at 49 Yonge Street (now the Canadian Imperial Bank of Commerce) was finished in 1875, not long after the General Post Office and Government House, and is in the same Second Empire style. There are numerous houses in the Annex, shops on Yonge Steet, and churches across the city that are as worthy of preservation as those that are illustrated here. Finally, the lack of Jarvis Street mansions in this book can in part be attributed to the perhaps surprising fact that a good number of the best still survive—albeit in a precarious state.

Lost Toronto is not meant to be a depressing tale of woe and destruction. It is rather a filling-in of the gaps in our streets and of the blanks in our understanding of the city. I hope it will encourage all public-spirited efforts in favour of preservation, and make unnecessary a subsequent volume continuing the litany of demolition and loss.

Acknowledgements

I would like to begin by expressing my warm appreciation to Professor R.M.H. Shepherd and Norma Bliss, without whose help and support I would probably never have come to Toronto in the first place.

Of the many people whose knowledge and assistance have been invaluable to me in the writing of this book, my special thanks go out to Edith Firth and John Crossthwaite and the staff of the Baldwin Room and the Fine Art Department of the Metropolitan Library; to Scott James, Anthony Ross, and Linda Price of the City of Toronto Archives; to Marion Macrae; and to Douglas Richardson, my former teacher.

My work on this book also benefited from my three-year association with the Toronto Historical Board and its staff, under Brigadier J.A. McGinnis, and from the various forms of help generously granted by Jane Noakes of the Bank of Nova Scotia; Stephen A. Otto; Sybille Pantazzi; Mildred Pulleybank and Roman Sawk of the Toronto-Dominion Bank; Margaret Van Every; Colonel F.N. Ovens; and F.H. Armstrong.

Finally I would like to thank my editor, William Toye, for his considerable help, and Jack Bell. Without their constant encouragement this book would never have been finished.

WD

LOST TORONTO

2

THE BANK OF MONTREAL
1845 by Kivas Tully

THE CUSTOMS HOUSE
1876 by R.C. Windeyer
Yonge Street at Front Street West, c.1876

Lower Yonge Street developed in the 1830s and 1840s as Toronto's main commercial street. Never as fashionable as King Street, it had a vibrant life of its own (only palely reflected today), with the Great Western Railway Station (plate 3) and the city's principal public wharf at the south end, and wholesale and retail establishments spreading out along Front and the streets running north.

The Bank of Montreal—on the right in this photograph—was designed by Kivas Tully in 1845. The bank had established itself in Toronto in 1841, in a converted town house at the northwest corner of King and Bay.* When it commissioned Tully to design a new Toronto Main Branch that would reflect its importance, the intersection of Front and Yonge was the natural location and the new bank was erected on the northwest corner. Described in a contemporary guide to the city as a 'handsome cut stone building in the Palladian style of architecture',[1] the form of the building was decisively influenced by the London clubs and mansions designed by Sir Charles Barry in the style of the Italian Renaissance. All its details—the smooth columns of the portico, which steps out to the street to frame and monumentalize the entrance; the horizontally channelled masonry of the main floor; the overhanging cornice; and the architraves supported on brackets that shadow the windows of the main floor—emphasize the dignity, prudence, and wealth of the corporation. The crest, with flanking volutes above the cornice, was a traditional element of banks, derived from the detailing of Sir John Soane's Bank of England in London.

By the 1880s Tully's Bank of Montreal seemed hopelessly old-fashioned, especially by comparison with the neighbouring Customs House and other commercial buildings in the city. In 1885 it was decided to rebuild the Toronto Main Branch in an opulent and freely classical style. Designed by Darling & Curry and completed in 1886, this is the building that dominates the intersection of Front and Yonge Streets today.

On the southwest corner of Front and Yonge, across from the Bank of Montreal, stood the Customs House, which was completed in early 1876 at a cost of $200,000 to designs by R.C. Windeyer.[2] It is seen here with William Irving's Examining Warehouse (1876) behind. (See also plate 1.) Both buildings were in the 'modern

French style', better known today as the Second Empire style. With its high roofs, prominent dormers, and an almost obsessive layering of classicizing detail (generally executed in light-coloured materials), the Second Empire style was a sophisticated European conception of grandeur that dominated public architecture in North America in the 1860s and 1870s. The frontispiece of the Customs House above the arched main entrance had the palatial scale and elegance associated with the imperial reviewing balconies of Napoleon III's Paris (seen today in Canada in the balcony of the Montreal City Hall). Like the General Post Office of 1869-73 (plate 65), it was a federal building that consciously symbolized the hoped-for prosperity of the young Dominion of Canada. Irving's Warehouse, behind the Customs House, was appropriately simpler, eliminating much of the classical detail but retaining the basic arrangement of a basement storey, with the windows of the three upper floors grouped under a wide arch.

After the First World War the federal government began planning a new Customs House. Windeyer's building was demolished in 1919; but Irving's Warehouse was not demolished until construction began in the late 1920s of the present Dominion Public Building, which fills the entire block from Yonge to Bay.

---

*Where its Toronto Head Office, 'First Canadian Place', now stands.

THE GREAT WESTERN RAILWAY STATION
Yonge Street at The Esplanade (SE)
1866 by William G. Storm

The Great Western was the second railway to be built from Toronto. It was chartered in 1834 as the London & Gore Railway Company, and reorganized in 1845 as the Great Western to serve western Ontario. The line was opened to Hamilton in 1854, from the first Union Station at Front and York Streets; but it was not until March 1866 that it had its own station.[3] The architect, William G. Storm, had been the partner of Frederic William Cumberland, who was very active in the speculative building of railways and left this project with Storm when the partnership was dissolved in 1865.

Romanesque in style, although constructed in wood, the station was divided into two units: a long train shed and a low building that filled the angle between the shed and the street intersection and housed both offices and a waiting-cum-refreshment room. As in most English stations of the period, the grouping was dominated by the train shed, which adapted to a smaller size the barrel-vaulted wooden-beamed construction and the multi-windowed lunette-shaped end that were part of such stations as King's Cross, London. The roof was covered with tinned metal: it had none of the airy lightness of English train sheds, with their greenhouse-like glazing. The great arch of the shed probably suggested the use of Romanesque-Italianate detailing in the waiting-room, where small arches over the windows echoed the main arch, and the deep overhanging roof on scroll-sawn brackets sheltered waiting passengers.

In 1882 the Great Western amalgamated with the Grand Trunk to form the line that eventually became the Canadian National. In the 1890s the railway began to use the second Union Station (which had been built in 1871-3 at York Street and The Esplanade, plate 14) when the Yonge Street station became a freight depot. It was used as such until early in this century, when it became a vegetable market associated with the wholesale warehouses on Front Street East. It was destroyed by fire on 17 May 1952[4] and the site is now a parking lot.

4

THE AMERICAN HOTEL
Front Street at Yonge (NE), c.1875
c.1844; altered 1873

The American Hotel was built on the site of the house of Chief Justice Scott, for whom Scott Street was named. (After the house was demolished, a whole ox was roasted in the abandoned foundation to celebrate the coronation of Queen Victoria.)[5] About 1840 the corner was bought by a Mr Rennie, who then erected a building that was advertised for rent in *The Globe* of 10 April 1844:

HOTEL TO LET
That large BRICK BUILDING on Front Street and Corner of Yonge Street, has been converted into a HOTEL; the situation is the very best in the City being in the vicinity of all the Wharves, and the accommodation is second to none in the city. It makes up about forty beds, with a corresponding number of good Parlours, a Dining-room Fifty feet by Twenty, a large Bar-room, Kitchen, and Servants apartments, etc., etc.

Rennie himself ran the hotel until 1849, and it prospered because of its location near the railways, markets, and wholesale houses on the waterfront. In 1873, shortly before this photograph was taken, the hotel was closed for renovations that added a complete floor, with 35 bedrooms.[6] As remodelled, it catered specially for 'Commercial Men and Country Merchants'. The building was simply detailed, with Renaissance-style flat architraves and triangular pediments over the windows, probably made of pressed metal (like similar details still surviving at 36-40 Yonge Street). There was little of the high-style detailing found above the cornice in the Queen's Hotel (plate 10), which had pretentions as an elegant hostelry: the building was ornamented only with a parapet that raised its name into visibility across the harbour. During the 1880s the American Hotel was run by William Mackie and his son James—who at the same time ran the St Lawrence Hotel in Port Hope and, after 1883, the Hotel Hanlan on Toronto Island (plate 21). Finally it was bought by the Toronto Board of Trade, and in 1889 it was demolished to make way for the first Board of Trade Building (plate 7).

This view shows, on the right, the foundation shoring for the Customs House (plate 1), which was completed in 1876; and on the left the large flowering chestnut that stood in front of Kivas Tully's 1845 building for the Bank of Montreal (plate 2).

THE A.R. McMASTER WAREHOUSE
12 Front Street West, c.1930
1871

Plate 5 shows the intersection of Front and Yonge Streets about 1930. The McMaster Warehouse is on the left. In the centre is the 1885-6 Bank of Montreal, which replaced Kivas Tully's building of 1845 (plate 2), and beyond it is the Board of Trade Building (plate 7).

William McMaster founded his wholesale dry-goods firm in 1844 on the southwest corner of King and Yonge Streets. In 1850 it was moved first to 32 Yonge Street (since demolished) and then into this building on Front

Street. McMaster was one of Toronto's merchant princes, as well as a member of the Legislative Council. He was appointed to the Senate in 1867, the same year that he founded the Bank of Commerce. In 1878 he endowed the Toronto Baptist College (later McMaster University). His nephew and successor in business, A.R. McMaster, helped found the Toronto, Grey and Bruce Railway (and built the house at 515 Jarvis Street, better known as the home of Hart Massey).

The new building on Front Street, the most palatial of Toronto's warehouses in the Second Empire style, was built for A.R. McMaster in 1871 and was possibly designed by Henry Langley. (Plate 6 is an unsigned architect's drawing that was published in 1872.) The firm was justifiably pleased with it, and proudly pointed out that it was

> constructed with all the modern improvements and of the most durable materials, the object being to erect a serviceable structure, adapted to the wants of the firm, present and prospective, and having a due regard to ornament without special reference to cost.[7]

The building was three storeys high and was faced with honey-coloured Cleveland sandstone, at this time the most popular material for Toronto's large public and commercial buildings and houses. With a ground floor over 17 feet high inside and an overall height of 80 feet (including the bulbous mansard roof), it established a new and much larger scale in Toronto's commercial architecture and towered above Front Street. (It was serviced by an Otis steam-driven elevator.) Below the mansard and the bracketed main cornice, the front and side façades were divided into three layered sections by strong horizontal cornices marking the floor levels, and were dominated by the huge windows that were necessary for safe interior lighting. The basic structure was clothed in a decoratively French classical façade, with tall Corinthian columns on the ground floor; paired columns on the second and third levels supporting deeply framed arches with scrolled keystones; and bonnetted dormers and oval windows. This extravagant use of height and detailing proclaimed the success and civic importance of the company and its owners. It could be said to amount to conspicuous display, but the first-quality materials, the careful craftsmanship, and the flamboyant yet beautiful combination of historical forms made the McMaster warehouse a generous gift to the city.

The company continued to occupy the McMaster Building until the firm was dissolved in 1896/7. On 19-20 April 1904 the building was seriously damaged in the second Great Fire of Toronto; when rebuilt, the façade was doubled in width, but the extension reproduced the original design almost without change. (In the photograph only the right half of the façade is original.) The warehouse was used for light manufacturing and office space until 1960, when it was vacated and demolished. Today the site is a parking lot. A gaping hole has been left in the streetscape where the McMaster Warehouse had been one of its principal decorative features.

7

THE BOARD OF TRADE BUILDING
2-8 Front Street East at Yonge (NE)
1888-91 by James & James

On the right in plate 5 stands the Board of Trade Building, occupying the angled site where the American Hotel (plate 4) had stood prior to its demolition in 1889. The Toronto Board of Trade was founded in 1845[8] to express the views of the city's business community on trade, railway development, tariffs, and other matters, and to try to protect the interests of the community. Its first suite of offices was in the Mechanics' Institute on Church Street (plate 78); in 1866 it moved to larger

rooms in the Toronto Exchange (plate 46). Given the ambitious prosperity of its members and of the city it represented, it was not unexpected that after the board amalgamated with the Toronto Corn Exchange in 1884 it would decide to build for itself a large, conspicuous building whose significance would be unmistakeable.

To get the best possible design the Board decided to hold an architectural competition. It was open to Canadians *and* Americans (a sore point with Toronto architects, who had become intensely nationalistic as a result of the incursions of American architects into the city). Eight American and eleven Canadian designs were submitted and the appointed assessor was Professor Ware of Columbia University; he picked two by Toronto architects and one by an American firm as the best of the group, and then left it to the Board to make the final decision.[9] When the commission was given to the firm of James & James—British architects who had moved to New York in 1887/8—a scandal erupted. It was shown in the *American Architect and Builder* (21 June 1890) that the Board had unfairly opened the letter naming the architects for each design before making their final decision and had chosen the American design over one by the Toronto firm of Darling & Curry, although the latter was considered to be of higher quality.* The discussion clearly suggested that the Board was prejudiced against the Canadian firm principally because it was Canadian, and opted instead for the greater prestige of having an American firm, implying at the same time that it would be better able to execute a complex design. Criticisms were poured on the James & James design for being too small and too expensive for the $200,000 budget; for including poorly lighted and ventilated offices, halls, and stairwells. The architects, of course, protested; but local apprehensions were in part confirmed when, during construction, three storeys of completed brickwork collapsed because a single supporting beam was unable to bear the weight. At this point the city entered into the controversy and, with the local newspapers up in arms, declared the building unsafe. The architects then fired the builder; the Board of Trade replied by firing the architects and calling in a local builder to clean up the mess. Finally, on top of all the bad publicity it had received, the building came in at $140,000 over budget.

In spite of the controversy, however, even the most nationalistic of the critics acknowledged the general excellence of the exterior design. James & James had modelled it on the Boston Chamber of Commerce Building by Shepley, Rutan & Coolidge, erected in 1890-2 but designed earlier. In fact the Board of Trade Building was almost a copy. But it was a superb solution to the irregularity of the site, with its rounded corner at the intersection of Yonge and Front that rose like a great tower in three levels to a corona-like ring of gabled arches. The building was capped with an arcaded parapet and a steeply conical roof with a cupola on top. The Darling & Curry design included a similarly emphatic rounded corner; but there is no denying that the James & James building, with its Gothic and Romanesque Revival touches and the onion-domed cupola,

*The designs had been identified by pseudonyms to ensure an impartial decison; the real names were not supposed to be revealed until after the final decision had been made.

was picturesque, especially when seen from Front Street or the harbour area. It stood like a medieval tower adorning the entrance to Yonge Street. In their original designs, James & James faced the vertical piers of the façade with rough masonry and included much decorative carving (plate 7). In execution, most of the carving was omitted and the piers were faced with smooth-cut Credit River sandstone and fine brick. The change lessened the monumental appearance of the load-bearing piers and the contrast between them and the lighter infill of large windows and sleek colonnettes.

The Board of Trade remained on Front Street, occupying a rotunda-like room in the corner of the top floor, until 1914, when it moved to new premises in the Royal Bank Building (on the northeast corner of King and Yonge Streets). In June 1921 the newly founded Toronto Transit Commission took over the building as its head office[10] and remained there until 1957-8. After this it stood vacant for a short time and then was pulled down. Its demolition was part of a misguided scheme for urban renewal that destroyed all but one building in the blocks bounded by Front Street East, Wellington Street East, and Yonge, and left nothing but an enormous parking lot and a miniscule area of grass (known officially as Berczy Park).

THE WILLIAM WARREN BALDWIN HOUSE
44 Front Street West at Bay (NE), c.1885
1835 by Dr W.W. Baldwin

William Warren Baldwin (1775-1844) came to Upper Canada with his father in 1798 and in 1802 arrived in York, where—as doctor, lawyer, architect, and politician—he became one of its leading citizens.[11] In 1818 he built Spadina House three miles from York, on a huge estate that had originally belonged to the Hon. Peter Russell, administrator of Upper Canada after Simcoe's return to England in 1796, and to William Willcocks, Baldwin's father-in-law, who had settled in York in 1793. This property—which extended from Queen Street to Eglinton Avenue—had been inherited by Baldwin's sister-in-law, Maria Willcocks, and his wife, Phoebe Willcocks Baldwin. When Miss Willcocks died in August 1834, Baldwin acquired control as executor

and trustee. His wife's estate, and other investments in land, gave him the freedom to exercise his talent as an amateur architect and planner, which had already been demonstrated in several important buildings, including the Bank of Upper Canada of 1830 (plate 52). In 1836 he laid out the 132-foot-wide Spadina Avenue, from Queen to Bloor Streets, and Spadina Crescent, as the centrepiece of a new residential district.

Spadina House burned down early in 1835. Though Baldwin would soon rebuild it, he had already begun construction of a residence on Front Street West. When completed in September or October 1835,[12] it was the most up-to-date house in Toronto. More monumental and urban in character than its neighbours—such as

Holland House (plate 12) and The Palace (plate 13), which tended to be suburban rather than city houses—it had the austere simplicity and solidity of the Greek Revival style that was popular in the United States at the time. Baldwin had experimented with simplified details in the Bank of Upper Canada, but there the result was still recognizably Georgian in character. The finest element in the design of the bank—the chaste Roman Doric portico—was repeated in the house, apparently also in stone. The rest of the design shows an American influence in the geometrical purity of the shape and the mass of the brick walls, which is emphasized by the shallow vertical panels that cut into their thickness. These panels left vertical piers between the windows, which are a simplified form of the full-scale columns and pilasters in cut stone that were beloved by the Revivalists but too expensive for Baldwin's resources. The horizontal elements of the order—the entablature that visually crowns the verticals—are also revisions of the classical model. The lowest section, the architrave, is reduced to a simple brick band that joins the piers and completes the panels. The top section, the cornice, has been thinned out to a spreading eave that casts a dark line of shadow—even when most of the façade is brightly sunlit—to complete the composition. The intermediate element, the frieze—the decorative feature of a classical order—is surprisingly composed of vase-like balusters, probably worked in stucco, interrupted by small horizontal attic windows. Instead of lighting the attic with dormer windows, Baldwin inserted small windows in the frieze below the eaves—a common trick of the Greek Revival, widely used in Ontario. The use of balusters, or a balustrade, as a frieze instead of as a decorative element on the roofline of the building is perhaps a solecism, as Eric Arthur has described it; but the re-use of a form that Baldwin knew as traditional, within the context of his well-thought-out Greek Revival scheme, is completely consistent with the way in which he rethought other classical details. In its elegant simplicity, the final design is impressive evidence of Baldwin's creative approach to the classical style; it reveals his appreciation of the expressive power of these forms, even when stripped of elaborate decorative details and executed not in stone but in locally made brick.

As in many houses in the Greek Revival style, the basic planning was traditional, or Georgian, in character.[13] There was a central hall, with the stair at the far end and two main rooms on either side—an arrangement found in Late Georgian houses in the city, such as The Grange; the kitchens and service rooms were located downstairs in a full basement, as befitted a town house. In spite of choosing the fashionable Greek Revival style for the exterior of his building, Baldwin found the old patterns of interior arrangement acceptable: he provided for the same necessities and pleasures that were found in the more traditional houses of his friends.

Baldwin's town house was a visible symbol of the family dynasty that he hoped to found, conceived in terms of the Anglo-Irish establishment from which his family had come to Canada. His house, like the Dublin town houses of Ireland's landowners, was also the urban expression of soundly based landed wealth.

When Baldwin died in 1844, only two of his five sons were living: Robert (1804-58), the Reformer, and William Augustus (1808-83). Robert had shared his father's house on Front Street—in January 1836 his young wife Augusta died there—but the frequent moves of the capital of the Canadas after 1841 took him away from the city. Upon the death of his mother in 1851, he inherited both the Front Street house and Spadina (which had been rebuilt in 1836). When he returned to Toronto, after resigning from the legislature in 1851, he retired to Spadina, though he still owned the Front Street house when he died in 1858. By then the area could no longer be considered a fashionable residential district. In the City Directory for 1868-9 the house is listed as the Military Hospital of the 29th Regiment. The following year it is the office of the Toronto, Grey and Bruce Railway and of the Toronto and Nipissing Railways.

The house stood vacant for three or four years until 1889, when it was demolished. In its place rose two wholesale warehouses, which were destroyed in the fire of 1904. They were replaced about 1920 by the present Foy Building.

SWORD'S HOTEL
Front Street West, east of York (N), c. 1857
1838

Sword's Hotel was opened in 1856 in a row of four fashionable town houses built in 1838 on a large lot between the gardens of H.J. Boulton's Holland House (plate 12) on the east and York Street on the west.[15] These were the only row houses among the mansions built by the Boultons, the Baldwins (plate 8), and Bishop Strachan (plate 13) that lined the north side of Front Street, looking out across the harbour. They were quite simple in design, following the standard English Georgian town-house plan, with a side hall and two principal rooms on each floor. In the house on the west end of the row the plan was varied by introducing thirteen windows in the side façade—which in the normal row would butt against the next house—to take advantage of the garden view. The window lintels, with splayed ends and raised central keystones, follow a pattern more common in the 1790s or early 1800s than the 1830s; the persistence of such details in Ontario architecture is characteristic of its relatively isolated

condition in these years. A comparison of the original lintels with those of the later additions made for the Queen's Hotel (plate 10) will indicate the different taste for more elaborately decorative forms in the late 1850s and 1860s.

In 1844 the houses were remodelled as the first permanent home of Knox College, which had just been founded. The College remained in this location until 1856 (when it moved to the more secluded site of Elmsley Villa, near the corner of Bay and Grosvenor, close to the re-established University of Toronto). With renovations, and the addition of the north wing seen in this lithograph, the houses were run as Sword's Hotel. Sword's specifically catered for the needs of members of the peripatetic legislature of the United Canadas. When the capital was moved to Quebec City in 1859, Mr Sword sold the business to B.J.B. Riley, who renamed it the Revere House. In 1862 it was again sold, to Captain Thomas Dick, who renamed it the Queen's Hotel.

10

THE QUEEN'S HOTEL
100 Front Street West at York (NE), c.1886

Sword's Hotel (plate 9) became the Queen's Hotel in 1862, It was operated by Captain Dick and, after May 1874, by Messrs McGaw and Winnett, who were also the proprietors of the Queen's Royal Hotel in Niagara-on-the-Lake. Extensive additions, including the east and west wings, were made by 1865.[16] The centre cupola, added later, was designed as a scenic outlook for guests. Identifying the hotel on the skyline and in the long streetscape of Front Street West, it was markedly similar to the tower of Government House on Simcoe Street (plate 29). In this view of about 1886, the four houses that had formed Sword's Hotel are still recognizable at the centre of the building, although raised one storey.

The Queen's could boast of a fine cuisine and staff, 210 'boudoirs', seventeen private parlours, total accommodation for 400 guests, and a private garden east of the hotel, 'which in summer is made doubly attractive by the silvery spray of playing fountains and the fragrance of many flowers'. (Plate 11 shows the hotel garden with its cast-iron fountain and carefully tended gravel walks. Overlooking the garden is the south front of Holland House [plate 12].) In the opinion of the management, its location was both convenient and quiet, 'situated on an isolated island in the commercial sea of Toronto'.[17] The hotel remained fashionable for over sixty years, unaffected by the building of the King Edward Hotel in 1899. It served guests as diverse as Lord Dufferin; Grand Duke Alexis of Russia; Jefferson Davis, the president of the Confederacy; and General Sherman (who burnt Atlanta in 1865). The Queen's remained in use until the new Union Station was opened in 1927, when the CPR purchased the site and demolished the hotel. In 1929 the railway built the Royal York Hotel on the site as the largest and most important of its chain of hotels.

11 LOOKING NORTH FROM THE GARDEN OF THE QUEEN'S HOTEL TO HOLLAND HOUSE, C.1880.
SEATED WITH THE GUESTS IS MRS THOMAS MCGAW (SECOND FROM THE RIGHT), WIFE OF
ONE OF THE PROPRIETORS. HER SON IS IN THE LEFT FOREGROUND.

HOLLAND HOUSE
61 Wellington Street West (S), 1904
1831

Holland House was built by the Hon. Henry John Boulton (1790-1870) as a suburban residence on a large lot, at the corner of Wellington and Bay, that extended south to Front Street and allowed the house an unobstructed view across the harbour. The north half of the site was purchased in 1820 from his father, D'Arcy Boulton Sr, two years after Henry's appointment as Solicitor-General for Upper Canada; the south half was not purchased until 1827.[14] But he delayed the start of his new house until his fortunes and political position were consolidated, first by his appointment in 1829 as Attorney-General for Upper Canada, and then by his winning the seat for Niagara in the Assembly in 1830.

He named his residence for a suburban London mansion built in 1606-7 and later owned by Charles James Fox, to whom the Boultons were related. It was

there that Henry Boulton was born, and Holland House was probably his second home while he studied law in England. (He was called to the Bar in 1815 and returned to York in 1816 to practise.) But there was no resemblance between the London mansion and Boulton's house. More surprisingly, there was no resemblance between it and The Grange, the house his older brother, D'Arcy Boulton Jr, had built in 1818. Instead, just as Henry is reported to have followed the fashions of Regency dandies in his dress, so in building Holland House he was influenced by the taste for gentlemen's villas created by English architects such as Sir John Soane, John Nash, and James Wyatt. More than in any other period of British architecture, the Regency had a passion for the exotic and the picturesque. Villas were designed in Indian, Moorish, Italianate, Greek, and medieval styles, according to the client's fancy. The Gothic style that Boulton chose was popular because it was both picturesque and immediately identifiable as English, while implying that the owner had a distinguished lineage dating far back into history.

Like most contemporary examples of the Gothic style, Holland House was not an archaeological recreation of a baronial castle. Built of brick covered with stucco, lined in imitation of stone blocks, it was designed to be seen as part of an evocative landscape. The photograph shows the south-facing garden front of the house, its centrepiece a three-storey curved tower.* With the deep shadows of the Gothic-arched loggia on the ground floor giving it an air of monumentality, it was meant to establish the importance of the gentleman owner (like the classical porticos and pediments of The Grange and The Palace [plate 13]). Most of the other details, though derived from genuine Gothic sources, were more fanciful in character, especially the circular turrets that hid the chimneys on the sides of the house and the crenellations around the parapet of the second-floor balcony at the roofline, which broke up the horizontal lines of the design and created interesting shadow patterns. The tower dominated the plan of the house, as it dominated the exterior, and the resulting curved rooms on each floor—a popular architectural device of the period—probably served as the drawing room and principal bedroom.

It is not known who designed Holland House. However, like many English gentlemen of the eighteenth and early-nineteenth centuries, and like William Warren Baldwin in Toronto (see plate 8), it is possible that Boulton was his own architect, providing a local builder with a fairly specific scheme for execution. There are many possible sources for the design in British buildings of the period that Boulton would have known directly, or through illustrations. The two most likely are

Windsor Castle, as remodelled for George IV by Sir Jeffrey Wyattville in the 1820s, and (more likely) James Wyatt's castle for the Duke of Rutland at Belvoir (begun in 1801), which has a very similar, although much larger, tower. But however much Boulton's Holland House was indebted to English examples, it was a novel and well-executed expression of the newest fashion in architecture and a landmark in itself (as Casa Loma was to be in twentieth-century Toronto). The line of picturesque Regency villas in Ontario is usually seen as beginning with John G. Howard's Italianate Colborne Lodge of 1836. But both the basic plan and the style were established with Holland House, one year before Howard's arrival in Canada.

Boulton had lived in the house for only two years when, in 1833, he lost his official position for criticizing the British government. A direct appeal to friends in England got him the office of Chief Justice of Newfoundland. He lost this post in 1838, also for political reasons, and returned to Toronto and Holland House. In later years he sat in the Assembly for Niagara and then Norfolk, while retaining a strong connection with the Establishment as solicitor for the Bank of Upper Canada. Boulton lived at Holland House until his death in 1870, sharing it for the last five years with his daughter and her husband, Clarke Gamble. After Boulton's death the Gambles moved to a new house called Pinehurst on Beverley Street, near The Grange— the last of the original families to leave their Front Street mansions. Holland House was sold to Alexander Manning, a leading contractor in the city and later its mayor. The Mannings lived in the house until 1886; but as early as 1870 part of the property had been subdivided for building along Bay and Front Streets. From 1886 to 1889 the house was occupied by the Ontario Reform Club; thereafter it stood vacant, except for a brief period in 1892-3. The fire of 1904, which destroyed so many of the buildings in the area, did not damage Holland House; but in the massive redevelopment that followed, it was demolished. The site was rebuilt with warehouses that stood until the construction of the present Royal Bank Plaza.

*Holland House was originally approached through the garden by a carriage drive from Front Street; but in 1846 it was entered from Wellington. This façade was also ornamented with Gothic details, including a porch to one side, but otherwise had little of the picturesque character of the garden front.

13

THE PALACE
Front Street West, west of York (N), c.1890
1818

The house of John Strachan (1778-1867), the first Anglican Bishop of Toronto, was built in 1818, when he was rector of York, at the centre of the block bounded by Front, York, Wellington, and Simcoe. One of the four most important houses in York[18]—with Spàdina, Russell Hill, and The Grange—it far outshone even Elmsley House, the official residence of the Lieutenant-Governor. Dr W.W. Baldwin, laird of Spadina and an amateur architect of considerable talent, described it as 'magnificent' and estimated that it had cost five to six thousands pounds because it had been built of brick.[19] In 1819 it drew the celebrated comment of Strachan's brother James: 'I hope it's a' come by honestly, John.'[20]

The design of the house is clearly based on the traditional form of small Georgian mansions of around 1750 in Britain—one that remained popular, especially in Strachan's native Scotland, well into the early eighteenth century and was brought to Canada as part of the standard repertoire of immigrant builders. The design has so much in common with that of The Grange (1817), particularly the T-shaped portico—here executed in wood, as it was originally at The Grange—that

the same craftsman or designer was very likely responsible for both houses.

When Strachan became Bishop in 1839, the popular name of the house, The Palace, was confirmed, although it was never formally connected with the diocese. Front Street, with its lake view and breezes, was a favoured location at the time, and several villas and town houses were built nearby. Strachan himself subdivided his lot in 1833 and the eastern half went to his son-in-law, Thomas Mercer Jones, who built there a villa designed by John G. Howard.

Strachan lived at The Palace until his death on 1 November 1867. The area had lost much of its fashionable tone with the coming of the railways in the 1850s and the building of factories and warehouses along the south side of Front Street. Not long after his death the house became the Palace Boarding House, and as such it survived most of the other Front Street villas until it was demolished, almost without comment, in 1896. Warehouses were built on the site, some of which were demolished in 1931, when the extension of University Avenue was pushed through to Front Street.

THE SECOND UNION STATION
South side of Station Street, west of York, c.1875
1871-3 by E.P. Hannaford

Toronto's first railway station was a frame shed built by the Northern Railway in 1853 on the south side of Front Street, opposite the Queen's Hotel (plate 10).[21] From there, on 16 May 1853, the first train to leave Toronto departed for Aurora. During the next five years several makeshift depots were built, particularly by the Grand Trunk Railway, which had entered the city in 1855-6. The flurry of development culminated in May 1858 with the opening of Toronto's first Union Station at the southwest corner of York and Station Streets. A shed-like building on a quay at the edge of the harbour, it was owned by the Grand Trunk, but was also used by the Northern and the Great Western.

The next fifteen years was a period of incredible expansion for the railways in distances covered, freight and passengers carried, and actual profits earned. In 1866 the Great Western chose to leave the Union Station and build for its own use a new station at the foot of Yonge Street (plate 3). Finally, in 1871, the Grand Trunk began to build a new and larger station a little to the west. It was formally opened on 1 July 1873.

In the early 1870s public and commercial enthusiasm for the railways knew no limits. In response to this, E.P. Hannaford, the British-trained chief engineer of the Grand Trunk system,[22] built a new Union Station for Toronto that was more ambitious in scale and design than any other station in Canada to date. In plan it was relatively simple. Because the tracks passed through the city instead of ending there (as they did in Montreal), the freight and passenger facilities were arranged in a long row on the south side of the tracks. But instead of the simple wooden shed and open platforms of the 1858 station, the new station, constructed in buff brick, was palatial in design. The three tracks were sheltered within a long gabled shed, open at each end through three tall arches and lit by a skylight along the ridge of the roof as well as by arched windows in the side walls (plate 15). Unlike many designers of the period, Hannaford integrated the shed into the total design, grouping the triple arches under a larger arch and a wide pediment-like gable surmounted by a sculpted coat of arms. But the design was dominated by the long block of ticket

15   THE SECOND UNION STATION: THE SHED, c.1880

offices, waiting and refreshment rooms, and other facilities on the south side of the tracks.

Although the façade was over 200 feet long, the great length, and the bulk of the train shed behind, were balanced by three towers with pointed mansard roofs and fanciful cupolas; the taller central tower, with its four-sided clock, marked the main entrance to the station. (Such towers were an almost inevitable feature of large stations of the period, as was the rather coarse Italianate detailing of the building.) The towers, the repeated paired arches of the windows, and the horizontal rustification of the lower storey of the façade caught the eye with strong rhythms, contrasts of horizontals and verticals, and rich effects of shadow and light that were tremendously impressive. Hannaford's design was brash, and in its self-confidence it typified much of what was best in the city's Victorian architecture.

More unusual than the design was the siting of the station so that the façade, with its towers and main entrance, faced the harbour and lake rather than the

city. This must have been inconvenient, since all traffic to and from the station had to cross mainline tracks. However, to those who approached the city by water and saw the towers reflected in the harbour (as they were when the station opened in 1873), the building was lifted out of the congestion of the city as an almost iconic symbol of the importance of the railways to Toronto.

The new Union Station must have seemed more than adequate for the future of the city, but with the completion of the Canadian Pacific system and the growth of the city as a manufacturing centre, its facilities were taxed to the limit. In 1893-4 the station was doubled in size by the addition of a three-track trainshed in glass and steel on the quay in front of the original façade. At the same time, to improve the passenger and freight facilities, a seven-storey block, designed by the Toronto firm of Strickland & Symons, was built on the south side of Front Street. (It is illustrated here in a contemporary reproduction of the architects' drawing (plate 16), which omits the earlier buildings on the south side of the street.) It was connected to the 1873 station by a long concourse that bridged Station Street, because of the fall of land between Front and the harbour. The Romanesque Revival design of the new block, with its tall corner tower, was modelled on that of the Illinois Central Station in Chicago (1892-3 by Bradford L. Gilbert), though it was neither as spectacular nor as interesting for its time as Hannaford's design. The immense semi-circular arch through which travellers entered and left the station presented for the first time the role of the station in the architectural form of a gateway to Toronto. (The same image is central to the character of the present Union Station.)

By the turn of the century the facilities were again strained beyond efficiency. However, conditions were such that only a total rebuilding would solve the problems. Not only was there no more space on the site for new tracks, but the arrangement of the tracks at grade level was causing severe problems for traffic between the city and the harbour. The opportunity to rebuild came when the fire of 1904 levelled the buildings on the south side of Front Street between Bay and York. The land was owned by the city, and the Grand Trunk—taking up a lease—agreed to build a new station by 1908. In the end, construction did not begin until 1915 and the present Union Station, the third to be built, was not opened until August 1927. In October 1927 Hannaford's Union Station was demolished. Today the site is occupied by railway tracks and a CN office building. Only the name Station Street commemorates the location.

16 THE SECOND UNION STATION SHOWING 1893-4 ADDITIONS: ARCHITECTS' DRAWING, 1892

THE BOATHOUSES AT THE FOOT OF LORNE AND YORK STREETS
c.1900

Toronto's site on the ancient alluvial plain beside Lake Ontario lacks most of the grand natural elements that grace Vancouver, Montreal, or Halifax. And systematically, as the city expanded, the many small ravines and watercourses were buried under a regular grid of streets. But from the beginning the lake, the Island (actually several islands), and the lagoon-like natural harbour between the Island and the shore, were recognized as redeeming features and were consciously developed as the focus of the city's recreation, which they remained until after the Second World War. The harbour especially attracted all types of 'messing about in boats'—sailing, rowing, sculling, canoeing—among all classes and ages in Toronto. The craze for boating was summed up by C.S. Clark in his book, *Of Toronto the Good* (1898):

> In spite of all its drawbacks . . . Toronto is a delightful place to live. Its boating is unsurpassed. The bay on a summer night is one mass of skiffs and sailboats, and there is scarcely a youth in the city who has not experienced the delights of rowing, and a large number are owners or part owners of boats . . . . All the waterfront comprises interminable lengths of boat houses both private and public and the houses owned by organizations such as the Royal Canadian Yacht Club are perfect palaces in their way. Aquatic sports comprise very largely the principal diversion of Toronto's men and boys, and there is scarcely a boy in the city whose sympathies are not enlisted in some of the great summer events.[23]

This illustration shows only a small portion of the waterfront, between Lorne and York Streets, southwest of the second Union Station (plate 14)—the westmost tower of which can be seen on the right. Each of the main boathouses was built on an extended pier that stretched out from the shore. The effect was not unlike that of a Venetian palazzo on its canal-side site, as reconceived by a late-nineteenth-century architect of country houses. The design of each building was dominated by the need for wide first- and second-floor verandas to serve as grandstands for the frequent regattas in the harbour. Rowing shells and canoes were launched from the broad landing stages in front of the Argonaut Rowing Club (the parent body of the Argonaut Football Club in the Canadian Football League) on the right and the Toronto Canoe Club in the centre; behind the Canoe Club are four ranges of small storage boathouses for members. On the left is the Harbour Clubhouse of the Royal Canadian Yacht Club (plate 18).

Although a great deal of attention was lavished on the design and building of these clubhouses—in particular so they would stand out when seen from the water—they were built of wood and stucco and were vulnerable to storms, winter ice, and fire. However, it was the rapid extension of landfill and development of the harbour area that led inexorably to their removal. For at the same time as the increasingly busy harbour became dangerous for small boats, the wharf space became expensive to maintain and too valuable not to sell. As a result, the clubs scattered—to more protected sites on the Island or along the lakeshore.

HARBOUR CLUBHOUSE OF THE ROYAL CANADIAN YACHT CLUB
The foot of Lorne Street, c.1897
Rebuilt in 1896 by Dick & Wickson

The Royal Canadian Yacht Club set the standard for grand clubhouses in Toronto, just as it dominated both racing and pleasure yachting on Lake Ontario, as the largest inland yacht club in the world. Although a proposal to form a sailing club was discussed as early as 1850, the RCYC was not founded until 20 March 1852.[24] Official support for its becoming the 'Royal' Canadian Yacht Club in 1854 may even have arisen from the colonial administration's natural desire to have some sort of sailing flotilla for the training of a strong naval reserve.

Until 1869 the RCYC used as a clubhouse a large scow from 1853 to 1858, followed by the stripped-down lake passenger steamer *Provincial* from 1858 to 1869, both moored at Rees's Wharf just west of the foot of York Street and south of Station Street (an area that has long since been covered by landfill and railway tracks). These barges were both cheap and convenient but suffered from a distressing tendency to float away in storms; a permanent building erected on the wharf in 1869 represented a definite advance. The lakeshore facilities were supplemented by a suite of rooms on King Street and, after 1877, by a brief period of social affiliation with the Toronto Club. These town facilities became especially important when the RCYC located its anchorage on Toronto Island in 1880-1 (plate 19). The Rees's Wharf building was then sold to the Grand Trunk Railway for expansion of the railway yards. But when the RCYC amalgamated with the Toronto Yacht Club (founded in 1880) in 1889, the TYC's building at the foot of Lorne Street was retained as the mainland extension of the facilities and as a terminal for the private ferry that sailed to the Island.

The Toronto Yacht Club had built its clubhouse in 1882, but after it was severely damaged by fire in 1896 it was rebuilt to designs by Dick & Wickson.[25] An active member of the RCYC, Norman Dick was a logical choice as architect. (The *Zelma*, Dick's first-class 55-foot cutter, won every race she entered in 1893, including the Prince of Wales Cup, the Lansdowne Cup, and the Queen's Cup in Hamilton.) The new building was a spirited piece of Classical architecture, very much in the manner of the Southern Plantation/Colonial Revival style that was popular in American and Canadian suburbs and resorts at the time. It was quite blatantly an example of façade architecture, designed to be mirrored, white and shining, in the lake as a proud expression of the club's importance, for there was little requirement for interior space other than a sheltered waiting room for the ferry. The entire building was really conceived as an elaborate grandstand, with extensive space for watching regattas under the pedimented main portico; on the second-floor balcony that slides behind the columns to swell forward as a reviewing balcony in the centre; and probably also on the balustraded roofs of the twin towers that balance the lightness of the portico.

For all the flair and grandeur of the design it was, unfortunately, executed in wood and stucco (like the other clubhouses) and weathered badly. The RCYC used the building as a ferry terminal until about 1906. But judging from surviving photographs, it became steadily more frayed around the edges until it was replaced by a city ferry terminal at the harbour end of the Canadian Steamship Lines building, on its wharf. In 1951 the RCYC took over the simple (though still decoratively Classical) ferry building that stands today on Queen's Quay at the foot of York Street.

19

THE ROYAL CANADIAN YACHT CLUB
Toronto Island, c.1900
1880-1

The RCYC's first clubhouse on Toronto Island was very much like the fashionable summer cottages of the period. The lakeside verandas and a tall tower provided extensive space from which to view events on the harbour. But with lounges and dining rooms and some residential accommodation looking across the spacious tennis and croquet lawns to the lagoon anchorages, it was more like the private resorts and fishing clubs that developed around northern American cities and in the Laurentians near Montreal. The lightly framed wooden architecture of the building, with open verandas and large windows, was in studied—and intentional—contrast with the solid stone and brick Toronto houses of the eighties and nineties and defined the different atmosphere of the Club and the Island. This rustic character was like that of the park pavilions of the period, and especially appropriate to the still natural, though hardly wild, feeling of the Island in the 1880s, before the extensive cottage developments appeared in the last years of the century. This clubhouse was destroyed by fire in 1904.

THE ROYAL CANADIAN YACHT CLUB
Toronto Island
1905-6 by Sproatt & Rolph

As the RCYC entered the twentieth century and grew, its character changed. It remained devoted to the tradition of sailing on Lake Ontario (as it is today). But like many similar American and British organizations, it evolved into a true country club, offering its members a social centre equipped for many different activities. This was especially important in the years before Toronto society accepted hotels and small restaurants as the locus for dignified entertainment. The 1881 clubhouse, which had been destroyed by fire in 1904, was replaced in 1906 by a new building that clearly expressed the developed character of the club.[26] Gone was the rustic background of the old clubhouse. It was replaced by the white Georgian Classicism of long, cool verandas and easy formality that echoed the romantic image of the ante-bellum South—the ideal of country living in the period. This was the other, perhaps more personal, side of the prosperous and self-confident Classicism of Edwardian Toronto—a carefully designed 'soft-focus' environment for the men in white flannels and blue blazers and the women in flowing white organdy who

people the long summer evenings of Fitzgerald's early novels.

Sproatt & Rolph were versed in many styles— designing in collegiate Gothic for Victoria University, in monumental Classicism for the Canada Life Assurance Company, and in Georgian for clients in Forest Hill and Rosedale. This clubhouse was one of their best designs, made all the more effective by the sense of suspended reality that comes from the gradual approach to it across the harbour. So successful was the design and its atmosphere that when this building too was destroyed by fire, on 9 May 1918,[27] it was rebuilt almost exactly. The fire came just before the opening of the summer sailing season, destroying most of the club's possessions—though fortunately not the trophies or silver service. But even under wartime conditions, the disaster was not allowed to delay the opening—a response typical of the way in which the RCYC preserves, even today, its own traditions, and the atmosphere and character of its architectural setting.

THE HOTEL HANLAN
Hanlan's Point, Toronto Island
1874

The protection that Toronto Island—originally called the Toronto Peninsula—gave the harbour is said to have been a major factor in Governor Simcoe's decision to locate his capital at York.[28] The Island is actually an extended curving sandbar that is broken into a number of large and small islands. Until storm erosion opened the Eastern Gap in 1858, it was connected to the mainland.

When York was established, the Island was reserved as Crown land and most of it remained in the government's possession, with only the Ward and Goodwin families established as permanent homesteaders.[29] The first large house on the Island was a three-storey brick-and-frame summer residence, built in 1837 by Lord Sydenham, which in 1843 was converted into a hotel. In 1846 John G. Howard surveyed the area for building, but there was little development. When the Crown land was granted to Toronto in 1867,[30] the area of 400 acres was mostly semi-parkland. (The Ward property, including Ward's Island, was purchased by the city in the 1920s.)

From the early years of the city, the Island provided an escape from the summer's heat and humidity; by the 1860s it was easily reached by steamer from the mainland. Several hotels were established during the nineteenth century and of these the most popular and best known was the Hotel Hanlan, opened in 1874 by John Hanlan, at what was then called West Point and is now known as Hanlan's Point.

The building, shown here in a lithograph, was constructed of wood, like the churches, summer houses, and most of the other buildings on the Island. It was the cheapest of materials and the most easily transported and worked, while also being light in weight—an important factor, since most of the buildings on the Island were built on piles rather than on standard foundations of brick and stone. The hotel might be described as Second Empire in style because of the high pavilion roofs that rose above the main front of the building. But its real character derived from its light framework of horizontal and vertical milled timbers—usually known as a 'balloon frame'. The technique was developed in the United States, and because of its low cost and the ease with which it could be put up, it became very popular in North America for houses, small churches (plate 129), and commercial buildings. The exterior of the frame was sheathed in wide boards, with the joints covered by narrow protective strips known as battens; hence the

22 THE HOTEL HANLAN, 1907

term board-and-batten was often used to describe such buildings. But in the 1870s it became fashionable, especially in large summer houses and—as here—in hotels, to leave the principal elements of the frame exposed and to use the sheathing only as infill panels in the grid of horizontals and verticals. In some examples the grid pattern was obtained by applying wide strips of wood across the surface, which echoed the real frame that was concealed underneath. The use of an exposed framework became especially decorative in the light cage-like constructions of balustraded verandas and balconies, which covered wide areas of the façades, as they do in the Hotel Hanlan. This manner of building, which now is usually called the Stick Style—for its emphasis on thin, stick-like verticals and horizontals—can be compared to medieval half-timbering, but there were few intentionally historical references in these buildings. Where more traditional elements were used, such as the brackets under the eaves and between the arches of the veranda of the Hotel Hanlan, the details were jig- or scroll-sawn, or turned in a way that left no doubt about the material and had no pretensions to historicism. Other features that were borrowed from more historical styles, like the hotel's Second Empire roofs, were picturesque elements or accents: the graceful lightness of the building, which comes from the skeletal structure, and especially from the repeated verticals of the board-and-batten sheathing, was not affected. The contrast between the essential character of this building and that of the more solid buildings in the city itself demonstrates the variety that can be found in Victorian architecture and that is too often missed by its critics.

The Hotel Hanlan was later operated by Ned Hanlan (1855-1908), John's son and Toronto's legendary oarsman of the nineteenth century. In recognition of his achievements the city granted him the lease on the site free of charge.[31] The hotel was enlarged in the 1880s: first by the addition of a full third floor and more extensive balconies (plate 22), and then by two look-outs with fanciful roofs like pointed domes. By the turn of the century the area around the hotel had been developed as a full-scale amusement park—with a merry-go-round, a roller coaster, boat rentals, and a baseball stadium—proudly compared to New York's Coney Island. Everything except Durnan's Boathouse and the merry-go-round was destroyed by fire in 1909.

23

THE SWEATMAN COTTAGE
390 Lakeshore Avenue, Toronto Island, c.1885
1884 by A.R. Denison

In the 1880s City Council finally recognized the Island's unique importance to the city, and to prevent what the period saw as rowdyism it revoked permanently in 1883 all public liquor licenses on the Island and formally dedicated the approximately 400 acres it owned as a public park. At this time there were plans to lay out ornamental gardens, build temperance coffee houses and a low-cost family hotel, and connect the park to the mainland by a carriage drive and a street-car line;[32] but only a small section of the area was actually developed. Most of the park development occurred on the north side of the Island. On the south side, and at the east end, an area was laid out as leasehold property for the building of large and small summer cottages.[33] (Residential developments like this were a common element in the park schemes of the nineteenth century: the ground rents helped to support the public areas, and the houses did not materially interfere with the free enjoyment of the beaches and meadows.) Development began in earnest in the early 1880s and a wide variety of cottages of all sizes were erected at about the same time as the first boat clubs were being built on the Island.

Lakeshore Avenue, on the south side of Centre Island, was the most fashionable of the several streets, where George Gooderham, Casimir Gzowski, the Masseys, and later E.J. Lennox all maintained houses that looked south across the lake. At the physical and social centre of the community stood St Andrew's-by-the-Lake, built in 1884 by A.R. Denison as a chapel of ease to St James' Cathedral (though it functioned as an interdenominational church for the whole Island[34]). It stood at the corner of Cherokee Avenue and Lakeshore, and next door was the rectory—both seen here in a photograph of about 1885. The principal force in the establishment of St Andrew's, and later the minister in charge, was the Right Reverend Arthur Sweatman (1834-1909), who came to Toronto in 1879 as Anglican Bishop. (In 1906 he was made Archbishop and Primate of all Canada.) The lease for the property was in his name, and when the church was built, he commissioned Denison to build the rectory—at a cost of $1,500—at the same time. Bishop Sweatman was an enthusiastic believer in the benefits of the Island, and the house that he christened 'Happy-Go-Lucky' became his summer residence.

Although 'Happy-Go-Lucky' was strikingly similar to the church in profile, even to the belfry-like tower that crowned its roof, its design was typical of the summer houses built on the Island in the 1880s and 1890s. They, like the church and even the large hotels, were built of wood, on piles. All the houses, even the small ones, opened onto wide verandas that were both sleeping porches and living space. Verandas and porches were popular in city houses; but in summer cottages they frequently wrapped around the entire front and side façades, and were treated as an integral part of the design. The main roofs of the cottages swept forward over them to create outside rooms defined, as here, by an exposed framework of posts and beams, ornamented with fretwork and turned wooden details. In the church, the appearance of a similar wooden skeleton is outlined in chocolate-brown trim against white stucco panels; the effect is one of appropriately Gothic or 'Olde English' half-timbering. The cottage is more whimsical and beautifully toy-like.

The Church of St Andrew survives today—although moved away from its original site on the beach front and completely painted white. The houses on Lakeshore Avenue, including Sweatman's cottage, suffered a fate that was more unkind. Some were destroyed by fire or by neglect, but most were systematically demolished by the Metropolitan Toronto Parks Department in the 1950s and early 1960s. A decision had been made to expand the park area, and the new plans blithely called for the removal of most of the buildings from the Island. The hotels, the last remaining section of the amusement park, and the cottages on the south side all disappeared. In their place was built an ersatz children's town, and along what had once been the main street of the Island a formal garden of mind-numbing banality. Only the more isolated communities of Ward's and Algonquin Islands held out in opposition to the Metropolitan Council's determination to eradicate one of the city's most distinctive communities. At this time the conclusion of the controversy over the Island houses cannot be written.

24

THE LAKESIDE HOME FOR LITTLE CHILDREN
Lakeshore Avenue, Toronto Island, c.1912
1891 by S.G. Curry

The Lakeside Home stood at the west end of the Island, not far from the Gibraltar Point Lighthouse, facing west across the lake. It was founded in 1883, on land donated by the city, as the summer accommodation of the Hospital for Sick Children, which then occupied crowded quarters on Elizabeth Street. The convalescent hospital on the Island, as described in the Hospital's 1882 *Report*, was to be a place

> where the little ones so long prisoners of their rooms and beds, could lie on a broad veranda, breathing the delightful breezes of our lake, watching the boats go by, while we watched the long-vanishing roses returning to their cheeks.[35]

The first building, designed by Mark Hall, opened on 5 July 1883 and was entirely paid for by John Ross Robertson, publisher of the *Evening Telegram*. Robertson was President and Chairman of the Board of the Hospital for Sick Children and its principal financial supporter. In 1891, as the Hospital's new main building at College and Elizabeth Streets was being completed, he paid $70,000 to have the Lakeside Home rebuilt and enlarged.[36]

The architect was probably G.S. Curry. (As a partner in the Toronto firm of Darling & Curry, he managed the construction of the College Street building and later did other work for Robertson.) The new Home was built of wood. The high roof, with its prominent dormers, and the shingles that sheathed the walls and corner towers as smooth, curving surfaces, clearly showed the influence of the large summer houses and hotels that were built in the United States at this time, in what has been aptly called the Shingle Style. It expressed the flexible character of shingles and the thin surfaces they formed over buildings, just as the Romanesque Revival expressed the massive solidity of brick and stone. The dominant features of the exterior of the Lakeside Home were the wide screened verandas, supported on Doric columns, that stretched across the façades in front of the wards, and the round, almost medieval-looking corner towers, with their conical roofs. The inclusion of towers like these in hospital design was supported by the most up-to-date medical theory of the day, which believed not only that corner wards offered the best ventilation and lighting, but that rounded inside walls eliminated the possibility of germ-laden dirt accumulating unseen in corners. Most importantly the towers, like the wide verandas, gave the hospital the gentle picturesque beauty of a summer cottage or hotel, which was as appropriate in this children's hospital as in any summer retreat for those who were more fortunate.

The Lakeside Home stood on about one acre that stretched down to the beach and included a boathouse and another pavilion. Each year when the Home opened for the summer at the beginning of June, the city watched as the children were paraded, in a long line of carriages led by Robertson's own, from College Street to the Island ferry docks; and again at the end of September when the children returned to the city.[37] The 1891 building stood until 22 April 1915, when it was destroyed by fire—fortunately before the spring opening.[38] A new building was opened in 1917, but it remained in use only until 1928, when a new convalescent hospital north of the city replaced it.

THE THIRD PARLIAMENT BUILDINGS
Front Street West (N), between Simcoe and John, c.1900
1829-32 by J.G. Chewett

These Parliament Buildings on Front Street at the western edge of the town of York were preceded by two earlier structures that had been built in 1797 and 1818 on the east side.[39]

Upper Canada, from which the Province of Ontario traces its descent, was established—with Lower Canada, now Quebec—as a separate colony within British North America by the Constitutional Act of 1791. The earliest sessions of the colonial Parliament were held in temporary quarters in the first capital, Newark (now Niagara-on-the-Lake). When the capital was re-established at York in 1793, a site southeast of the present intersection of Berkeley and Front Streets was set aside at the eastern end of Governor Simcoe's town plan, approached from the north by Parliament Street and from the west by Front Street (then called Palace Street because it was planned to build a government house on the same lands). Simcoe's Executive Council first met in York on 31 August 1793. But the first Parliament Buildings were not begun until the next year; they were finished in 1797, after Simcoe had returned to England. These two red-brick buildings, connected by a covered walkway, must have been unpretentiously Georgian (a contemporary illustration

does not exist). They were part of the English vernacular manner of building brought to Upper Canada by the first settlers and especially, as here, by the British Army Corps of Engineers, the colony's first and long its best-trained architects. The balanced symmetry of the design was less a choice of the designer than an expression of the colony's governmental system, which provided for seven Legislative Councillors in an 'upper house' and a maximum of 16 members of the Legislative Assembly in a 'lower house'. While the constitution remained so structured, the two later buildings followed the same basic plan. (Only the Queen's Park buildings of 1886-92 are fundamentally different, acknowledging the unicameral system that was established in Ontario in 1867.)

During the War of 1812 the first Parliament Buildings were destroyed on 27 April 1813 by the American troops that had occupied York. After the war the Assembly moved from building to building until, in 1818, it settled in a new one on the site of the old. Also built of red brick, two storeys tall, and as plainly Georgian as the first, it survived until 1824, when it was destroyed in a fire caused by an overheated chimney flue. Although there was a proposal to rebuild in the original location, using the remaining walls—primarily

26 THE THIRD PARLIAMENT BUILDINGS, C.1890

in order to save money—the site was turned to other uses.* In 1825 the government moved west to take over the new buildings of the General Hospital at John and King Streets (NW), as yet unoccupied, with the residence of the Lieutenant-Governor nearby at King and Simcoe (SW). To this developing government quarter was added in 1829-31 Upper Canada College on the north side of King between John and Simcoe (plate 32). In 1829-32 the third Parliament Buildings, illustrated here, were built by J.G. Chewett two blocks to the south, on relatively open and uncrowded land in the block bounded by Front, Simcoe, Wellington, and John.

Chewett's design was the grandest of the city's public buildings to date, even though the intended portico over

*On this site in 1840 John Howard built the city's third jail, which remained in use until 1865, when William Thomas's Don Jail was opened. In the late 1870s the Toronto and Nipissing Railway built a yard (on the site of the second Parliament Buildings) and a passenger depot at the southwest corner of the block. By 1878 the Consumers' Gas Company had begun to build on the northwest corner of the block; its facilities expanded, replacing the old jail building by 1890, until they covered much of the block. Today the block is vacant and awaits redevelopment.

the main entrance was never built.[40] There were three separate blocks, two storeys high, of red brick with stone trim, facing south across Front Street to the lake. The east block was built by Messrs Ewart and Parkes, the centre by Mr Priestman, and the west wing by Joseph Turton[41] (who completed the centre block first of all in 1830, after Priestman accepted the contract to build Upper Canada College). The east and west blocks were seven bays wide, dignified by a slight projection of the end bays, a sill course that divided the two storeys and echoed the strong horizontal of the long cornice, and a central door framed by oddly belted Tuscan pilasters. These blocks were used from the beginning as offices. The centre block was nine bays wide. Chewett had intended a full-height portico of stone columns to shelter the central three bays that marked the main entrance and the central hall; but while everything else was completed, this was omitted, causing a discordant shift in scale in the centre of the design.

East of the main hall was the Legislative Assembly; on the west was the Legislative Council—each chamber two storeys high and lit by tall, stone-framed, and pedimented windows across the front and along the side

27 THE THIRD PARLIAMENT BUILDINGS: ASSEMBLY CHAMBER, 1892

wall. At the north end of the hall was the main stair-way[42] to the upper floor and the galleries of each chamber. The stairs rose in two flights, with an elegantly curved bannister, and were separated from the front part of the hall by a broad semi-elliptical arch—an arrangement similar to the stairhalls found in houses of the period at Niagara-on-the-Lake.

The Parliament of Upper Canada remained in comfortable residence in Chewett's buildings until 1841. Then, in the wake of the 1837 Rebellion and Lord Durham's *Report*, Upper and Lower Canada were combined by the Act of Union to form the Province of Canada, with a single legislature. The capital was then moved away from Toronto and the buildings were left vacant until they were given to King's College (plate 94) in 1846 as temporary quarters while its own building was being erected in Queen's Park.[43] For King's, a one-storey dissecting room with two skylight monitors was built next to the west wing, and the chamber of the Legislative Council was remodelled by Thomas Young as an Anglican college chapel. In 1848-9, after King's had left, the buildings were used as a temporary mental asylum until the first section of John G. Howard's Asylum on Queen Street West was completed (plate 91).

The government camped out briefly in the old buildings in 1849-51, after rioters protesting the Rebellion Losses Bill burned the temporary Parliament Buildings in Montreal. It then followed its peripatetic course to Quebec City. Not until 1855 did it return in full force to Toronto. With the possibility that Toronto might become a permanent capital, extensive alterations were made to all the former government buildings (including the old General Hospital and Government House). The alterations were carried out by William Hay in 1855-6,[44] but with considerable difficulty, for not only had the bureaucracy grown, but with the growth of population the membership of the Legislative Assembly had become too large to be accommodated in the old chamber. Hay solved part of the need for office space by filling the openings between the centre and side blocks with projecting blocks three bays wide, designed in a simple Late Georgian vernacular idiom. Housing the enlarged Legislative Assembly, however, was his main problem. He shifted the Speaker's dais from the north side to the east, where the long windows had already been blocked by the new office addition, and then extended the room to the west into the space of Chewett's central hall. New galleries were built at the

28 THE THIRD PARLIAMENT BUILDINGS: LEGISLATIVE COUNCIL CHAMBER AS CONVERTED TO A LIBRARY, 1892

west end for spectators and visitors from the other House, and at the east end for the Press. Plate 27, a photograph taken shortly before the move to Queen's Park in 1892, shows the members of the Ontario Legislature in their accustomed places. The east wall is dominated by the Speaker's dais—Chewett's original was probably re-used by Hay—and to either side are the cramped press galleries, with railings of cast iron in a naturalistic Gothic Revival style.

Hay's additions also included the erection of a series of rooms around two sides of the rear yard, designed to house the 30,000 volumes of the Parliamentary Library. (This collection, probably the finest in the colonies at the time, formed the nucleus of the Library of Parliament in Ottawa.) Hay's rooms connected with Chewett's original galleried Library on the second floor of the short wing behind the Legislative Council chamber and included a long stack room on the north side of the court, raised on a Tuscan colonnade to keep the books from the damp.[45] Though the Parliamentary Library did not stay in Toronto, and another collection had to be formed for the new Province of Ontario, the space provided by Hay was quickly outgrown. Plate 28 shows the Legislative Council chamber—which became

unnecessary under the new provincial system—as it was converted to provide additional library space prior to 1892. Its galleries effectively hid all the architectural detail except the semi-elliptical arches along the north wall, which had once set off the throne of the Lieutenant-Governor.

As early as 1853 there was a discussion about the building of a new legislative complex in Queen's Park, probably inspired by hopes that the capital would settle permanently in Toronto.[46] However, it was not until 1886 that the present buildings were begun. The Legislature moved to Queen's Park in 1892 and the following year the old buildings on Front Street were completely vacated. They stood unused until 1900, when they were demolished. Like nearly all of the government-owned land downtown, the property was transferred to the railways, in this case the Grand Trunk, which built freight sheds on the site. Today the railways have moved south of Front Street and the site of the third Parliament Buildings stands empty, without any indication of its historical significance. At present it is reserved for a new studio and office complex for the Canadian Broadcasting Corporation, promised several years ago.

GOVERNMENT HOUSE
Simcoe Street at King Street West (SW), c.1885
1866-70 by Gundry & Langley

In 1866, shortly before Confederation, the Toronto firm of Gundry & Langley was commissioned to draw up plans for a new Government House. The chosen site was that of Elmsley House,* occupying the whole of a city block from Simcoe to John, and from Wellington to King. In Henry Langley's words, the new house was 'designed in the modern French style of architecture which has been adopted largely in American cities and is rapidly getting into favour in England.' The charac-

*Built by John Elmsley in 1798 at the northwest corner of Wellington and Simcoe Streets, this was the first residence provided by the government for Lieutenant-Governors and Governors. The house was purchased after the War of 1812 and remained in use until 1841, when the government moved to Kingston. After being put to many temporary uses, it was destroyed by fire on 10 January 1862 (the day after it had become an officers' barracks).

teristic picturesque tower, steeply sloped mansard roofs, and prominent bonnet-topped dormers—which Langley called 'segmental domes lighting the third story apartments'—were considered very fashionable in Toronto in the 1870s. (Examples can still be seen in such formerly exclusive districts as Beverley Street and the Sherbourne-Jarvis area.) Government House was built in red brick with dressings of Ohio limestone. Its form and details combined high style in which 'effect was sought...by grouping, by large simple treatment of the openings and by contrast of colour, rather than by elaborateness of detail'. A strong note of Methodist economy encouraged the use of 'galvanized iron strings and cornices painted and sanded to imitate stone. The main cornices are heavily bracketed in the same material. This material has been much more suitable to our client than stone, and at the same time is exceedingly economical.'[47]

The exterior view shows the main entrance, with its 'large, handsome carriage porch' facing Simcoe Street, and the south façade of the house, from which the drawing rooms on the ground floor and the state bedroom suite on the second looked out towards the lake over landscaped gardens that occupied most of the very large site. Beyond the house on the right is the main building of Upper Canada College (plate 32), as remodelled and extended in the 1870s.

The two interiors were photographed in 1912, shortly before the house was demolished. The impressive reception hall (plate 30), 65 feet long by 21 feet wide, was dominated by the main staircase, which rose through three storeys to similarly spacious halls on each of the two upper floors. The ground-floor hall opened on the north into the Lieutenant-Governor's offices and the state drawing room, on the west into the ballroom (behind the stairs), and on the south into a suite of drawing rooms. Although fashionable taste in interior decoration had changed dramatically by 1912, the hall retained much of the rich, dark atmosphere characteristic of the 1870s. The walls were hung with flocked paper, probably not unlike that originally installed by the John Edwards Company. The floor was 'laid with Minton's encaustic tiles of a rich design', visible to the left of the stair, and the heavy woodwork of the walls and stair was painted and grained 'in imitation of fine woods'. The interior was flooded with light from the first landing of the stair, coloured by the 'exceedingly rich glass' of a window* made by Joseph McCausland.

The main drawing room on the south side of the main hall (plate 31) opened onto a garden veranda through the french doors on either side of the square bay window on the left. The three rooms in the suite—the morning room to the east and the original private dining room to the west, later the conservatory drawing room—were, in contrast with the hall, painted by the John Edwards Company with the 'finest gloss of white', 'papered in the most elegant manner', and lit by gas fixtures 'of crystal of the most chaste and elegant description' hanging from ceilings panelled and enriched in gilded plaster, 'which will afford ample scope for the decorator'. By 1912 much had changed in these rooms, notably the replacement of the gasoliers by nearly invisible electric fixtures, such as that in the upper-left corner of the photograph. The floor was covered with a Victorian Axminster carpet in a pink and green floral design. But much of the original furniture (by the well-known local firm of Jacques and Hay) remained, arranged in the seemingly random conversation groupings that went out of fashion after the turn of the century. This suite connected with the conservatory by

*Now in Branksome Hall, a private girls' school.

30 GOVERNMENT HOUSE: MAIN STAIRCASE, 1912

sliding doors at the rear of this view, and with the ballroom and hall. It formed the ceremonial heart of the house and was intentionally planned so that 'an unbroken view of the 160 feet can be obtained from the front vestibule to the end of the ballroom, or from the morning room to the end of the conservatory, and a promenade of 1/16 of a mile is thus obtained.'

The house cost $105,000 to build,[48] but in the Ontario Parliament—controlled by economy-minded rural representatives—money spent on repairs, new furniture, servants, and social events for the Lieutenant-Governor was deplored as an unnecessary extravagance. In *Toronto: Past and Present* (1884) C.P. Mulvaney makes his reformist sentiments about the use of the building very clear:

Government House is the residence of the Hon. Beverley Robinson, at present nesting in the last year of his term of office as Lieutenant-Governor. . . . The apartments . . . are well and elegantly proportioned, and if ever the conviction gains ground with the tax-

31 GOVERNMENT HOUSE: THE MAIN DRAWING ROOM, 1912

payers of Ontario that a grievance which costs them $50,000 a year had better be abolished, this sumptuous edifice, the people's property as it is, built and maintained by the taxpayer, would serve admirably for a State Hall or People's Palace. Still better, it might be converted into a public library and industrial museum, the grounds, now selfishly appropriated by sinecure officialism, being utilized as a park, free forever to all our citizens. Meanwhile the unsightly board fence, which spoils one of the finest views on King Street and shuts out a view of the gardens, ought to be removed.[49]

However, it was really changes in the area that led to the demolition of the house. Upper Canada College moved to its present site on Avenue Road above St Clair in 1891, and its lands on the north side of King Street were gradually redeveloped with warehouses and industrial buildings. A description in the 1910 *Report of the Minister of Public Works* sums up the changes:

When the present building was erected in 1870 the surroundings and conditions were different from what they are now. The railway tracks were much farther south and fewer in number. The traffic has immensely increased. On the streets surrounding the building the traffic was nil compared with continuous movement of vehicles of all kinds, day and night. To the west, on King Street, there were no commercial houses of any kind on the south side. Opposite, on the north side, the entire block from Simcoe to John Street was occupied by the old Upper Canada College. The land is now entirely built over with mostly manufacturing establishments, and the whole neighbourhood has become the centre of commerce.

In 1912, after planning had begun for a new Government House at Chorley Park (plate 122), the property was sold to the Canadian Pacific Railway and the old house was demolished.

UPPER CANADA COLLEGE
King Street West (N), between Simcoe and John, 1868
1829-31 by J.G. Chewett

When a charter was granted in 1827 for a university at York, Upper Canada—mainly through the efforts of Archdeacon John Strachan—there were strong objections in the Assembly to its 'sectarian tendency'. In 1829 the new Lieutenant-Governor, Sir John Colborne, called a halt to the establishment of a university and took steps to found a preparatory school, modelled on the pattern of English public schools, for which he felt there was a much greater need. With such a college, boys would no longer have to be educated in the United States, returning 'troublesome and discontented' and imbued with 'a bad spirit against England'—a persistent concern of the Tory establishment.[50] Upper Canada College was founded in 1829 under a Royal Charter granted by George IV. It opened for classes on 4 January

1830 in the Blue School, formerly the Home District Grammar School on the north side of Adelaide Street East, near Church. It stayed there until the autumn of 1831, when its new buildings on King Street West were completed.[51]

This site—bounded by King, Simcoe, Adelaide, and John, and known as Russell Square after the Hon. Peter Russell (Administrator after Simcoe's departure)—was relatively large and had the advantage of being across King Street from Government House, where Colborne resided, and a short distance from the third Parliament Buildings (plate 25), which were then being erected. The designs were by J.G. Chewett—a logical choice, since he had designed the new Parliament Buildings. The project was completed in the summer of 1831 by Mr Priestman

33 UPPER CANADA COLLEGE, WITH EXTENSIONS, 1884

(who also worked on the government buildings) at a cost of over £20,000. This figure is given in Alfred Sylvester's *Sketches of Toronto* (1858), and though it seems exorbitant for the time, it may be correct, given the many difficulties of building in Toronto.

Plate 32—from one of the original prints illustrating *Toronto in the Camera* (1868)—shows the College substantially as completed in 1831, set at least 100 feet back from King Street, with a gravelled drive or square in front. Chewett's design provided a two-storey block, with two simpler two-storey pavilions ranged symmetrically to the east and west. The composition is similar to the arrangement of the three blocks of the Parliament Buildings complex. But the grouping was systematic and heirarchical, for it placed the most important element in the College—the block housing the classrooms, prayer hall, and offices—at the centre and ranged the buildings of lesser importance—the masters' and students' lodgings—on either side.

All the UCC buildings were of red brick. Only the main block had much architectural pretension, with its large porch supported on stone piers and the windows ornamented with flat, ledge-like architraves supported on scrolled consoles—again, details related to those of the Parliament Buildings. The centre block measured 80 feet wide and 82 feet deep and contained offices and classrooms opening off a central hall on both floors; in the northwest corner of the second floor there was a 'prayer room', with a dais for the masters and box pews for each of the seven forms. At various times before becoming rector of Holy Trinity, Henry Scadding, one of UCC's early students who was to become Toronto's first historian, taught in the front rooms west of the hall on both floors. The first-floor front room on the east

side of the hall was the studio of John G. Howard, one of Toronto's first professional architects and drawing master to the College from 1833 to 1856.

The two blocks on either side of the main building were each double houses for masters and boarding pupils. They were linked by units set back from the south front, containing separate entrances and stairways. The entrances—with plain but elegantly moulded frames forming transoms and sidelights—faced north into the College's private quadrangle, which gave an appropriate air of college seclusion.

In 1876-7, under pressure for a growing enrolment and an expanding curriculum in the College, the Senate of the University of Toronto (which also formed the College's board of governors) voted the expenditure of $50,000 for enlarging the buildings. The extensions (plate 33) were completed by April 1877 according to plans prepared by G.W. Lloyd of Sandwich, Ont.—an otherwise unknown figure—under the supervision of Kivas Tully as Provincial Architect.[52] The most obvious change was in the centre building, which was expanded by the addition of a mansarded block 85 feet wide by 44 feet deep directly in front of the old main building. The lower floor contained a principal's classroom east of the hall and a study room to the west, each 33 by 42 feet. The entire upper floor was occupied by a chapel-assembly hall (plate 34) that rose 28 feet to a beamed roof with a ribbed and diagonally boarded ceiling, described as Gothic. The whole room had a natural wood cornice and wainscot finished in matching fashion. The character of the exterior is more difficult to describe. C.P. Mulvaney in 1884 saw it as an example of 'the Queen Anne style of architecture, now so much in vogue'; John Ross Robertson in 1888 referred to it as

34 UPPER CANADA COLLEGE: THE CHAPEL-ASSEMBLY HALL, 1890

'modified Elizabethan'. Both descriptions suggest the consciously English atmosphere.[53]

The addition to the main block was built in red brick to match the original buildings. Horizontal bands in white stone formed a grid pattern with the two-storey piers that grouped the tall windows. The front entrance stepped forward, and was framed by banded columns—an eccentric touch of Jacobean classicizing detail—as a tall frontispiece. Above this, in the centre of the roof, rose a high octagonal cupola, matched by thin pinnacles topping piers at the corners of the block, which actually concealed chimneys and ventilators. The inspiration of the cupola and the ventilators was probably Kivas Tully's own design for similar cupolas in Trinity College (plate 86). But the design as a whole, like much Victorian work of the period in Canada, makes a virtue of individualized and inventive detail: a basic medieval picturesqueness achieved with French and Italianate classical detail. Elsewhere in the renovations, the French Second Empire style—present in a purer form in Government House across the street (plate 29)—dominated: in the mansard roofs added to the old buildings, in the elaborately moulded and crested window heads of pressed metal and cast iron added to the front windows, and in the new front entrances to the residences, with their high stoops and porches.

The renovation was not a permanent solution to the space problems of the College, and by 1888 arrangements had been made to move it to a new site on part of the Baldwin estates in Deer Park, at the top of Avenue Road, where it is still located. The principal reason for the move was undoubtedly the crowding of the College into a nine-acre site where there was little room for the extensive playing fields that were associated with such schools, and where cloistered seclusion, considered equally desirable, was no longer a characteristic. Arrangements were made with the University of Toronto Senate by which UCC received a new building, thirty acres of land, and an endowment of $100,000. In return, the University gained control of the old site, conservatively valued at $750,000 in 1888, and the remnants of the College's original endowment for an estimated net profit of at least $800,000 (according to John Ross Robertson). The College abandoned the old buildings in 1891. As publisher of the Toronto *Telegram*, Robertson was not opposed to the move itself, but he was against the commercial redevelopment of the grounds. C.S. Clark's *Of Toronto the Good* (1898) quotes an editorial in the *Telegram* on the subject—probably by Robertson:

> Toronto ought to outbid every private tender and secure the use of the old Upper Canada grounds for the city's children during the summer months. It is a small thing, but civic statesmanship could afford to stoop to conquer those convenient acres for the use of boys and girls who have no play ground but the street. Spite of high taxes, the city is rich enough to rent the property from the University trustees. The few hundred dollars which it would cost at most, would be small price for the boon which such a play ground would be to hundreds of children.[54]

The buildings were demolished in 1900 and the grounds were redeveloped commercially. One of the new buildings erected was the Royal Alexandra Theatre.

THE JOHN GORDON HOUSE
303 Wellington Street West at Clarence Square (SE), c.1912
1874-5

In the 1830s the street system of Toronto was extended west, from Peter Street to Bathurst south of Queen, and a new area was planned as a distinctive and high-quality residential district. Wellington Street (at first called Market Street), Clarence and Victoria Squares, with Wellington Place between, were laid out following the spacious patterns long established in Britain. However, except for a few houses like Lyndhurst, built in 1837 by Vice Chancellor Jameson (husband of Anna Jameson) and enlarged after 1844 by Frederick Widder of the Canada Company, development was very slow and scattered. The houses on the north and south sides of Clarence Square were not completed until the late 1870s. But the construction of Government House in 1866-70 (plate 29) encouraged the building of several fashionable houses on Wellington Street close to the Square. Hugh John Macdonald, son of Sir John A. Macdonald, built at 304 Wellington Street on the east side of the Square, and in 1874-5 John Gordon built his mansion, one of the finest in the city, across the street.

Gordon was a senior partner in the dry-goods importing and wholesale firm of Gordon, Mackay & Co., founded in 1850, and also president of the Toronto, Grey and Bruce Railway.

The basic form of his brick house was Italianate, with paired front gables, wide eaves on scrolled brackets, and a multi-windowed monitor at the crest of the roof to light the central stairhall. But these regular shapes were ornamented with carved stone details that were in keeping with the taste of the period for richly decorative effects, especially of light and shadow. The most important of these decorative elements is the columned portico, formed distinctively as a series of tall, narrow arches. The unusual banded columns, with bracket-like supports at the bases, are typical of the experimental detail used by architects of the period seeking a new 'modern' style. The grouping of the arches concentrates and climaxes the strong undulating rhythms of the round-arched windows of the façade. The panelled quoins emphasize the corners of each of the vertical

36 THE JOHN GORDON HOUSE: THE DRAWING ROOM, C.1912

sections of the façade, and on the side (at the right of the photograph) the rolled mouldings and cresting of the window frames complement the smooth curve of the wall that forms a large bay.

The same orchestration of detail into large complementary patterns can be seen in the interior of the drawing room that occupied this bay, illustrated here in a photograph taken about 1912, when the Victorian interior was still unchanged (plate 36). The curving wall, with its central fireplace, established an oval design of plaster mouldings on the ceiling that dominated the entire room, disguising the actual rectangular plan. Heavily outlined curves were popular in the interiors of the period. Here they are seen not only in the ceiling mouldings but in the deeply carved marble mantel, the arched frame of the overmantle mirror, and even in the scrolled legs and backs of the upholstered furniture.

The architect of John Gordon's mansion is not recorded, but it was likely designed by either William Kauffman or William Irving and Joseph Sheard.

Kauffman continued to practise in Toronto until 1874/5, and the portico and window frames of the house resemble similar details in his Bank of Toronto (1863) on Wellington Street East (plate 44). On the other hand, the overall treatment of the rich carving can be compared with Irving and Sheard's Ontario Bank (1862), also on Wellington Street East (plate 48).

John Gordon lived on Wellington Street until 1879/80 and the house stood vacant until after his death in 1883. In 1884 it was bought by his brother-in-law, William Mortimer Clark, who lived there with his family until 1912, except for the period 1903-8, when he served as Lieutenant-Governor of Ontario. In 1912 the house was destroyed to clear a right-of-way for CPR tracks that led to the new express building being erected on the site of the recently demolished Government House. At one stroke the extension of the railway tore the heart out of one of Toronto's most interesting residential neighbourhoods and destroyed two of the city's finest Victorian mansions.

THE PALACE OF INDUSTRY
North of King Street West, west of Shaw, c.1868
1858 by Sandford Fleming and Collingwood Schreiber

The Canadian National Exhibition traces its lineage beyond its official establishment in 1879, back to the series of agricultural fairs established in 1846 by the Provincial Agricultural Association and the Board of Agriculture of Upper Canada.[55] The first of these fairs was held on 21 and 22 October 1846 in the grounds of Elmsley House, at Wellington and Simcoe Streets. From the beginning the fair was not intended to be sited permanently in Toronto because it was designed to encourage agricultural improvement in the province at large. It was held in Hamilton (1847), Cobourg (1848), Kingston (1849), Niagara-on-the-Lake (1850), and Brockville (1851), before returning to Toronto in 1852. Inspired by the successful Great Exhibition of 1851, the 1852 fair was the largest and most diversified one yet, with a midway of sideshows outside the main gates (on the present site of St Andrew's Presbyterian Church). In 1855 the commissioners visited the Paris Exposition, where there was a Canadian exhibit, and it was probably this experience (and perhaps a visit to London) that encouraged the decision to build a permanent hall in Toronto for the 1858 exhibition.

A new site was chosen on the military reserve south of the Asylum (plate 91). Speed of erection and low cost were crucial factors in the design of the new building, to be called the Palace of Industry. With this in mind, and influenced by the example of Sir Joseph Paxton's remarkable exhibition building in London, the committee had called for a glass and iron building when they announced the competition for designs. But the design by Fleming and Schreiber that won the competition was rather more conservative in character, with far more sense of the cast iron used for support than of glass, which had given the 1851 exhibition building its revolutionary lightness (and its popular name, the 'Crystal Palace'). It is very likely that traditionalists on the committee would have been reluctant to accept a building fully designed according to Paxton's principles, even had such a structure been buildable in Canada at

the time. More influential in the character of the final building were other halls derived from Paxton's work, such as the Dublin Crystal Palace and the New York version, both of which had only partially glazed roofs. Certainly, as G.P. Ure's 1858 *Handbook of Toronto* indicates,[56] Dublin provided the model for the thick translucent plate glass that was used, while the New York design seems to have been the direct inspiration for the fan-shaped window used decoratively over the carriage porch of the front entrance—although both features were present in different form in Paxton's designs.

Like most of the Crystal Palaces, the Palace of Industry was cruciform in shape and the visitor entered through the short arm. At the centre of the plan was a two-storey space, 64 feet square, lit by a square skylight in the otherwise solid roof. To the right and left in the long wings were similar rectangular spaces, and around the whole interior at second-floor level was a wide gallery that provided additional exhibition space. As in Paxton's design, the basic framing of the walls was in cast iron—with a horizontal and vertical module of 16 feet. The panes of plate glass in the infill were amazingly large for Toronto at the time and were imported from Birmingham. The roof rose in a flattened curve to a height of 54 feet. Except for occasional skylights, it was built of wood on an iron frame and covered on the outside with tin plate. The solidity of the building—ostensibly dictated by the Canadian climate—gave it a low, heavy, frumpishly conservative appearance that nullified the lightness of the glass-and-iron walls. To contemporaries such as Ure, who knew the London Crystal Palace well, this was the chief failing of the design. Still, as it was built in only three months, with iron and wood elements that had been mass-produced and prefabricated in the city rather than imported, it was an important example of modern building technique for Toronto.

The Palace of Industry was opened with great pomp

and ceremony by Sir Edmund Walker Head, the Governor-General, in late September 1858, and celebrated with a Choral Society presentation of Haydn's 'The Heavens are Telling', races in the harbour, a bazaar on King Street, and a parade of the fire brigades of Toronto, Hamilton, London, and Cobourg. Inside, the exhibits included a bookcase with 100 Bibles in different languages and models of HMS *Niagara* and *Agamemnon* laying the first Atlantic cable. In the centre of a main court was a fountain with statues of Chinese mandarins and John Bull; a jet of water supported with its pressure a continuously spinning gilt sphere. Among the prize-winning exhibits was a collection of native plants formed by Catharine Parr Traill, author of *The Backwoods of Canada* (1836).[57]

Though the exhibition was a great success, the directors decided to continue its yearly travels. The Palace of Industry was used until 1878, when it was disassembled and rebuilt as the Crystal Palace (plate 38) in the present Exhibition Grounds. At this time the land on which it had stood was sold to the Massey Manufacturing Company. (Massey-Ferguson still occupies the site.) Even though the design was only a partial and short-lived success, it was an important landmark in Toronto architecture, using extensively for the first time an industrialized system of building, with standardized component parts, that foreshadowed both cast-iron construction in the 1860s and 1870s and high-rise design in our own century.

THE CRYSTAL PALACE
Built from parts of the 1858 Palace of Industry in the present Exhibition Park, 1889
1878 by Strickland & Symons

By 1878 the Agricultural Association decided that the Palace of Industry (plate 37) was too small, and that unless a new building could be provided, the exhibition would not come to Toronto again. With this in mind, and as part of a plan to capture the fair for Toronto permanently, the city council offered to provide a new site and buildings. Although two public referendums defeated money by-laws to fund the new construction, Council decided to continue with the project, funding it from general tax revenue.[58]

The new site—60 acres of fairly level land west of the present Stanley Barracks (the Marine Museum, then called the New Fort)—was more easily accessible by water, rail, and street-car than the old King Street site; and at the main, or Western Gap, entrance to Toronto harbour, it was more conspicuously located. The Crystal Palace was designed to exploit its new position with a tall angled cupola—which, though handsome in itself, was unrelated to the rest of the building—that effectively replaced the Gibraltar Point Lighthouse on the Island as the main landmark at the harbour entrance. Most of the ironwork was re-used from the earlier Palace of Industry, with new sections copied, where necessary, from the old patterns. To provide more space, the wings were lengthened and the central transept extended north by 85 feet to house a new art gallery. These changes—and the addition of a third storey, raised skylights, and the cupola—corrected the heavy effect of the original roof, but the result was still very close to the design of the 1858 Palace of Industry.

Inside, the central court of the building was much higher than in the old Palace of Industry, but it was dominated by four cast-iron columns, 18 inches in diameter, 66 feet high, and set at the corners of a 22-foot square that supported the rooftop cupola. Mounted between the columns at the level of the second gallery was a bandstand, and the pavilion-like space below was filled with a complex arrangement of cast-iron fountains and drinking fountains set in artificial rockwork.

The new Crystal Palace was only the centre-piece of a large group of display buildings and a railway station—constructed in wood in decorative and sometimes fanciful Carpenters' Gothic and Queen Anne forms—that were built by Strickland & Symons for the 1878 fair at a cost of over $100,000.[59] When, despite the expense and the lavishness of the accommodation, the Provincial Agricultural Association held to its belief in a travelling exhibition, City Council organized the Industrial Exhibition Association, and opened the first Toronto Exhibition on 5 September 1879. For the next twenty-six years the Crystal Palace was both the focal point of the grounds and the symbol of the Exhibition. In 1906 it was destroyed by fire and in its place rose the Horticultural Building by G.W. Gouinlock (1908).[60] A spreading multi-columned design in the Edwardian Baroque style, its glazed dome is a clear reminiscence of the old building.

THE DUFFERIN GATE OF THE CNE
The foot of Dufferin Street, c.1927
1910 by G.W. Gouinlock

By the first years of this century the Exhibition had evolved from a fall agricultural fair into a large-scale expression of the new industrialization and cosmopolitanism of Toronto, of Ontario, and of Canada. A massive rebuilding program was begun, and the Horticultural Building, which rose on the site of the Crystal Palace in 1907, was only one of a group of new buildings that began with the Manufacturers' Building in 1902, and included the Art Gallery and Administration Building in 1905, a new Grandstand in 1907, the Railways Building in 1908, and the Government Building in 1911.[61] Though they were classical in basic design, the architect, G.W. Gouinlock, took advantage of a relative freedom from strict functional requirements (most of the buildings simply contained open halls of varying sizes, with metal-framed roofs) to create an architecture that was festive in character.

The introduction to the new Exhibition was the Dufferin Gate at the foot of Dufferin Street. (Until the late 1920s this was the principal entrance to the grounds, served by both a railway stop and streetcars.) In front of the entrance Gouinlock laid out a semi-circular forecourt, facing the railway tracks and the streetcar terminus, with one-storey curving wings that ended in pavilions. At each corner of the two pavilions were fantastic baroque domes ornamented with fat ribs, draped garlands, and arched rows of light bulbs. (Only one of the domes can be seen in this photograph.) The wings gently funnelled the crowd towards the central gate, whose tall piers with flag staffs on top framed a long perspective of trees and new buildings leading to the lakeshore. The whole design was deliberately theatrical and grandly scaled to arouse anticipation and make coming to the 'Ex' an unforgettable event. This photograph is undated but probably shows the Dufferin Gate in 1927, decorated for the 60th anniversary of Confederation. The space above the metal gates was filled for the occasion with a radiating pattern of electric lights and two huge maple leaves. In the background on the right can be seen the Government Building, with its central glass dome and one of its towers.

The Dufferin Gate was demolished in 1959 to make way for the Gardiner Expressway. In its place was erected a 'modern' parabolic arch of concrete that seems meagre, cheap, and trite compared with the picturesque and festive gate that Gouinlock designed.

THE SECOND CITY HALL
103 Front Street East at Jarvis (SW), 1868
1844-5 by Henry Bower Lane;
rebuilt 1851 by William Thomas; renovated c.1870 by Henry Langley (?)

When the City of Toronto was incorporated in 1834, the council offices were located in cramped and makeshift quarters on the upper floor of the Market Hall at King and Jarvis, where St Lawrence Hall now stands. In 1843 the city council decided to build a new city hall having the style and presence they very much desired. A large market was to be included in the project, because the growth of the city had caused serious overcrowding in the old market facilities. There was no available site on the north side of Front, which had been reserved for public use when the city was laid out; but to keep the new market and City Hall close to the centre of the city (then focused roughly on King and Jarvis), Council voted to purchase the water lot on the southwest corner of Jarvis and Front, which was occupied by the Home District Farmers' Storehouse. Immediately to the west was a water lot already owned by the city and used since 1834/5 as a municipal fish market. Together these properties became the site for the new building.[62]

Early in 1844 City Council advertised for 'plans and specifications' for the new City Hall. Projects (both Gothic in style) were submitted by Henry Bower Lane and John G. Howard; and by John Tully (brother of Kivas Tully) and William Thomas. Both Lane and Howard submitted alternate designs in a Classical style. The committee that had been appointed to judge the designs concluded that the Howard and Lane submissions were of equal merit, but chose Lane's Gothic design, considering it better suited to the needs of the city. When the designs were presented to Council, however, this decision was rejected and Lane's alternate Classical proposal was chosen instead.[63]

The second City Hall was begun in 1844. Plate 40 shows the building approximately as Lane completed it in the summer of 1845. In both layout and style it was very much in the Late Georgian tradition that dominated Toronto architecture in the first half of the nineteenth century. The façade, facing Front Street, was 140 feet wide and arranged with a three-storey pedimented centre and two flanking two-storey wings, each with six narrow round-arched shops on the ground floor. Above the pediment Lane placed a two-stage clock tower with a low, square, podium-like base—ornamented with quoins, rounded pediments, and scrolls at each corner—that housed the city's public clock and supported a diminutive domed cupola with a weather-vane on top. Although not large, it rose proudly above the surrounding buildings to mark the City Hall as the most important and conspicuous landmark in the city. A door in the centre of the façade led to a hallway from which spiral staircases gave access to the council offices at the front of the second floor, and to the council chamber in the rear. This was two storeys high, with a gallery at the north end that was reached from the third floor and was lit by three elegantly arched windows at the south end.* There were further offices in the wings above the shops, and Police Station No. 1 was located in the basement. On either side of the main entrance an arched corridor led through the building to the market court behind. This was bounded on the east and west sides by rows of two-storey shops, with arcades in front, devoted to fruit, vegetables, and poultry. Cellarage and an ice house were provided below the shops and there was a yard at the south end of the court for loading and unloading carts. Beyond this yard, at the edge of the lake (where the Esplanade was later built on landfill), was the city's principal fish market, with docking for the boats at the Market Wharf just to the west.[64]

The detailing of Lane's building was rather simple, because his small budget did not allow much in the way of ornament. The ground floor of the central block was faced with rusticated masonry; the main entrance was sheltered under a simple porch with Roman Doric columns; and the windows of the upper floors were framed with simple but crisply executed mouldings. For the rest, Lane depended for decorative effect on the colour contrast of the red brick walls, with the grid of horizontal and vertical strips executed in buff or 'white' brick, approximating a classical vocabulary of cornices, string courses, and pilaster strips.

In its basic arrangement and most of its details Lane's City Hall was a thoroughly competent design, very much up to the standard of the Toronto church designs he prepared in the 1840s: St George the Martyr, Little Trinity, and the Church of the Holy Trinity among others. However, in the arrangement of the shops and the façades of the wings that flanked the central block, Lane surprisingly disregarded all the period's basic design and planning tenets having to do with symmetry and alignment. In each of the wings there were six impractically narrow shops with arched shopfronts. Above each shop was a mezzanine level, lit incongruously by five (rather than six) windows, spaced

_____
*The windows are still visible on the inside of the north wall in the South St Lawrence Market, which was later built around the central portion of the second City Hall.

40

between the lower arches; and above these windows were four more windows, divided by vertical pilaster strips of white brick, that lit the City Hall offices on the second floor of the wings. This arrangement was completely incoherent and violated the principles basic to the Late Georgian tradition in which Lane had been trained and that influenced the rest of his work. It is not hard to believe that the division of the wings into six shops—instead of the four that would have matched the pattern of the second-floor windows—was forced upon Lane (probably after the designs were complete and possibly after construction was well advanced) by a city council eager to have more rental income from the new building. But whoever was at fault, it was Lane who was criticized. (He left Toronto in 1847 and was in no position to defend himself.) The most celebrated judgement of the design comes from W.H. Smith's *Canada: Past, Present and Future* (published in 1852, but possibly written about 1850, before the later changes to the building). Smith concluded that the City Hall was

a very strange looking building and it was unfortunate for the reputation of the architect that he had not left the province before he completed the building instead of afterward.[65]

41 THE SECOND CITY HALL: COUNCIL CHAMBER, 1898

However, there were more serious problems with the new City Hall and market in these years. Not long after the building was opened, merchants began to complain that the new shops were too small; and by 1849/50 there was serious deterioration in the building's fabric. John G. Howard was called on, in his capacity as City Surveyor, and reported to City Council on 2 December 1850 that in his opinion the building needed an almost complete reconstruction. He cited in particular the need for a new roof and a rebuilt porch. At the same time he presented four different schemes for the reconstruction, all of which included the rebuilding of the market stalls and a redesigning of the shops in the side wings.[66] City Council commissioned Howard to rebuild the market area, but William Thomas (who was then completing St Lawrence Hall) was given responsibility for the new shops in the wings.*

*There is evidence that in this period Howard shared certain commissions with Thomas and that he did not regard Council's choice of Thomas, in this instance, as a slight to himself.

The changes Thomas made in the building were not nearly as extensive as those Howard had proposed. He completely rearranged the police station and cells in the basement of the building; but on the exterior—though he must have made extensive repairs—his hand was apparent only in the new shops. Among Thomas's drawings preserved in the Metropolitan Toronto Library, there is one, signed and dated 17 January 1851, that shows the new shops in plan (no elevation drawing survives). This corresponds with the arrangement of the shops as they are shown in plate 40 and indicates that the six shops Lane had provided were gutted and rearranged as three larger areas. The new shop fronts were built in front of Lane's façade—as can be seen in plate 42—leaving the quoins that had originally ornamented the corners imbedded in the wall. Each of the shops was framed with a wide arch that was ornamented with mouldings and a keystone carved as a human head and supported on half columns banded with the vermiculated pattern frequently used by

Thomas. Each shop also had its own multi-paned display windows, a recessed entrance to one side, and a mezzanine above lit by a window that filled the curve of the arch. Executed in stone and framed with side piers and a crowning architrave, the new fronts of the wings were grandiose and decorative—more in keeping with the scale and finish of St Lawrence Hall than with Lane's smaller and simpler City Hall. Functionally Thomas's work seems to have been successful, but the relation of the three new shop fronts with the four windows above is in itself no better than in Lane's design. In fact Smith's comment might be applied just as well to the revised façade as to the original.

Plate 40 shows the City Hall substantially as Thomas left it. In the interval between 1868 and the streetscape photograph of about 1872 (plate 42) it was again renovated, apparently by Henry Langley. The shops facing Front Street were closed, the windows altered, and the space probably given over to the offices for the expanding civic bureaucracy. At the same time, doors were installed to passages that led to the market court behind; and, inexplicably, the rusticated banding with which Thomas had decorated the columns of the shop fronts was cut away, leaving standard smooth shafts. In this period the scrolled volutes at the corners of the tower were also removed.

Through the various rebuildings and renovations the interior arrangements of the City Hall remained largely unchanged. Plate 41 shows the council chamber as it was in 1898, as viewed from the gallery. The plaster-work, with the heavily bracketed cornice and geometrical ceiling mouldings, probably dates from the Lane or Thomas periods, as does most of the furniture. Drawings surviving in the Metropolitan Toronto Library indicate that Henry Langley's office designed the two mantels (not seen in plate 41), the wainscot panelling, and probably the columned dais that blocks Lane's beautiful arched window. Hanging from the ceiling are long ventilators, like stove pipes, that were intended to draw off the stale air of the room and the fumes and heat from the gas lighting fixtures.

When the civic offices moved to the third City Hall in 1898-9, it was decided to reconstruct the old building as a larger and more efficient market. A project was prepared in 1898 by W.L. Symons that included a rebuilt version of the market behind St Lawrence Hall, as well as new construction on the site of the second City Hall, and that covered both markets with a great arched shed.[67] The earlier shops and stalls of both markets were to be eliminated and a great roof was to stretch across Front Street to provide an enormous covered loading area. This project formed the guidelines for a competition (Canadian architects only), held in early 1899, for precise designs for the section south of Front. The commission was won by John Wilson Siddall, architect of Holy Blossom Synagogue on Bond

Street (1895) and several other buildings in the city. His scheme eliminated the cupola, pediment, and side wings of the Lane-Thomas building, rebuilt the first level of the centre with a wide central arch and a passage through the building, and destroyed the council chamber by raising the floor level to provide more height below. Siddall's shed, which submerged the remains of the City Hall, did not span the width of Front Street as originally projected, but there was something eloquent and confidently Edwardian in the way in which the arch was made to leap over the former City Hall. Unfortunately, shortly after work began the piers of the shed were found to be too weak for the load and City Council appointed Beaumont Jarvis as co-architect with Siddall (who really lost control at this point). There were no further problems, and the South St Lawrence Market, as it has since been known, opened for business in 1901. It became one of the city's principal wholesale centres, and as completely renovated in 1975-7 it continues in use today.

During the last renovation the matter of what to do with the remains of the City Hall was considered. In spite of certain obvious faults, the Lane-Thomas building was an interesting and dignified one, with some beautiful details and great historic significance. After considerable discussion, however, it was decided that there was simply not enough information to restore the building completely. Instead it was decided to renovate the remains of the old building and include in the plans a reworking of the upper floors to house the city's large art collection, which has not been properly displayed since the move to the fourth City Hall in 1965.

42 THE INTERSECTION OF FRONT AND WELLINGTON, SHOWING THE SECOND CITY HALL
    AND THE COFFIN BLOCK, *c*.1872

THE COFFIN BLOCK
Between Front Street East and Wellington at Church (W), c.1872

Front Street* was laid out to follow the line of the lake shore and the harbour front. East of Jarvis it ran parallel to King. But west of Jarvis the street curved south, at an angle to the other streets of York, following the shoreline. This created a series of oddly shaped sites at Jarvis, Market, Church, Scott, and Yonge Streets. The most interesting of these is a sharply pointed wedge of property where Front, Church, and Wellington all intersect. It is seen in the centre of plate 43, showing the Coffin Block, and in the distance (beyond the second City Hall) in plate 42. Both photographs were probably taken at the same time, in 1872.

The Coffin Block was a very simple brick building, erected in the early 1830s,[68] with unornamented windows, broad eaves, and string courses dividing the storeys. In spite of its simplicity, its odd triangular shape—which was likened to the end of a coffin—made it a local landmark. The building was actually divided into three separate units. The smallest of these, at the intersection, was originally the booking office and terminus for the stage lines that connected Toronto with the cities and towns to the east and west, before there were adequate train connections. In later years this section, like the rest of the building, was occupied by a

variety of concerns; but in the 1840s and 1850s both upper floors were converted into an annex to the Wellington Hotel, which was at the corner of Church and Wellington. (The much-weathered sign for the hotel can be seen above the parapet of the building.) The Coffin Block stood until 1891, when it was demolished to make way for the Gooderham Building (better known today as the Flat Iron Building, again because of its shape) by David Roberts.[69] The triangular shape of the new building was specially designed with a turret-like tower at its apex, to make it as prominent and as recognizable a local landmark as the Coffin Block had been.

At the right in this photograph is a clear view westward along the length of Wellington Street at a time when it was the banking and financial centre of Toronto. The first building on the right, Ontario Chambers, was built about 1866; it was the headquarters of the W.R. Griffith grocery wholesaling firm. The next building, on the northwest corner of Church and Wellington, is the Bank of Toronto, with its arched portico (plate 44). Further along the north side of Wellington are the Toronto Exchange (plate 46) and the Ontario Bank (plate 48). On the north side of Front Street can be seen the high cornice of the Royal Canadian Bank (plate 49) and beyond it the three-storey block of the Bank of Montreal (plate 2), at Yonge and Front, and the McMaster Warehouse (plate 5) behind it.

---

*Originally called Palace Street, Front Street was intended as the principal approach to a government house that was planned but never built, at the eastern edge of the Town of York.

THE BANK OF TORONTO
58 Wellington Street East, at Church (NW), 1868
1863 by William Kauffman

The Bank of Toronto was chartered by the Province of Canada on 18 March 1855. Earlier attempts had been made to found the bank as the Millers, Merchants, and Farmers Bank of Canada West, a name that indicates its support and explains the prominent role played in its affairs by the Gooderhams, whose family business (Gooderham & Worts) was at the time involved in both milling and distilling. The first office was in a rented building at 70 Church Street. (Though altered, it still stands.) So successful were the first six years of operation that in 1862, with the paid-up capital increased eight times over what it had been in 1855 and the shares fully subscribed, the directors announced the construction of a new head office at the intersection of Church and Wellington.[70]

The new building, designed by William Kauffman, cost $46,590, but there can be no doubt that the bank received an impressive home rivalled by few of the other banks that crowded Toronto. Three storeys high, 64 feet wide on the Wellington Street façade and 100 feet on the Church Street façade, it was impressive in the streetscape for its sheer bulk alone. It was designed in the Italian Renaissance style, faced with Ohio sandstone, but was not so chaste as Kivas Tully's Bank of Montreal of 1845 (plate 2), which was also inspired by Renaissance forms. There is the same use of horizontal rustication on the ground floor; but the framing of the windows is much more complex and ornamental, with acanthus-leaf scrolls supporting the sills, garland-like floral mouldings around the arches, and carved keystones. The same comparisons can be made with the second- and third-floor windows, where Kauffman chose sculptural richness—layered curves, individual architraves, carved capitals and keystones—instead of the crisp, ordered clarity that was basic to Tully's work. The decorative qualities of the design, very much to the taste of the period, extended to the ordering of the entire façades with the slight projection of single end bays on Wellington Street and paired end bays on the side façade, with each projection marked on the skyline by short chimneys above the main cornice. By defining emphatically the ends of each façade, an effect of impressive solidity was obtained, which was crowned by the strong shadow line of the bracketted cornice that ran around the roofline.

The most striking feature of the exterior was the double-arched portico that sheltered two principal entrances on Wellington Street. Normal rules of architectural composition dictated an odd number of intervals in a portico to permit an opening on the central axis of a symmetrical façade. Not only did Kauffman use just two arches; he also constructed twin columns on the centre axis, and on the upper levels of the façade paired the window frames to match the portico. However, the unique design is completely explained by the planning, which divides the building into two separate units, with the Bank of Toronto on the east side, next to Church Street, and the Quebec Bank on the west.

The exterior richness and detail were continued inside in the decoration of the banks' offices.* All of the ceilings of the main rooms and ground-floor offices were richly detailed with plaster mouldings of interlocking roundels, ovals, and rectangles in a vaguely seventeenth-century style. These rooms were finished with massive and heavily moulded oak woodwork and the settings were completed by the surfacing of the walls with a thick layer of scagliola—a mixture of plaster, marble dust, glue, and a variety of colours, polished to imitate marble or granite—with a Sienna pattern in the banking room, white-veined marble in the Directors' Room, and green Syenite granite in the corridors and cashier's office. These interiors were conceived, like the exteriors, as an ensemble to impress the public and demonstrate the importance of this bank among the many other banks in the city. As he had done in the Masonic Hall (plate 60) and other buildings, Kauffman succeeded in creating work that was richly detailed, finely crafted, and personal.

As the Bank of Toronto grew, it took over more of the building. In 1884 the Quebec Bank moved out and a three-unit warehouse was built on the land to the west (designed by A.G. Macklin); it was connected to the Kauffman building to provide offices for the president, George Gooderham, and for his company. When the Gooderham & Worts Building (the 'Flat Iron' Building) was completed in 1891-2, the entire space was altered by Knox and Elliott for the bank.[71] By 1901, however, the building was again too small, and because further additions were not possible, the bank began to plan a new head office at King and Bay (plate 72). This was opened in 1913 and the old building became a branch bank and then a records centre, with some sections rented. Finally in 1961 the bank—known as the Toronto-Dominion Bank since a merger in 1955—demolished the 1863 head office and replaced it with a pavilion-like building that opened on 1 August 1962.

---

*The original specifications for the interior and exterior construction are preserved in the Premises Department of the Toronto-Dominion Bank.

4

55

THE TORONTO EXCHANGE
34 Wellington Street East at Leader Lane (NW), 1868
1855 by James Grand; altered 1877 by Henry Langley

The principal landmark on the north side of Wellington Street was the Toronto Exchange, seen here on the right in this photograph, taken in 1868. It was established, on the model of the Royal Exchange in London, to provide both co-operative office space and a forum for the speculative sale of produce, a type best represented today by the various grain exchanges of western Canada. The 'Association of Merchants Millers and Business men' that built the Exchange was established in 1854 by an Act of Parliament, and their building, which ultimately cost £14,200,[72] was conceived as much for the air of dignified and even palatial grandeur it presented as for the provision of useful space. The large scale of the building, the quality of the detailing throughout the design, and the fine limestone used were meant to testify to the prosperity of the Exchange as an institution and to its importance in the commercial and public life of the city.

Basically Greek Revival in style, the Exchange had a 54-foot frontage on Wellington Street—properly in the heart of Toronto's wholesale district—and 140 feet on Leader Lane* at the side (plate 45). The recessed portico on Wellington was dominated by two Greek Doric columns, which framed steps leading up into a semicircular porch that sheltered the main entrance.

---

*Leader Lane was named after *The Leader*, a Tory newspaper that was published in Toronto from 1852 to 1878.

(On either side of these columns, steps led down to the basement entrance.) On Leader Lane there was a frontispiece of four half columns, also Doric, and large piers framing a large centre door and two shorter side doors. The order supported an entablature—with a frieze ornamented with carved wreaths—that ran round the building. This divided its height and made the lower storey an effective base for the more elaborately finished upper two storeys. An impressive twenty feet high, the character of this lower level was intentionally different from that of the neighbouring buildings, both in scale and in the solidity of its rusticated masonry.

The windows of the two upper floors were grouped vertically between unfluted closely spaced Ionic pilasters. With the round-arched second-floor windows, they created a compressed up-and-down rhythm across the façade. The wall surfaces between the windows were decorated with recessed panels, while the panelled and balustraded parapet that concealed the roof was accented by the Royal Arms and originally by ornamental vases (gone by 1868). The total effect was consciously decorative: the building had little of the severity that is characteristic of the Greek Revival as a style.

The plans for the building, which survive in the Baldwin Room of the Metropolitan Toronto Library, show that on the ground floor there was originally a central corridor, 130 feet long, lined with offices.[73] From this, two main stairs rose to the second floor, the

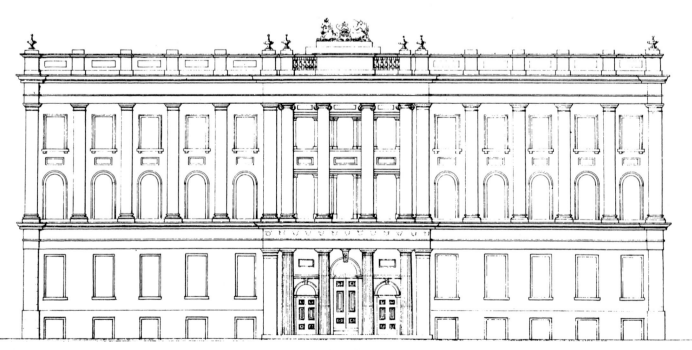

45 THE TORONTO EXCHANGE: SIDE ELEVATION BY JAMES GRAND, 1855

front of which, facing Wellington, was taken up by a spacious reading room supplied with newspapers and periodicals for the use of members. In the centre of the north half of the building was the Exchange room itself, 50 by 30 feet, oval in shape, and rising 40 feet to a circular dome of glass and iron. This was the first major use of ferrovitrious construction by a Toronto architect—in this case to produce a spacious, well-lit interior.

In 1877 the Imperial Bank established its offices in the Exchange, taking over the front half of the main floor. At this time the façade was altered by Henry Langley. The framework of James Grand's ground floor was retained, but the Doric portico was removed when the front section of the building became a banking hall. The ground-floor façade was transformed with a series of round arches on banded columns and a curved pediment over the centre. When the Board of Trade moved into its new building in 1891 (plate 7), the Exchange was renamed the Imperial Bank Chambers. Further alterations were done by Darling, Sproatt & Pearson in 1894.[74]

The low two-storey clapboard house in the centre of plate 46 is the Coopers Arms Hotel, on the northwest corner of Wellington and Scott Streets, later to be replaced by the Western Assurance Building. Just to the right of this is the Ontario Bank at 24 Wellington (plate 48).

On the right in plate 47 can be seen part of the row of shops at 36-42 Wellington, erected in 1855-7 on land that in the 1840s had been the wintering home of George Bernard's Circus. The basic style of the row is Greek Revival, with the slight peaks in the stone lintels of the windows imitating in a simple manner the pediments that were popular in more expensive buildings. This block still survives, although 42 has been altered; 36-8 is the Graf Bobby Restaurant.

The other buildings on the street have been less fortunate. The Exchange was severely damaged by fire in the 1930s and demolished in 1940/2. Today nothing remains of the warehouses and commercial buildings between Leader Lane and Scott Street. The site is used as a parking lot.

THE TORONTO EXCHANGE, c.1891

48

THE ONTARIO BANK
24 Wellington Street East at Scott (NE), 1868
1862 by Joseph Sheard and William Irving

In 1862 the Ontario Bank commissioned the firm of Joseph Sheard and William Irving to build its head office at the corner of Wellington and Scott Streets. (Irving, Sheard's son-in-law, was in charge of the design.)[75] Although the site was a corner lot with a long frontage on Scott, it was quite narrow—only 34 feet wide along Wellington, the principal front. The width was not a problem in terms of planning, since the standard patterns of bank architecture, borrowed from England and at the time universally popular in North America, had established a simple plan of a long, usually narrow, suite of rooms running back from the banking room at the front of the building. But in purely architectural terms the narrow façade allowed little scope for the grand effects demanded by the image- and status-conscious directors of the bank. Where William Kauffman and the Bank of Toronto solved the problem, in effect, by putting up two buildings in one (plate 44), Sheard concentrated on providing luxuriously carved detail that would attract and hold the viewer's attention.

The façades of the new bank were constructed in Cleveland sandstone, and Sheard's work shows great sensitivity to its sculptural possibilities. The quoins that frame each façade, and the heavy blocks around the arched windows of the ground floor and the Wellington Street entrance, are finished in contrasting textures alternately: some are smooth-cut, others are vermiculated (roughly carved to look like worm-eaten masses). The window arches are prominently ornamented by keystones carved with classical heads.

On the narrow Wellington Street façade there is an air of heavy extravagance in the profusion of detail, particularly in the swags of carved stone flowers, leaves, and fruit that droop from the volutes supporting the balustraded balcony over the main entrance. On the ground floor the two windows that light the banking room balance the heavily decorated main entrance. On the upper floors, however—which include triplets of deep-set windows and an empty niche above the entrance—the arrangement is cramped and unbalanced. (Some sense of order is maintained by the horizontal mouldings—belt courses and string courses—that divide the 50-foot height of the building into three levels, topped by a closely bracketed cornice.) The side façade facing Scott Street is much more successful. Here the 88-foot width allowed more freedom in the creation of a symmetrical and balanced organization of the windows. The wide areas of plain masonry effectively set off projecting bands of carved work as well as the shadowy recesses. Here too the horizontal courses become part of a comprehensible hierarchy in the graduated storeys of the façade. The ground floor, with its rough vermiculated masonry, appears as an impressive and substantial base for the smoother, more elegant second floor (which housed the manager's residence); and the third floor, with its smaller windows, is clearly shown to be subsidiary space. The building is not without delightfully eccentric details, such as the two rusticated panels expressing, yet disguising, the chimney flues as they rise through the main cornice of the building, becoming stubby chimney-stacks and squeezing other details between them: first a narrow balconied window, and then a row of small arches. Such details, whether 'correct' or not, were highly valued by architects and patrons alike for the picturesque and individual distinction they gave to buildings in the streetscape.

The Ontario Bank prospered on Wellington Street. In 1888-9, after several branches had been opened, a large addition was built along Scott Street, north of the original building, in the style of the old one. In 1905/6 the Bank of Montreal took over the Ontario Bank, and for two years this building housed its Wellington Street branch. After 1908 it became a general office building and in 1950-1 was vacated and demolished. The site, like the entire block from Scott to Leader Lane, is now a parking lot.

THE ROYAL CANADIAN BANK
36-8 Front Street East (N), c.1872
c.1871 by Smith & Gemmell

The Royal Canadian Bank was founded in August 1865, during the boom that accompanied the American Civil War. It quickly opened fifteen branches and in 1867 five more. But in 1869 the same over-investment in land that had caused the collapse of the Bank of Upper Canada in 1866, and the Commercial Bank of the Midland District, forced the Royal Canadian Bank to suspend operations, though it was still technically solvent. In 1870 it was drastically reorganized; but without the influential social and commercial backing that supported the Dominion Bank, the Canadian Bank of Commerce, and the older banks, it finally closed its doors in 1876.[76]

The bank's first offices were on Toronto Street. But about 1871 a new head-office building was begun, to a design by Smith & Gemmell, a Toronto firm that produced both commercial and religious architecture.[77] The new site was on Front Street East, within the triangular two-block parcel running back to Wellington known as the gore. In the heart of the wholesale district, it was chosen to attract the commercial clients the bank needed. The building itself was grandly designed in the ornamented French Renaissance style, sometimes described as the Modern Classic style, that banks of the period often adopted to express their progressiveness and their conservatism simultaneously: taste and security, to inspire confidence in customers. With three tiers of attached Corinthian columns supporting a bracketed cornice, which was mounted with the Royal Arms, the design was also conceived as a dominant element in the streetscape—an architectural advertisement for the bank. However, the façade was not carried out in carved and cut stone but in cast iron, with side walls of red brick. Cast iron was common in the United States at this time and was a thoroughly respectable material. (Several of the best architects designed specifically for it.) But in Toronto, although many buildings had iron columns inside or iron elements in the ground-floor portion of the façade, iron was rarely used for full façades. This may have been partly because of insecurity about its stability after numerous cast-iron buildings had been destroyed by fire in the United States. In spite of this, the material had definite advantages for the bank: it was far cheaper than stone, and the savings permitted a second similar façade on Wellington Street. Cast iron was also quickly erected; and, as in today's steel-framed skyscrapers, it permitted large areas of glass in the façade—an important factor before the development of safe, high-quality artificial light.

This photograph, taken shortly after the building was completed, shows the bank's Front Street office. (The offices on Wellington Street were from the beginning designed as rental space and were only partially occupied by the bank.) Next door, to the west, is the Newbigging House, a small businessman's hotel, established in a house built between 1840 and 1855 and run by W. Newbigging (demolished in 1882). The contrast in scale between the two establishments—each having three levels above grade and one below—is remarkable.

When the Royal Canadian Bank collapsed, the building was first taken over by the Consolidated Bank, then by Toronto General Trust, and finally by the Gooderham companies. During this period the addition of a fourth floor caused the removal of the semi-elliptical central pediment and the Royal Arms, but the building survived largely intact until 1964/5, when it was demolished. Unlamented by Toronto's architectural community, which at the time was wedded to architectural 'modernism', this demolition was especially disastrous. Of all the buildings in Canada built with cast-iron façades—the direct ancestors of the present steel-framed skyscrapers—only a handful remain in Canada, which means that an essential link in the development and understanding of contemporary architecture is rarely to be seen. There are only three in Toronto, almost directly across from this site: at 45, 47, and 49 Front Street East.

49

50

THE JOHN MACDONALD & CO. WAREHOUSE
21-3 Wellington Street East (S), c.1872
1862

John Macdonald (1824-90) was a Scottish-born merchant who became, in the words of C.P. Mulvaney, 'the Canadian dry goods king'. He founded his wholesale dry-goods company in 1849, just as the new railroads were about to make Toronto the emporium for western Ontario and western Canada. One of the keys to the firm's success was his introduction of a departmental organization within his business—the first in Canada—and his practice of sending buyers to England and the continent twice a year to purchase the most up-to-date fabrics and clothing directly. Once established in his wealth, he used it as a springboard to politics, holding the provincial seat for West Toronto from 1863 to 1867 and the federal seat for Centre Toronto from 1875 to 1878. His career was capped by an appointment to the Senate; he was the only Liberal that Sir John A. Macdonald ever sent to the upper house.[78]

Macdonald began business at 30 Wellington Street East (then number 17, and to be seen in plate 46 when occupied by R. Jordan & Co.); the building shown here was built in 1862. It was in a variation of the Venetian Gothic style that had seized the popular imagination after the publication of John Ruskin's *The Stones of Venice* (1851-3) and that was fashionable in British commercial buildings at the time. The design should probably be attributed to William Kauffman. Probably to please his client's conservative taste and ideas of economy, it is simplified in detail, especially in the carving of the corbelled cornice, the pointed Gothic arches over the windows, and the use of pale gold Ohio limestone rather than the vibrant polychrome patterns Ruskin advocated. But it satisfied the Victorian merchant's desire for a building that aptly represented prosperity, and to which Macdonald could proudly point as his personal contribution to the beautification of his city.* Indeed, the building was proudly used in the firm's advertising.

In 1870-1 the company expanded south, into a warehouse at 30 Front Street East, and in 1878 the building on Wellington Street was extended in the same subdued Gothic style, doubling the façade. In 1882, at a cost of $25,000, the Front Street premises were rebuilt and doubled in size again. This expansion gave the firm two acres of sales space on six floors and permitted a logical development of the departmental system.[79]

Senator Macdonald was succeeded by his son John and the firm continued on Wellington Street until it closed in 1897. After this the buildings went through a series of owners, but they were largely intact when, in 1964-5, under the auspices of the City of Toronto, all the buildings on the Wellington-Front blocks between Church and Yonge Streets, with the exception of the Gooderham ('Flat Iron') Building, were demolished. Today the site of the Macdonald warehouses and the Royal Canadian Bank (plate 49) is Berczy Park—one of the more useless and ill-conceived of Toronto's new open spaces—which does not compensate for the destruction of a major section of the city's commercial and architectural history. Sadly, had the demolition been proposed in 1975 rather than 1965, it would probably never have occurred. Instead, like the Griffith's and Perkin's Building on the south side of Front Street, the two main buildings in the block would have been lovingly restored as part of the city's living heritage, instead of being included in the litany of its lost landmarks.

---

*Macdonald devoted the same interest to the building of Oaklands (1860), his suburban estate that still stands at the top of the Avenue Road hill (it is now De La Salle College). It is also possible that Gundry & Langley, the same architectural firm that designed Oaklands, was responsible for Macdonald's Warehouse.

THE EDINBURGH LIFE ASSURANCE BUILDING
17-19 Wellington Street West (S), 1868
1858 by Cumberland & Storm

This photograph is dominated by two major financial buildings. In the centre, and still standing today, is the Commercial Bank of the Midland District, built in 1845 by William Thomas. Grandly designed in the style of the Greek Revival, it—like Kivas Tully's Bank of Montreal of the same year (plate 2)—could have strayed from the streets of the City of London.

The Edinburgh Life Assurance Building to the right of the Commercial Bank, built in 1858 by Cumberland & Storm, is as grandly conceived, but richer in detail and even exotic in its overall design. Where the Commercial Bank was properly conservative, Cumberland's design shows the influence of the new and experimental attitude towards historical style that was found in Victorian London. A contemporary description of the building (apparently by a Toronto resident), published on 20 August 1858 in the *Building News* (London), described Cumberland's design as 'somewhat peculiar', though embracing some very interesting features, 'the Norman or Early English prevailing'. It was, however, 'one of the most beautiful buildings which has yet been erected in Toronto'.[80]

Cumberland was proficient in many styles. His most important Romanesque or Norman design was University College (begun in 1856 and still under construction in 1858), which was conceived in richly sculptural terms but with fairly historical detailing. The historical elements in the Edinburgh Life Assurance Building are combined more freely, as much Venetian as Norman in form and associations. The high ratio of window to wall, the layering of the façade, the corbelled freize at the roofline, the twisted colonnettes at the corners of the ground floor, and especially the smooth arches framing the windows that rise to points at the keystones (although the windows themselves are round-arched) are all more or less Venetian. The keystones stand out in high relief and reach upwards to link in succession the first-floor cornice, the emphatic horizontal of the balcony (which is purely decorative), and the main cornice of the building. The architectural details are linked, as if they were a free-standing structure, in honey-coloured Ohio cut stone in front of the plain brick mass of the building. This was emphasized with red stone highlights to create polychrome patterns. With its tension between horizontal and vertical elements, the design tries to resolve the problems of articulating a tall, narrow façade in the thoughtful manner of contemporary High Victorian 'street architecture'.

The first building on the left in the photograph, at 5-7 Wellington Street West, is the warehouse-showroom occupied by Charles Moore & Co., importers of groceries, wines, and liquors (built about 1861). The warehouse between Moore's and the Commercial Bank, 11 Wellington, was occupied by Thomas Lailey, an importer and manufacturer of ready-made clothing (built about 1855). Both these buildings still stand today, although the ground-floor fronts have been altered, and show the larger scale and greater height in buildings that came to Toronto's side streets in the 1850s, replacing smaller, Late Georgian buildings, such as the house on the right, at 25 Wellington, occupied by G. Capreol, the railway engineer.

The Edinburgh Life Assurance Building was taken over by the Union Bank and in 1899 was extended and completely refaced by Bond & Smith in an Edwardian Baroque style, with richly chromatic rustication that was the latter-day counterpart of Cumberland's Neo-Romanesque.[81] Renamed The Union Bank Chambers, it continued as office space until 1914, when it was again remodelled for the American Club. Unfortunately the Club moved out in 1916 and the building stood vacant until 1929, when it was demolished for a parking lot—an early example of the fate of so many of Toronto's distinctive buildings.

C.MO
IMPO
GROCERI

1

52

THE BANK OF UPPER CANADA
232 Adelaide Street East at George (NE), 1872
Dr W.W. Baldwin, 1830

William Warren Baldwin's design for the Bank of Upper Canada, shown here with additions to the north and east, was modelled on the elegant and dignified Georgian town houses of London in the late eighteenth century. The Roman Doric portico sheltering the main entrance, the solid stone construction, and the location of the building in what, in 1830, was a fashionable residential street, were all intended to impress potential customers and depositors with an appearance of substance and regularity.*

The bank was founded in 1821 to aid the development of the province and opened in 1822 in a converted but handsome shop on the southeast corner of King and Frederick Streets (now demolished), from which it moved to this building on Adelaide Street (originally Duke Street). In the eyes of the province's populist movement, the bank was inextricably linked with the governing oligarchy of the Family Compact. However, in spite of opposition from William Lyon Mackenzie and others, it prospered sufficiently so that, about 1855, it added additional space in the north wing in the Greek Revival style (on the left in the photograph).[82]

By the late 1850s the building's Georgian good taste had become old fashioned. The best that commentators could say about it was that it was 'plain but substantial' while acknowledging, in apology, that, though it was designed 'at a remote date, ere yet the little town boasted of Architects "cunning in their craft" ', it was

still 'a fair evidence of what good sense can accomplish even in cases requiring skill and art'.[83] By this time the location of the Bank of Upper Canada was inconvenient and out of the way, since the City of Toronto had grown far to the north and west of the Town of York. After rumours of a move to the lower end of Church Street, the bank re-established itself in an existing building at the southeast corner of Colborne and Yonge, in the heart of the westward-moving financial district, where it remained until it collapsed in 1866, over-extended by investments in unsaleable land and mortgages.

The 1830 building was bought by the Christian Brothers and rededicated as the De La Salle Institute. The block east of it, in the Second Empire style, was added in 1871; and further extensions were made later, including the addition of a dormered mansard roof to the original bank building. After De La Salle moved to Senator John Macdonald's house, Oaklands, on Avenue Road, the building passed through many hands, becoming most recently an egg-grading station.

This building, the oldest in Canada designed as a bank, still stands today, much changed and threatened by neglect and redevelopment. It is one of the very few buildings included here that are still standing, because Baldwin's original design has been so denatured that it is almost unrecognizable. The need to preserve the building, which is unoccupied at present, is immediate, because in June 1978 the bank and the De La Salle buildings were damaged by fire. (Most of the damage was confined to the additions made in 1871 and later.) Such fires are never entirely accidental: they are a direct result of neglect and lack of supervision. This fire serves to underline the necessity for a firm policy concerning an owner's, or the state's, obligation to maintain in a secure condition a building of great importance.

*In this photograph, taken in 1872, the bank building is without the panelled and balustraded parapet that conceals the roofline in the vignette of the building in Sandford Fleming's map of Toronto (1851), which was the basis for later graphic reconstructions of the bank. However, the low sloped roof, with wide eaves, of the bank shown here is comparable to the roof that Baldwin designed for his own house on Front Street (plate 8). The roof of the bank may have been altered and the parapet removed between 1851 and 1872; but it seems more likely that the parapet Fleming shows was an intended, not an executed, addition to Baldwin's design.

53

THE QUETTON ST GEORGE HOUSE
204 King Street East at Frederick (NE), c.1885
1807

When Laurent Quetton St George built this combined house and store on King Street East, the only other brick buildings in York were the Legislative Buildings of 1794-7. Laurent Guéton (1771-1821) was a French royalist émigré who escaped to England in 1796—where he anglicized his surname and added 'de St George' to commemorate his arrival—and in 1798 settled in Upper Canada on lands in the royalist colony at Windham, Markham Township. Unlike most of the émigrés, he made a success of the move by opening a dry-goods and provisions business which, based on imports and the Indian trade, expanded into a chain of stores between Fort Erie and Amherstburg and north into the Lake Simcoe region. After 1802 his headquarters was in York, close to the lake shipping routes and friends in government, on which profits and success depended.[84]

Although it was not the grandest residence in York, Quetton St George's brick house had an air of permanence and dignity in a town of log, frame, and stucco buildings. Brick was in use elsewhere in Upper Canada by this time, but the Davenport and Don Valley clay pits that supplied the city later in the century had not yet come into use, and the expense of using imported bricks was enormous.* Although digging the cellar for a house might provide sufficient clay for brickmaking, brick remained a conspicuous sign of prosperity and style into the 1820s. In St George's house it had the added advantage of making the building where he also stored and displayed his stock more fireproof, and therefore much safer, than any other building in town.

The St George house is Georgian in style, but it is even more severely rectangular than Strachan's 'Palace' (plate 13) because it lacks the decorative front pediment that would have been normal in Britain but, in 1807, was too expensive for the owner's resources. There is, in fact, no ornament in the masonry; even the window lintels are flat arches of brick—the simplest possible form. Instead, the sparing ornament of the exterior was provided by the carpenter's skills, especially the three-part Palladian window in the centre of the second floor, Thin pilasters support short sections of entablature over the sidelights and frame the round-arched central section, which has a decoratively scalloped pattern of glazing bars around the curve. There is a similar arch over the front door, concealed here by a wooden porch that repeats the Palladian motif, with Ionic columns supporting a semi-elliptical arch in the centre. The great skill and effort put into the creation of these wooden details suggest that the design and building of the house were controlled by an accomplished carpenter rather than a mason, using forms having the slim, elegant proportions that were popular in the St Lawrence and Hudson River Valleys.

Nothing is known of the plan or interior detailing, although it is reasonable to assume that the arrangement was very similar to the centre-hall plan of The Grange. The use of part of the house as a shop for storage seems to have made little difference in the design.

Quetton St George remained in York until the defeat of Napoleon brought a restoration of the Bourbon monarchy in France; his business was then carried on by John Spread Baldwin, brother of Dr W.W. Baldwin (a friend of St George), and by Jules Quesnel of Montreal. The house later belonged to the Baldwin family and it was rented to the Canada Company (founded in 1822 to settle the Crown lands in western Ontario) as its Toronto headquarters. The Canada Company remained there until 1895, when it moved to new offices in the Toronto Exchange Building (plate 47). With the westward expansion of the city, the area east of Jarvis Street had lost its status as an important commercial area, and after the Canada Company moved, the house became first a drug factory, then a boarding house, and finally a junk shop. So it remained until about 1904, when it was demolished and replaced by the brick warehouse/factory of the Adams Harness Company that still stands on the site.

In spite of its delapidation, the house was recognized in the 1890s as an important historical monument, and the publication of a measured drawing of the porch in the February 1892 issue of the *Canadian Architect and Building News* was a major step in the appreciation of Toronto's architectural heritage—as important, at the time, as the construction of the house in 1807.

---

*According to John Ross Robertson, the bricks for the St George house came from Rochester and Oswego.

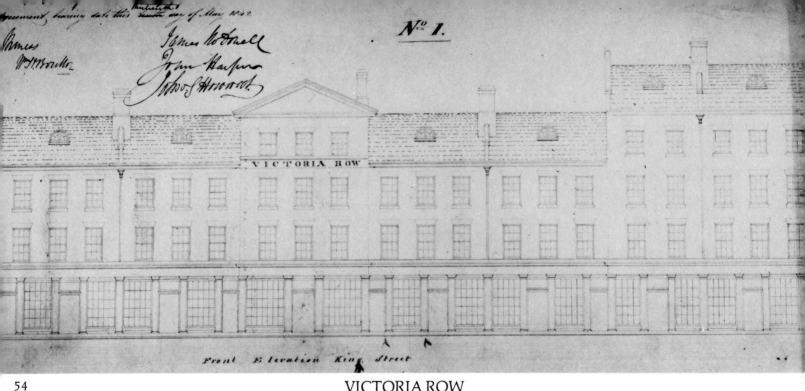

54

VICTORIA ROW
87-97 King Street East (S)
1842 by John G. Howard; altered c.1866

Nineteenth-century Torontonians were proud of their city, often to the amusement of their neighbours, and commentators were particularly fond of praising King Street. In 1858 Alfred Sylvester apostrophized it by saying it was 'What Oxford Street is to the cockney of London, what the boulevards are to the muscadin of Paris, what Broadway is to the denizen of New York.'[85] Even the usually level-headed C.P. Mulvaney could hardly restrain his enthusiasm for

> the most brilliant and long extended series of first-class stores of which Toronto can boast, her Palais Royal, her Regent Street. On the south side, the 'dollar,' or fashionable side, of King Street, continuously from York Street to the Market, are the spacious plate-glass windows, glittering with jewelry, with gold and silver plate, with elaborate china and bric-a-brac, with sheen of satin-shining tissues for Toronto's brides . . . with more sober-hued, but still beautiful and elaborate materials for the adornment of Toronto's golden youth. Here are restaurants, where men and ladies can dine in comfort, and as luxuriously as in any in New York or London, photographers, art warerooms. Is there any luxurious taste you desire to gratify, any decorative art you would pursue? In that case, o reader, 'put money in thy purse,' (for that is an indispensable condition), and take a walk along the south side of King Street.[86]

Some of the praise lavished on King Street was justified, for there were several co-ordinated rows of shops along its length that gave the street the simple elegance that characterized the best Late Georgian and Regency developments in Britain. John G. Howard built

up a considerable practice in this type of commercial architecture, and designed several rows. Victoria Row, on the fashionable south side of King, was designed for James Macdonnell. Plate 54, reproduced from Howard's original drawing (now in the collection of the Metropolitan Toronto Library), shows the five units of this brick row, plus two shops to the west, for which Howard also prepared designs. He drew the composition together by raising the central unit one storey higher than its neighbours and finishing it with a simple triangular pediment. As in many of the houses of the first half of the century, the pediment was a symbol of style and elegance, and its character was matched by the semi-circular fan-like dormer windows ornamenting the side units, the flaring stone lintels over the upper windows, and the multi-paned shop fronts divided by severely simple piers.

About 1866 Victoria Row was altered in the Second Empire style, to keep up with the same fashions that affected residential, banking, and public architecture (plate 55). The basic fabric of Howard's block remained intact, but the changes were substantial. The central pediment was replaced by a higher, curved, tower-like mansard roof, ornamented by a double dormer with a richly moulded bonnet-like capping. Simpler straight-sided mansards with double dormers replaced the original shallow-sloped roofs of Howard's building, much increasing the useful space in the attics. The changes in the roofs were matched by a complete redecoration of the fronts. The units were separated by blocked pilasters topped by brackets, and the windows were grouped vertically in tall, arched frames of carved stone. The rich detail exploited the contrasts of light and shadow, and the varying textures of brick and stone, along with other coloured patterns made possible by the use of different kinds of slate on the roof. The façade was completed by a portrait statue of Queen Victoria in Court dress, set in an arched niche at the centre of the composition. No architect is recorded for the renovations.

Victoria Row was gradually eroded by later alterations. In 1898 the Albany Club occupied the central unit and the one to the right, altering the ground floor. Further changes occurred in 1930, when the club premises were rebuilt by D.J. Gibson. Today only one unchanged unit, at 87 King, indicates that Victoria Row once existed.

55 VICTORIA ROW, C.1890

THE GOLDEN LION
33-7 King Street East (S), c.1873

The busiest section of King Street was the block between Victoria Street and Leader Lane; here, on the south side, were concentrated the city's most fashionable shops and businesses. As on Wellington and Front, there was considerable rebuilding here during the 1860s and 1870s. Old shops, like Victoria Row (plate 54), were completely remodelled according to fashions that were as up-to-date as the gowns, furs, jewelry, and china sold inside. The new shop-fronts and buildings were not substantial and massive symbols of financial and commercial success, like the banks and warehouses on Front and Wellington. Instead they were frankly extravagant confections of plate glass, cast iron, and carved stone—glittering and ornamental showcases for the best that money could buy.

Cast iron was the key to mid-nineteenth-century commercial design, as steel was to be in office buildings later. Many of the new warehouses built at this time used cast-iron columns to replace thick masonry piers and walls and to open up large floor areas for efficient use. In the new shops, cast iron also made larger display windows possible through its use in great beams that carried the weight of the upper floors of masonry buildings across wide areas of plate glass, and in the framing of the glass itself.

The most impressive of all the new buildings was the Golden Lion at 33-7 King Street East, a four-storey building in which two storeys of heavy masonry seemed to float above great panes of glass 30 feet high and 8 feet wide.[87] The Golden Lion was a dry-goods store founded in 1836, on the south side of King Street East, by Robert Walker and Thomas Hutchinson. In 1847 Walker built two stonefronted shops a few doors to the east (at 33-7) at the immense cost for the period of $30,000. Hutchinson left the partnership in 1853, four years after a golden lion had been taken as the firm's symbol, and Walker assumed complete control. By 1868—having replaced both shops the year before with the store illustrated here—he owned the largest retail business in Ontario.

The name of the architect is not known. Joseph Sheard and William Irving may have designed it, but it seems equally possible that an architect was brought in from the United States to carry out the work. The King Street façade was 52 feet wide between narrow party walls of brick. The cast-iron framework—cast in Toronto at the St Lawrence Foundry at the cost of $4,000—consisted of seven thin piers, faced with twisted colonnettes, that supported a wide arch over the main entrance at the centre of the façade and two eight-foot-wide arches over the main display windows on either side of the entrance.[88] (A tall, narrow arch at the west end of the façade marked the service entrance.) Each of the arches rose 30 feet, and below the decorated iron beam that completed the shop front and actually supported the weight of the upper storeys the spandrels were filled in with cast-iron foliage. The principal ornament was a gilded lion that crouched on a bracketed shelf over the main entrance. Except for the spandrels, and the colonnettes and their capitals, the cast-iron frame was simply detailed, giving full prominence to the goods displayed in the windows. Above the shop front it was a different matter. The cut-stone façade was framed with panelled quoins and topped by an architrave ornamented with rosettes in the frieze and a row of lions' heads along the cornice. Above was a balustrade, with trophy-like urns on the piers, and in the centre was a lion rampant in stone mounted on a pedestal decorated with heavy garlands. Everything—including the paired windows, arched on the third floor and set in wide frames on the fourth—was calculated to attract the eye from a distance, just as the vast shop windows caught the eye of the passerby.

The richness of the exterior of the Golden Lion was matched by the most elaborate of Toronto's early store interiors. The building extended 210 feet back to Colborne Street. Behind the four-storey block facing King was a two-storey section with a light-well in the centre covered by a dome—again of cast iron and plate glass—45 feet in diameter and rising 55 feet above the level of the first floor. Nothing like this dome had been attempted before in a Toronto store, and it was not matched until the building of the first large Eaton's store in 1883-6 and the Simpson's store in 1895.

In its later years the Golden Lion seems to have been little affected by the growing power of Eaton's and Simpson's. In 1892 the store was doubled in size when a copy of the original building was erected immediately to the east of the earlier block. However, the store closed in 1898 because there was no one in the Walker family to carry on the business. The buildings were briefly occupied by another department store, but in 1901 the Golden Lion and the adjacent buildings were demolished to make way for the first section of the King Edward Hotel. For once the changes were not the result of a decline in the area because the hotel—designed by E.J. Lennox in an Edwardian Baroque style that was as exuberant, in its way, as the design of the Golden Lion—continued for many years to serve fashionable Toronto society, as the store had done before.

The building on the left in plate 57 was one of the first large cast-iron shop fronts in Toronto, built in

57 KING STREET EAST (S), SHOWING THE GOLDEN LION, 1884

1865-6 for J.D. Merrich's dry-goods and clothing business at 47-9 King Street East. Later known as China Hall, it had two storeys of plate glass (like the Golden Lion) framed in cast iron, supporting a two-storey façade of cut stone with a high balustraded cornice and windows framed with wide mouldings and strapwork designs. The cast-iron framing of the second floor was designed as a row of panelled arches supported on thin colonnettes above a three-bayed shop front. Though the effect was undoubtedly elegant, it was neither as dramatic nor as structurally adventurous as the design of the Golden Lion, because of the smaller size of the plate-glass panels and the use of two wide cast-iron beams to support and brace the structure of the building.

Between the Golden Lion and China Hall, at 39-43 King Street East, was the photographic studio of Notman & Fraser. Established by William Notman, probably Canada's greatest photographer in the nineteenth century, and John A. Fraser, it was the most important branch of Notman's Montreal studio. The Toronto studio, run by Fraser, was first established at 120 King Street East.[89] In 1872 Fraser rented a double shop between the Golden Lion and China Hall and had it completely remodelled. As part of the alterations the third floor was completely cut away and in its place was erected a studio 45 feet wide by 30 feet. The front wall was replaced by panels of plate glass framed in cast-iron arches that rose one storey and then sloped back between panelled piers of masonry to form a conservatory-like room. The new windows permitted the maximum amount of north light, considered desirable for photography at the time, to flood into the studio. The arched panel that filled the centre of the façade served as an immense billboard above King Street; on it was inscribed, in large letters, 'Notman & Fraser Photographers to the Queen'. The new studio, which opened in 1873, became one of the popular rendezvous of fashionable Toronto, not only because of the photographer but also as the location of the early exhibitions of the Ontario Society of Artists. The first showing was held here in March 1873; others followed, and the studio was for a long time the only acceptable gallery in the city. The firm continued as Notman & Fraser until 1882/3, when it was renamed Fraser & Sears; it closed in 1886/7 and the business was taken over by another photographer. In later years the premises served a variety of uses, until they were demolished in 1892 to make way for the extension of the Golden Lion.

TORONTO STREET
Looking north, c.1875

Of all the streets in the downtown area, Toronto Street—running north and south, west of Church Street—was the most elegant. At the south end was the fashionable shopping promenade of King Street East; at the north end were the law courts at 57 Adelaide, which attracted legal and commercial offices to the whole district. In 1851 Cumberland & Storm designed the Seventh Post Office at 10 Toronto Street (preserved today as the headquarters of the Argus Corporation). With its carefully designed Ionic portico and fine stone detailing, it set a high standard for the later buildings, such as the Masonic Hall next to it (plate 60), the first building of the Union Loan and Savings Company (plate 62), and the Consumers' Gas buildings on the east side of the street (plate 64). Finally, the grouping was completed, in conscious emulation of a dramatic vista in Second Empire Paris, by the General Post Office (plate

65), at the top of the street on Adelaide. The view of the Post Office looking up Toronto Street is shown in plate 59 (a photograph taken in 1891).

Plate 58 shows the west side of the street before the construction of the second Union Savings and Loan Building at 26-30 (plate 63) in 1876-8, in the space next to the Masonic Hall. In the foreground, on the left, is the Whittemore Building, which faced King Street. Erected in 1846-7 by Matthew Sheard for E.F. Whittemore,[90] it was a commercial and office block that shows the influence of the Greek Revival in Toronto architecture, especially in the simplified classical piers of the shop fronts. The northernmost shop in the building, with an entrance on Toronto Street, was leased to C.A. Backus, bookseller and newsdealer, and was the favourite resort of newsmen who had their offices on King and Yonge. It was also William Lyon Mackenzie's

59 VIEW OF THE POST OFFICE, LOOKING UP TORONTO STREET, 1891

favourite spot to sit and reminisce about his career in the years after his return to Toronto in 1849. The Whittemore Building was demolished in 1886 and replaced by the Quebec Bank building (shown at the left edge of plate 59), which still survives, although shorn of its cornice and mutilated on the ground floor.

The Rice Lewis and Son hardware store, on the right side of the earlier photograph (plate 58), opened on the corner—appropriately enough, at the sign of the Padlock—in 1847.[91] It was erected in 1840 as part of the Wellington Buildings, a long row of rental shops on King Street. This view shows it as it was altered in 1867-8 by the addition of an up-to-date metal-framed and arched plate-glass shop front. The firm remained at this address until 1888, when it moved to a new brick-and-iron building on the northeast corner of Victoria and King (since demolished). The old premises passed through several hands until they were demolished in 1957/8, to be replaced by one more offering to 'the

great god CAR':[92] a parking platform. Replacement by parking lots seems to be the fate of much interesting and fine architecture in Toronto; but this has to be the worst and most positive act of vandalism in the city, actively disfiguring what was once one of Toronto's most important streets—and its most beautiful—with an aggressively ugly concrete skeleton.

60

THE MASONIC HALL
18-20 Toronto Street (W), 1868
1857-8 by William Kauffman

North of Cumberland & Storm's Seventh Post Office on Toronto Street stood the Masonic Hall. Originally intended as a concert hall when it was erected by A. and S. Nordheimer, the piano makers and music sellers,[93] its fourth-floor assembly rooms were probably altered to accommodate the nine Masonic lodges of Toronto even before it opened. There were also shops on the ground floor and twenty double offices on the second and third floors. With its pronounced verticals and stepped roof line, the style of the building struck Torontonians of the period as rather strange, used as they were to fairly standard exercises in the Classic and Gothic styles. Kauffman described the style as 'Modern Munich', and Nelson's *Handbook to Toronto* (1860) noted:

Its elaborately finished front calls to mind somewhat of the exterior of the stately cathedral at Munich—to which city its style of architecture is said to be peculiar. The richness, variety and beauty of its numberless perpendicular lines carry the eye at once upward to its entire height, and give lightness and elegance to the whole structure.[94]

A certain Victorian practicality tempered the abstract concepts of art and style in this building. Not only do cast-iron columns make the ground-floor shopfronts possible, supporting the weight of the stone façade on thin piers between wide panels of plate glass, but G.P. Ure admiringly notes, in his 1858 guide to the city, that the architect 'purposely avoided all heavy projections on the front to avoid the effect of heavy rain or frost. The most of the carving is consequently sunk or fretted in the stone for the same reason.'[95]

The assembly rooms for the Masonic Hall included a main hall, with furniture designed by Cumberland & Storm and a central lighting fixture by William Hay; an armoury; a number of reception rooms and vestibules; and the Chapter Room illustrated here, with furnishings designed by William Hay. It was 35 feet long and 20 feet wide, apsidal, and divided into two sections by an arched screen that was panelled with crimson damask. The screen was continued around the curved wall of the room to form the backs of the stalls for the Chapter. In the centre of the apse was a throne topped with a crimson canopy that was lined in blue and had a crown finial. The vaguely Gothic design of the stalls and the throne, the trompe-l'oeil painting of the walls—suggesting a stone wall decorated with arched panels—and the metal pennants on standards in front of the stalls were appropriate to the romantically medieval associations of the Order. The gilded and coloured plasterwork of the ceiling was much more contemporary in style, using the wide plaster mouldings and complex patterns of panels common in Renaissance-inspired buildings of the 1850s and 1860s.

In the latter part of the nineteenth century the expansion of the Masonic lodges and the spread of the city led to the establishment of new lodges and buildings outside the downtown area. Although the lodge rooms of the Masonic Hall were being used in 1899, by 1901 the entire fourth floor had been converted to office space.

In 1886/7 the building was taken over by the Canada Permanent Building and Savings Society (now the Canada Permanent Trust Company), founded in 1885, and the head office remained there until the company moved to its present head office at 320 Bay Street in 1930. The old building was later taken over by the Excelsior Life Insurance Company, which already owned a building at the corner of Toronto and Adelaide. In 1964-5 the Masonic Hall was demolished. The high-rise office tower, occupied by Excelsior Life, that appeared on the site replaced a building that was of interest in its own period by one that is not. The old Masonic Hall was the single Toronto example of an eccentric style and important as one of the first buildings in the city to make height and verticality dominant elements in the design, like the early skyscrapers. The new building stands on a useless raised terrace that has destroyed the continuous line of the streetscape—the setting of the remaining buildings on the street.

The Munich-inspired Gothic style of the Masonic Hall was the direct ancestor of the Gothicism of the present Canada Permanent Trust Building, for Nelson's description of the verticality of the first applies just as well to the verticality of the second. In the foyer of the 1930 building on Bay Street the old Hall was raised to iconic significance: on the cast-brass elevator doors—designed in an Egyptianesque Art Deco style—two kneeling figures in low relief display models of both the old and new buildings.

61 CHAPTER
ROOM,
c.1875

62

THE TORONTO UNION BLOCK
32-40 Toronto Street at Adelaide Street East (SW)
1872-3; probably by Langley, Langley & Burke

This mansarded office building was the first Toronto Street home of the Union Loan and Savings Company (which was founded in 1865 as the Union Permanent Building and Savings Society and changed its name in 1876). Built in a simplified Second Empire style in 1872-3, it is a prime example of the superior private and speculative construction on Toronto Street that was encouraged by the building of the General Post Office, also by Langley, across Adelaide Street (plate 65). Its tower marks the corner in the streetscape and echoes the central tower and the basic stylistic features of the Post Office. It remained the principal office of the company until 1878, when they moved to their new Gothic Revival building next door at 26-30 Toronto Street (plate 63).

By 1899 much of the Toronto Union Block was occupied by the Excelsior Life Insurance Company. Prospering on the site, they demolished both Union Loan buildings to make way for the present Beaux-Arts Classical skyscraper, built in 1914-15 to designs by E.J. Lennox. Although the sheer height of Lennox's building was unprecedented on Toronto Street, the old and new buildings show in their patrons a common interest in fine, individualized, rather than faceless architectural design—an element conspicuously lacking in the modern building that replaced the Masonic Hall on the left and in which Excelsior Life is now a principal tenant.

63

THE UNION LOAN AND SAVINGS COMPANY BUILDING
26-30 Toronto Street (W)
1876-8 by Langley, Langley & Burke

The first home of the Union Loan and Savings Company was the Union Block at 32-40 Toronto Street (plate 62). After a period of success in the mid 1870s, it commissioned Henry Langley's firm to design a new building, at 26-30 Toronto Street, that would dignify its prosperity—and supplement its wealth by providing rental income.[96] Clothed in the High Victorian Gothic forms that were similar to the detailing of the church designs that were Langley's speciality (and suggested the Victorian belief in business morality), the design was centred on a tower, to give the building prominence in the streetscape. Inside were twenty suites of offices, well lit by generous windows that actually took up most of the wall area. All were designed with stilted heads—whether segmental, flat, or arched—popular in the

1860s and 1870s, that were carried on Gothic colonnettes (with characteristically exaggerated bases, capitals, and bands round the shafts). This detailing tended to obscure the fact that the façade of Ohio greystone was a grid decorated with carved work in New York brownstone, with column shafts of New Brunswick granite—both materials prized for their rich texture and natural colours.

The building later became the home of the Excelsior Life Insurance Company. With the Union Block to the north (on the left), it was demolished in 1914 to make way for the company's new skyscraper, designed by E.J. Lennox, which still stands at the corner of Adelaide and Toronto Streets.

THE EAST SIDE OF TORONTO STREET
Between Court Street and Adelaide Street East, c.1895

In the 1890s the east side of Toronto Street was lined with three-storey office buildings, all but one built in the 1870s. Displaying the wide range of architectural styles that characterized the eclectic taste of the period, each of these buildings was a direct result of the belief that a prosperous corporation had an obligation to build in a manner that would be a credit to the city as well as a symbol of commercial success. In spite of the differences in style, there is a sense of co-ordination in the appreciation of fine materials and craftsmanship, and in the general regularity of alignment and height. With the notable exception of the 1876 office of the Consumers' Gas Company (in the centre of this view), the buildings are more important to the streetscape as a group than they are individually.

On the right in this photograph is a section of the Building and Loan Chambers, built in 1879 and probably designed by Langley, Langley & Burke. Like the firm's Union Loan and Savings Company Building on the opposite side of the street (plate 63), it is Gothic Revival in style; but its fawn stone details, contrasting with the red brick walls, made it much more eye-catching.

On the left side of the photograph—and poles apart in style—is the Trust and Loan Building of 1871, at the southeast corner of Adelaide and Toronto Streets. It was designed in a plain but finely proportioned Renaissance Revival style, with the height of the block divided regularly by string courses and ornamented sparely by pedimented windows. It is a late example of the style used by Kivas Tully for the Bank of Montreal at Front and Yonge Streets (plate 2): its conservatism and reticence still satisfied the taste of some in Toronto's financial community at a time when more striking buildings had become popular. (The building survives today, with a porch added at the turn of the century, but unfortunately it has been shorn of the cornice and parapet that completed the design.) Next to the Trust and Loan Building stood Temple Chambers at 21-3 Toronto Street, another office building erected in 1873. Its façade was designed in a much more elaborate version of the Renaissance style, showing the influence on Toronto architecture of the richly detailed forms of Langley's General Post Office of 1869-73, at the head of the street (plate 65). The Trust and Loan Building and Temple Chambers were erected on the site of the Adelaide Street Methodist Church, built in 1833 as York's second Methodist Church and demolished in 1870. When the new buildings were put up on the site, they were set back slightly from the streetline and provided with an areaway. This not only allowed light

to enter the 'English basements', but also afforded a more generous view of the Post Office at the head of Toronto Street.

The two other buildings shown in this view, at 17 and 19 Toronto Street, were owned by the Consumers' Gas Company. It was founded in 1847 to take over a franchise to light the city that had been granted six years earlier to Albert Furniss of Montreal. By 1884 it was supplying Toronto, through 110 miles of main lines, with 240 million cubic feet of coal gas per year.[97] (This was manufactured in their plant, at the corner of Berkeley and Front, which still survives in part.) The first office, the brick building second from the right— the date of which is uncertain—was at 17 Toronto Street. It was small, compared with its later neighbours, but distinguished by the horizontally channelled rustication of the stone piers on the ground floor and the heavy stone lintels carried on scrolled consoles—more elaborate types of Renaissance detail that became popular in the 1850s and 1860s. However, the basic form, under the expensive stone detailing, is not very different from Late Georgian commercial buildings found elsewhere in Toronto. Indeed, the elliptical arches over the windows and the Rococo scrolls of the iron work on the second-floor balcony have the elegance and grace of Regency-influenced forms that remained popular in Toronto well into the 1850s.

In 1876 Consumers' Gas purchased the former York County Registry Office at 19 Toronto Street and built a new head-office building in its place.[98] It provided more space but was, above all, a solid and irrefutable statement of the company's strength even in times of relative difficulty. The design, possibly by Grant & Dick, is again Renaissance in inspiration; however, the emphasis is not on historical allusion but on opulence. The details form a logical pattern in a richly detailed tapestry of honey-coloured stone above the ground floor: fluted pilasters, paired and single; arched windows; carved keystones above the third-floor windows; a high cornice and parapet; and the heavy central cresting that rises above the façade. The street level is enlivened with polished red granite columns. In 1899 the façade was doubled in width when D.B. Dick built a large addition for the gas company on the site of Number 17.[99] This repeats the window patterns and cornice of the 1876 block (although the cresting of the earlier building was removed), but it is dominated by two doorways: one into the company's offices—wide, and framed by columns, with elaborate mouldings and a broad pediment in the Edwardian manner; and another, leading to rented offices on the upper floor, that is tall

64

and narrow for its height and surprisingly chaste in comparison with the other details of the façade. On each floor above the door, oval windows in monumental and rather tortured frames mark the rise of the stair and elevator.

The architecture of the Consumers' Gas Company dominated the east side of Toronto Street. Its visual importance was matched in fact as the company expanded into Temple Chambers, the Trust and Loan Building and, in 1903, around the corner into the remodelled west wing of Cumberland's Court House on Adelaide Street. After the rebuilding of Number 17 in 1899, the only major change was the replacement in the early 1960s of Temple Chambers by the one-storey bay

window of the 'Blue Flame Room', which jarringly broke the visual and historical continuity of the streetscape. But for the most part the Company has taken good care of its architectural heritage. The future of the Toronto Street buildings is not secure, however, for Consumers' Gas moved its head office out of the city core in 1975-6. Though proposals have been made for them, there has been no final settlement.

The Building and Loan Chambers to the south was demolished in 1961 and replaced by the present highrise, one of the most forgettable contributions of modern architecture to the city that seems to ignore, as if by definite plan, the high architectural standards of nineteenth-century Toronto Street.

THE GENERAL POST OFFICE
36 Adelaide Street East (N), opposite Toronto Street, c.1900
1869-73 by Henry Langley

The General Post Office was the majestic building that terminated the vista as one looked up Toronto Street. The eighth post office to be built in Toronto, it was the first major public building in the city to be commissioned by the federal government. It opened at the height of Toronto's economic boom of the 1860s and early 1870s and became a symbol of prosperity—both the Dominion's and the city's. The post office was the finest and most important public building of Langley's career and, like Government House (plate 29), it was Second Empire in style.[100] The three-storey frontispiece, with paired columns and crowned by a pediment, is derived from Perrault's seventeenth-century colonnade at the Louvre, while the high mansard roofs of the corner pavilions* and the bulbous dome over the centre recall Visconti and Lefuel's additions to the Louvre in the 1850s, giving the building more than a touch of Parisian grandeur. As light and shadow played across the stone of the decoratively complex portico and cornices, the recessed windows, and the channelled rustication, the façade took on a quality of vibrant life that was matched by few buildings in the city. This was enhanced by such fine carved details as the royal arms over the main entrance, and a keystone modelled on a human head in each of the arches.

It remained the central unit in the city's postal system and the principal federal office building in the city until the completion of the Dominion Public Building on Front Street West, between Yonge and Bay, in 1937. After the reorganization of the postal system made it secondary in importance to the new Postal Station 'A'; it was known simply as the Adelaide Street Postal Station. In 1958 this postal station moved to temporary quarters on Church Street and Langley's building was demolished, to be replaced by the present high-rise complex.[101]

The new building marked the beginning of the destruction of Toronto Street—not because it was modern, and not just because it replaced Langley's impressive building, but because it showed a complete disregard for the dramatic possibilities of the location. The connected towers of the new building do not terminate the vista: they simply block it. Their asymmetrical arrangement was apparently designed to be seen only from Adelaide Street: from Toronto Street one sees part of a featureless wall of glass and steel, without a single accent that might have climaxed the view. Given this example of the federal government's insensitivity to the special character of the location—an attitude that stands in remarkable contrast to that of the 1860s government—it is not surprising that private owners followed with the demolition of the Masonic Hall (plate 60) and other nineteenth-century buildings on Toronto Street, replacing them with equally characterless 'modern' buildings.

---

*The canopy on the left shelters the Ladies' Entrance.

5

THE WILLIAM CAWTHRA HOUSE
275 Bay Street at King (NE), 1868
1852 by William Irving and Joseph Sheard

This was without doubt the finest and most elegant town house built in Toronto. Torontonians, and writers on Canada in the mid-nineteenth century, were fond of comparing local buildings and streets with the finest in England and on the Continent. Much of this was simple puffery, but in the case of the Cawthra house there was more than adequate reason for such a comparison. The elegant balance of the design and the confident, extravagant detailing call to mind several great town houses not only in Britain, France, and Germany, but also in New York.

The Cawthra family, headed by Joseph Cawthra, came to Upper Canada from Geysley, Yorkshire, in 1803. Although he was granted land in Port Credit in 1804, he settled in York in 1806 and established the family fortune by supplying the British army during the War of 1812.[102] His son, William Cawthra, inherited a substantial fortune based on land holdings in downtown Toronto.[103] A financier who became very rich himself, he also took part in the public life of the city, being elected alderman to the first city council in 1834 and again in 1836 and serving later on the Board of Trustees for the Common Schools. It is quite possible that his view of himself as a commercial success influenced both the grandeur of the house and the choice of a very prominent site close to the centre of the city, especially as it is known that he later conducted his business affairs from the house. His lot, which originally measured 146 feet (along Bay) by 56 feet (along King), was purchased in 1851,[104] when the commercial district was already spreading westward along King east of Yonge.

The architect usually credited with the design of the house is Joseph Sheard. But there is good reason to believe that the design was actually drawn by William Irving, Sheard's younger partner.[105] Irving was trained in Edinburgh before he came to Toronto, where he married Sheard's daughter and remained in partnership with Sheard through the 1860s. In its Greek Revival detailing, the Cawthra house has several characteristics that were typical of work done in Scotland and Northern England in the 1840s and early 1850s: smooth wall surfaces, made possible by fitting the large blocks of light-coloured sandstone precisely; and contrasting sharply cut mouldings, with crisply and beautifully carved details, which frame doors and windows and (in pilasters and cornices) define the outlines of the building. It is possible that William Cawthra and his wife also played a part in the design of the house. Cawthra had strong commercial connections in New York, and the great marble mansions of that city's merchant princes might well have influenced his own taste.

The basic design of the façades on both Bay and King is fairly conventional: the walls are divided into three bays by tall panelled Corinthian pilasters, the centre pairs of which support a small pediment on each façade; the central pilasters on Bay frame a recessed porch with Corinthian columns, set *in antis*, and a decorated pediment.* The deeply shadowed forms of the carved detail bring the façade to life and markedly distinguish it from the drier, more linear, detailing of the Seventh Post Office on Toronto Street by Cumberland & Storm.

Construction of the house began in late 1851, but two years passed before the family occupied it. (The delay might have been due to the time required for the completion of the decorative carving.) William Cawthra lived there until his death. His widow continued in residence until 1884/5, when she moved to a new but equally palatial house on the northwest corner of Jarvis and Isabella. By 1885 King Street West was the centre of Toronto's commercial district and there was little question of the house's continuing as a residence. It was occupied from 1885 to 1907 by the Toronto branch of Molson's Bank and then from 1908/9 to 1924/5 by the Sterling Bank as its head office. The grandeur of the house provided an appropriate setting for both banks, although most of the interiors were completely renovated. Some time in this period the site was acquired by the Canada Life Assurance Company, whose head office was next door on King Street.

In 1929 Canada Life announced that it would be moving to a new building on University Avenue and the site of the Cawthra house was put up for sale.[106] It was bought by the Bank of Nova Scotia, which announced the construction, to begin in 1931, of a 27-storey skyscraper at King and Bay. The impending demolition of the house roused the first real concern for Toronto's disappearing architectural heritage. With considerable public and newspaper support, the Ontario Association of Architects and the members of the Cawthra family sought ways to save the building. It was accepted as inevitable that the house would have to be moved—although today a strong case could be made for preserving it on its original site—and the Cawthra family offered to meet the costs if a new location could be found and adequate funding for its maintenance ensured. Suggestions that the rebuilt house be used as a public library

---

*Owing to extreme foreshortening, a lower two-storey service wing set back from the Bay Street façade cannot be seen in plate 66 (the edge of its cornice is visible, however), Further north was the stable yard behind a high wall.

were rejected as impossible by George H. Locke and the city's library board, and proposals that it be used as a civic museum and a home for a local historical society fell through because of lack of money. However, by 1931 the need for an immediate solution was delayed when the Bank of Nova Scotia decided to postpone the construction of its new building because of the deepening Depression. After this came the Second World War, and it was not until late 1946, when work on the Bank of Nova Scotia building was begun, that the Cawthra house was again threatened. A solution could still not be found, although everyone seemed to agree on the need for preservation. Anthony Adamson, a member of the Cawthra family, offered to pay the cost of taking down the façades and re-erecting them at the Royal Ontario Museum. But his offer was rejected and demolition proceeded. Mr Adamson salvaged the mantel from the drawing room, the columns that flanked the entrance, and other fragments of the stonework. The stone details were re-erected as an ornamental ruin, first in the garden of Grove Farm, Joseph Cawthra's estate at Port Credit, and recently in the grounds of the Adamson home in Rosedale. Nothing else remains of William Cawthra's house. But the story of its destruction remains an object lesson in the need for strong, properly funded, architectural preservation legislation in Toronto.

67

THE WILLIAM LYON MACKENZIE HOUSE
194 York Street, between Richmond and Queen (W), c.1885
1830

At the same time as the élite of Toronto's establishment were building mansions along Front Street, a more varied and rather motley community was developing along York, Bay, Adelaide, and Richmond Streets. In this area large and small middle- and working-class houses were built, mixed with commercial and some manufacturing buildings. Many of the houses were built in rows, but a few had large gardens.

William Lyon Mackenzie (1795-1861) rented this red brick house on York Street in 1835,[107] and it was from an office behind the dining room that he published *The Constitution* (first issued on 4 July 1836) and no doubt made plans for the abortive Rebellion of 1837. The house was built in 1830 by Major Andrew Patton and was severely plain, in the Late Georgian tradition, with nothing but the basic symmetry of the front, the rectangular stone lintels over the openings, and the shutters on the windows to give it architectural character. Nevertheless it was a comfortable small house, built close to the street in the British manner. It was described by Mackenzie in an advertisement placed in *The Constitution* on 11 January 1837, when he was trying to sell the lease, as

> substantial and well-finished, with two storeys above ground and an underground storey, Cellars, Cellar-Kitchen, excellent Drains etc. — On the Ground Floor there are a Dining Room, Parlour or Library, with a Sitting Room and Five bedrooms upstairs.
>
> The Garden is spacious, in good order, and filled with currants, raspberries, gooseberries, grapes, with choice fruit trees. There is a stable for two horses, a woodshed and a yard. Also a well of the purest water to be found in Toronto.

Gardens were important at the time because they provided food and safeguarded the wells that supplied the houses of the city before the introduction of an efficient public water system.*

Mackenzie left the York Street house on Sunday, 3 December 1837, to join the other rebels at Montgomery's tavern on Yonge Street north of Eglinton Avenue. After the collapse of the rebellion he fled to the United States. Mrs Mackenzie remained with the family in the house, under constant supervision, until 29 December, when they joined Mackenzie in the U.S. Mackenzie had left all his files in the house, slung from the ceiling of a second-floor bedroom (unseen by the officers who repeatedly searched the house). On Sunday the 10th the family took advantage of the guards' absence at church to burn the lot.

The later history of the house is confused. When this photograph was taken it was in good condition, and some of the garden still survived. Apparently the house was taken down in the 1890s and replaced by a row of shops. These were demolished in 1952/3 and the site has long been a parking lot. Today Mackenzie is commemorated by the Mackenzie House Museum at 82 Bond Street, where he lived in 1859-61, after his return from exile. It is unfortunate, however, that nothing marks the site of the York Street house, where many of the events for which he is best known were planned.

---

*The gardens behind and on either side of such houses, separating them from their neighbours—made possible by the generous size of the original lot divisions (especially south of Queen Street and west of Yonge)—gave the city a spacious openness that can be seen in many of the early views and was very different from the closely built cityscapes of Britain.

68

THE UNITED EMPIRE CLUB
110 King Street West (N), west of York, c.1875
1874-5 by Grant & Dick

Two buildings marked the west end of fashionable King Street: the Rossin House on the southeast corner of King and York—the largest of Toronto's hotels and the principal competitor of the Queen's on Front Street (plate 10); and the United Empire Club, seen here in a photograph taken from the front balcony of the Rossin House.

The United Empire Club was founded in 1874—on the model of the Carlton Club in London—as the social and unofficial political headquarters of the federal and provincial Conservative parties in Toronto. There were several other men's clubs in Toronto organized in imitation of English clubs. The Toronto Club, founded in 1835, was the oldest and the National Club, founded in 1874, was the Liberal counterpart of the United Empire Club. Although the middle 1870s were not the best years for the Conservative party because of the Pacific Scandal, the new club began with more than 300 members from the cream of Toronto's old and new wealth and its rising professional class—including, of course, Sir John A. Macdonald. Each member was assessed an annual subscription of twenty dollars, and almost the first act of the trustees was to purchase a large site on King Street West (previously owned by the Baldwins, Liberals to the core) and, between April 1874 and April 1875, to build the large clubhouse illustrated here.[108]

The architects of the new building were the Toronto firm of Grant & Dick. (Both Robert Grant and David B. Dick were members of the club, as were other Toronto architects—all of whom would have found that it offered useful opportunities for meeting new and former clients.) It was easily the largest and best equipped of Toronto's clubhouses. Four large shops on the ground floor, flanking the pedimented entrance and with double-arched plate-glass windows, helped to support the cost of the building. The club occupied the second floor and possibly also the third, and used the large garden behind. The Carlton Club, which was undoubtedly well known to many of the members of the United Empire, was 'the King of Clubs', magnificently Venetian in its design. The United Empire Club could hardly afford to match its model; but in their design Grant & Dick avoided the polychrome Gothic Revival and the French-inspired Second Empire style that were so popular in Toronto at the time, choosing instead the rather old-fashioned ornamented Renaissance style. The round arches of the windows (with prominent voussoirs), the moulded quoins at the corners, and the bracketed cornice are all close in form to the basic patterns of British club architecture as they had been established by Sir Charles Barry and Sidney Smirke (the architect of the Carlton Club) in the 1830s and 1840s. (Even the second-floor bay window, opening from the club room, was a standard feature of London clubs, designed to allow the members to survey the passing scene from the comfort of their easy chairs.) At the same time the style of the clubhouse had obvious affinities with many of the banks and commercial buildings erected in Toronto in the 1860s and 1870s, such as the Ontario Bank (plate 48) and the Consumers' Gas Company office on Toronto Street (see plate 64). The whole design was very carefully set off in the streetscape, and distinguished from its neighbours, by its large scale and the two corner pavilions that rose above the cornice as short towers linked by a balustrade. These towers are reminiscent of the similar pavilions that were a basic feature of the Second Empire style and that ornamented the General Post Office (plate 65) and the Grand Opera House (plate 73) and may have been included intentionally to balance the mansarded corner pavilions of the Rossin House across the street.

The elegance of the new building, and of the furniture specially designed for it, was a nine-day wonder in Toronto. Unfortunately the expense strained the club's resources to the limit and poor management in the later years resulted in its being closed in 1881. (The Conservative mantle was assumed by the Albany Club, founded in 1882, which in the beginning made a conspicuous virtue of Spartan surroundings.) After standing vacant, the building on King Street was taken over about 1884 by the Canadian Express Company and the CPR. For a short time in 1893-4 the club rooms were occupied by the National Club; and in 1898 the building was purchased by the North American Life Assurance Company. The interior was altered at this time by Langley & Langley, but the exterior remained largely unchanged, until the building was demolished in 1932. North American Life then erected on the site a fine Art Deco office building designed by the Toronto firm of Marani, Lawson & Paisley, which stood until late 1975, when it too was demolished for the present First Canadian Place.

THE CANADIAN BANK OF COMMERCE
25 King Street West at Jordan (SW), c.1895
1889-90 by R.A. Waite

The Canadian Bank of Commerce was founded in 1867 by Senator William McMaster. By the 1880s its first office, on the southeast corner of Yonge and Colborne, had become seriously overcrowded and the bank purchased a larger site at 25 King Street West. The new building, shown here in a photograph taken in the 1890s, was designed by R.A. Waite,[109] the British-trained architect from Buffalo who designed the Legislative Buildings in Queen's Park (1886-92). Waite was not popular among Toronto architects because of his involvement in the controversy that had surrounded the design competition, but his success with the Legislative Buildings brought him several important commissions in both Toronto and Montreal.

The Bank of Commerce was one of a small group of new buildings designed at about the same time—including the Board of Trade Building (plate 7), Waite's own Canada Life Building at 40 King Street West (1890; demolished), and the still-standing Confederation Life Building (1889-90 by Knox, Elliott and Jarvis)—that established new standards of size and richness for office and financial buildings. Soaring (for so it seemed to Torontonians at the time) seven-and-a-half tall storeys above King Street, it dwarfed the neighbouring three- and four-storey commercial buildings dating from the late 1870s, early 1880s, and before, and clearly showed the influence of the first skyscrapers built in Chicago, New York, and other American cities. The height was made possible by the most modern of structural skeletons—steel and iron beams and columns—that actually carried the weight of the brick and stone walls and the fireproof terra-cotta floors.

In his design for the exterior of the building Waite outlined and emphasized the height with three towers that rose at each of the outside corners. The two on the right and left in this view appropriately marked the main and side entrances, and the stairs and elevators to the upper floors. The higher and much more prominent tower at the intersection of King and Jordan, which housed the offices of the branch and general managers, stepped boldly out into the streetscape and rose above the main cornice of the building to break the regularity of the skyline. Its strong verticality was echoed by the series of tall arches on either face that lighted the two-storey banking room inside, and by the vertical piers and pilasters that framed the windows of the upper floors. The lowest two levels of the tower, and of the main façades, were finished in light brown sandstone: cut in large, smooth blocks at the basement level and elaborately carved around the door frames and arches and in the spandrels. Above these levels the walls were finished in fine red brick, with only the trimming detail executed in stone. The change in colour made the lower storeys seem solid and strong enough to support the upper floors.

In Waite's design the corner tower gives the building a majestically picturesque character. Waite described the building as 'a modern example of the Italian Renaissance'. However, while he included several historical details—such as the broad cornice lines that wrap around the façades, seeming to tie the verticals together, and the patterns of pilasters and arches that frame certain of the windows—he did not intend to recreate a building of the fifteenth or sixteenth centuries and these details do not encumber his design.

When the building opened in January 1890, it was not its engineering or height that attracted the most attention but the costly materials used, and their elaborate detailing and finishes. Steps of polished black marble led from the street to a spacious vestibule with a wainscot of coloured African marbles. A second stair of Numidian marble, with polished metal and wooden detail, led from the vestibule to the raised banking hall, a galleried room 58 by 53 feet and 28 feet high. Above the ceiling were specially designed trusses that allowed a column-free interior in spite of the several floors above—a major innovation in Toronto at the time. Panelled in Santo Domingo and Mexican mahoganies and detailed with the polished art metal work that was very much the specialty of the period, the banking hall was the epitome of corporate magnificence—a selling point when the upper floor were rented and the building became one of Toronto's most fashionable office addresses. The 1885-6 Bank of Montreal (see plate 5) had been the first of Toronto's banks to achieve palatial scale and finish. Waite's Bank of Commerce Building was, if anything, *more* elaborate, and became a model for much of the office construction that followed; while its height and fine materials anticipated the towers built at King and Bay in the 1960s and 1970s.

During the life of Waite's building it was extensively renovated by Darling & Pearson, but it was demolished in 1928. In 1929-31 Darling & Pearson supervised the construction of the skyscraper that replaced it, which more than matched its predecessor in quality of design and finish.*

---

*Designed by the New York firm of York and Sawyer, this building has been renovated and is part of the Commerce Court complex.

69

THE BANK OF NOVA SCOTIA, TORONTO MAIN BRANCH
39-41 King Street West (S), c.1950
1902 by Darling & Pearson

At the turn of the century, bankers approached questions of architecture with a mixture of pretension and pride—pretension about their public importance, and justifiable pride in their success. In Canada, more than in Britain or the United States, the power of the handful of banks that were chartered by the federal government to operate nationally was real, and the pride of their owners out of all proportion to the size of the country. The architectural display of these qualities could easily have been heavy and humourless, in spite of all the fine materials used. Fortunately there were architects, such as Frank Darling of Darling & Pearson, who could temper pomp and circumstance with style and drama.

When the Bank of Nova Scotia erected this building on King Street West in 1902,[110] it was in effect moving the head office from Halifax to challenge the giants of 'Upper Canada'. Land was at a premium in Toronto's financial district. Without the possibility of either height or width on a narrow site in the centre of the block, Darling designed a façade that separated itself from its neighbours, rather theatrically, by stepping back to the swagged doorcase between tall proscenium-like side walls that defined a tiny forecourt (originally separated from the street by high iron railings with central gates). Above this lower storey rose a portico that enclosed the arched Palladian window of the boardroom under a bow-fronted balcony. The result was a succession of receding planes that dramatically exaggerated the effect of the perspective. The precedents are found in early eighteenth-century stage design and in the Neo-Baroque work of the British architect Richard Norman Shaw.*[111] The over-all effect is frankly grandiose—like Handel arranged by Sousa for a brass band. Although five such buildings in a row would be chaotic, one acts as a powerful antidote to the monotony and dryness of design in the average downtown streetscape.

Passing through the entrance, the customer entered first a low vestibule and then the spacious, finely detailed banking hall. Around this hall Darling placed a colonnade of paired Ionic half-columns on a high base that repeated the monumental dimensions of the exterior portico. The length of the ceiling was divided into three parts: a glazed dome over the centre, a glazed segmental vault at the front, and a more conventional plaster vault in the rear. Not only were the skylights an

*Shaw's Gaiety Theatre (1900) in The Strand may have been a direct influence on Darling's design, but it is the Piccadilly Hotel—begun in 1904, two years after Darling's building—which, though vastly larger in scale, most closely resembles the Bank of Nova Scotia in style and compositional principle.

71 THE BANKING HALL, c.1965

ingenious solution to the problem of lighting the banking hall, but they gave a sense of unroofed space that echoed the open forecourt. Mundane office space was stacked behind the main façade above the boardroom and in six floors over the rear section of the banking hall. In 1908 Darling & Pearson added a four-storey block behind the whole building (on Melinda Street).[112]

In 1929, seeking more space and probably a more contemporary image, the bank commissioned John M. Lyle to design an office tower at 44 King Street West (finally executed in 1946-51 by Mathers & Haldenby). When Lyle's building was completed, the Bank left 39-41 King Street. After a brief period as the downtown branch of the Toronto Public Library, the building was taken over by the Canadian Bank of Commerce. Finally in 1969 it was demolished to make way for Commerce Court.

THE BANK OF TORONTO
55-67 King Street West at Bay (SW), c.1913
1911-13 by Carrere & Hastings, New York; Eustace G. Bird, Toronto, associate

The Bank of Toronto began to plan a new head-office building in 1901. There was no thought of using the site of Kauffman's 1863 building at Wellington and Church (plate 44) because Toronto's business district was developing westward along King. The new site, with a frontage of 120 feet on King and 134 feet on Bay, was purchased in 1902. (It represented the largest land assembly for redevelopment in the city to that date.) As there were leases for existing buildings on the site that did not expire until January 1911, construction did not begin until January 1912.

The new building was designed by the New York firm of Carrere & Hastings, working with Eustace G. Bird of Toronto as associate architect.[113] The choice would not have endeared the bank to Toronto's architects, who were at this time very nationalistic and defensive in the face of intense competition from large American firms. But Carrere & Hastings was—with McKim, Mead & White (also of New York)—one of the two most accomplished and respected firms of the period. Any client of theirs could be certain that its new building would not only be an architectural event and have high prestige value, but would be well planned and meticulously detailed.* Carrere & Hastings were known in Toronto for their work in New York, and especially for their buildings at the Pan-American Exposition, held in Buffalo in 1904. That same year they prepared an unexecuted plan for a new Union Station in Toronto, and in 1905 established themselves in the city with the Trader's Bank (still standing) at 67 Yonge Street, followed by the first Royal Bank Building on King Street East in 1906 (demolished); and the Royal Alexandra Theatre (designed with John M. Lyle, who had completed his training in their office) in 1906-7. Before 1910 the firm produced several branch banks across the country for the Dominion Bank, the Royal Bank, and the Bank of Toronto.

In a period of varied and eclectic architecture, Carrere & Hastings were noted for the use in almost all their buildings of French Renaissance forms—particularly those of the late-seventeenth, eighteenth, and early-nineteenth centuries. The design of the Bank of Toronto was based on that of the Paris Bourse, built in 1808-26 by A.T. Bronigniart.[114] Both street façades—finished in grey Tennessee marble—were dominated by large-scale colonnades of fluted Corinthian columns (ten along King and eleven along Bay), which stood on a panelled pedestal separated by balustrades. They were elevated above the traffic on a smooth-faced plinth, taller than a man, that was interrupted only by the triple-arched entrance on King Street and small basement windows. (The high plinth expressed in the most direct terms the impregnable security of the building.) At each end of the two façades, smooth-surfaced piers framed the colonnades, emphasizing the corners and setting off the bank's modern Classicism from the older buildings next to it. With the strong horizontal lines of the plinth, the high entablature, and the parapet, and with the equally strong verticals of the corner piers and the colonnade, the building had a sharply geometric character. It stood like a magnificent pavilion—more self-confident than a temple—that was a complete work of art in its monumental elegance and in its balance of elaboration with simplicity.

One of the reasons the architects chose French Renaissance forms as the inspiration for their work was the ease with which contemporary needs could be adapted to the basic patterns of the style. Here the tall columns articulated the vertical elements of the bank's steel framework; and in the space between the columns there was ample room for the large areas of window that lit the space inside. The simple form is in fact rather deceptive, for the building actually contained five levels of offices and two full basements of vault and service space. Nevertheless, the soaring height of the colonnade and the double tier of windows—arched and square-headed—were a clear evocation of the splendid two-storeyed, galleried banking hall that formed the centre of the building. Roofed with a high coved skylight of bronze and glass and finished with multi-coloured marbles and polished bronze fittings, it was the largest, and easily the finest, of the city's many elaborate commercial interiors.

The new head office was completed in 1913 and remained the bank's principal building until 1955, when the Bank of Toronto amalgamated with the Dominion Bank to form the present Toronto-Dominion Bank. Shortly afterwards, the various business functions of the head office and the Toronto main branch were planned to be combined in one building. This culminated in the design of the present Toronto-Dominion Centre (1965). The Carrere & Hastings building was demolished as part of this scheme and replaced by the present glass-and-steel banking pavilion.

In the bank's search for the most modern of new cor-

---

*Similar considerations encouraged the appointment of Mies van der Rohe as consulting architect to John B. Parkin Associates and Bregman & Hamann, both of Toronto, in the building of the Toronto-Dominion Centre.

2

porate images, the architects received little, if any, encouragement to preserve the older building and include
it in a new scheme. The loss, which marked the beginning of a seven- or eight-year period of frenetic
redevelopment in downtown Toronto, has a poignant
aspect, because the new pavilion is uncannily similar to
the old bank in aims and methods, and in its attention to
fine materials and craftsmanship: it stands as a ghostly
reminder of lost splendour. Even though the Toronto-
Dominion Centre is a classic in its own right, it is very
difficult to regard the demolition of the older building—
at a time when its value as a work of art and as an element in the context of the city was widely
recognized—as anything but a prime example of
corporate vandalism.

THE GRAND OPERA HOUSE
9-15 Adelaide Street West (S),c.1875
1873-4 by Thomas R. Jackson

The Grand Opera House was the largest and best equipped of Toronto's nineteenth-century theatres. Several theatres served the city at different times, providing space for the troops of actors, musicians, and minstrels that toured Ontario and adjacent parts of the U.S. from bases in New York, Buffalo, and Montreal. Most of these theatres were makeshift conversions of earlier buildings, like the one that occupied the ballroom of Frank's Hotel, on the northwest corner of Market and Colborne Streets, from about 1820 to 1830. The first specially built theatre was John Ritchie's Royal Lyceum, which opened in 1848 on the south side of King, west of Bay. It was destroyed by fire in 1873 and in that year a company was formed to build the Grand Opera House; it was headed by Mrs Charlotte Morrison, a retired actress who had been managing the Lyceum at the time of its destruction.

The company appointed Thomas R. Jackson of New York as architect for the new theatre. Described as the architect of the Academy of Music in New York—that city's premier opera house before the opening of the Metropolitan in 1883—he probably directed the rebuilding of the Academy after it was burnt in 1866.[115] Though the Grand Opera House was considerably smaller than the Academy of Music, the Second Empire style of Jackson's brick and stone building had an undeniable air of festive and public grandeur, with its multi-layered frontispiece surmounted by the royal coat of arms and topped by a tower-like mansard and flagpole; this was framed by mansarded pavilions to either side. The front block—in which the first floor was rented as shops and the upper floors as offices—was simply a decorative and profitable façade that concealed from the passer-by the more irregular bulk of the auditorium and the stage, with its fly tower. The arched portal of the theatre entrance gave access to a corridor running back 50 feet to the main foyer, 65 feet wide and 24 feet deep, where the box offices were located. Theatre-goers passed straight through the foyer and a small lobby to enter the orchestra; stairs at the east and west ends of this foyer led up to the Dress Circle and two balconies. The domed auditorium seated 1,323. Patrons in the orchestra and balconies sat on folding seats—a relatively new development at the time—and those in the Dress Circle and the four boxes on each side of the stage sat in more comfortable arm chairs. Standing room and folding camp-stools accommodated an additional 500.

The most significant part of Jackson's contribution—and what distinguished the Grand from its older competitors in Toronto and the numerous 'opera houses' built across Ontario in the 1870s—were the stage and technical facilities. The stage itself measured 53 feet by 65 feet, about two-thirds the size of the auditorium. There was a sunken orchestra pit and a two-storey block containing dressing rooms, offices, and a green room. The entire building was heated by steam, and all the gas fixtures—a chandelier in the centre of the auditorium dome, chandeliers under the balconies, and wall sconces—could be turned on, and lit automatically by an electrical spark. (Without such control it was impossible to darken and then relight an auditorium, a practice introduced in new European theatres of the 1860s and 1870s.) Most important, Jackson provided the stage with two fire hydrants and the auditorium with a system of fire escapes that he believed could empty the entire theatre in two minutes.

The Grand Opera House was completed in the summer of 1874 and opened on 23 September 1874 with a gala performance of Sheridan's *School for Scandal* under the patronage of Lord Dufferin, the Governor General, with Mrs Morrison herself returning to the boards to play the role of Lady Teazle. The new theatre became one of the city's fashionable social centres; but it was not a financial success and in 1876 it was sold at auction to Alexander Manning. Three years later, on 29 November 1879, it was gutted by fire—in spite of Jackson's precautions. Manning immediately engaged George H. Lalor, of the Toronto firm of Lalor & Martin, to rebuild it. The fire had not destroyed the exterior walls, and Lalor's work, which began on 9 December 1879, was completed in February; the new building resembled Jackson's in almost every respect, except for an increase in the seating to 1,750. The theatre re-opened on 9 February 1880 with Adelaide Neilson starring in *Romeo and Juliet*.[116]

During the next twenty years the Grand was the focus of theatre in Toronto, presenting Sarah Bernhardt, Lily Langtry, Ellen Terry, Adelina Patti, Lillian Russell, and Henry Irving, among others. But in the twentieth century it declined in importance because of the competition from the Princess and the Royal Alexandra, both of which were linked to the major British and American touring circuits. The Grand booked instead Irish musicals, magic shows, and old-fashioned melodramas—one of which was played in real life when Ambrose Small, the last owner of the Grand, disappeared on 2 December 1919. It is usually assumed that he was murdered, but the mystery has never been solved. The theatre closed shortly after and was demolished the following year. A high-rise office building now stands on the site.

THE TEMPLE BUILDING
62-76 Richmond Street West at Bay (NW), 1899
1895 by G.W. Gouinlock

The first buildings in Toronto to explore the possibilities of skyscraper height in architecture were the large office buildings of the late 1880s. While transforming the character of King and Yonge Streets, they had conclusively proved that multi-floor elevator buildings were both profitable to build and very effective image-makers for the institutions that sponsored them. The Canadian Bank of Commerce (plate 69) and the Board of Trade (plate 7) were among the first generation of high-rises. The Temple Building, the North American headquarters of the Independent Order of Foresters, was the most important of the second generation—not only for its ten-storey height,* but also because it was completely designed by a Canadian architectural firm. (The earlier tall buildings had been designed by American firms, on the assumption that they were better qualified to execute such a commission.) The success of a local firm here marked a significant stage in the development of the architectural profession in Toronto.[117]

By the late 1890s fireproof steel-framed construction was standard in high-rise office buildings. Although the frame really carried the weight of the building, the slight contemporary distrust of steel led Gouinlock to design substantial walls of brick and stone. The foundation walls of the L-shaped building were 4'3" thick and the main floor walls 3'6" thick. Even on the ninth floor (originally the top floor), the walls were 18" thick.[118] The deep recesses these walls formed around the windows would have caused serious lighting problems on all sides if Gouinlock had not designed most of the windows on the lower floors as shallow bays to catch the light; there were more bay windows in the rounded corners of the building. As in the Bank of Commerce (plate 69), these corner features helped to break up and ornament the squared mass of the block. Gouinlock also varied the regularity of the layered façades (of red brick and Credit Valley stone) with strongly horizontal lines and deeply shadowed balconies, cornices, and tall arches. There was relatively little carved detail, except for acanthus-leaf ornament above the arches and the beautifully detailed corbels that supported third-floor balconies over the Bay and Richmond Street entrances. Carved by W.J. Hynes, each corbel was supported by a moosehead (the symbol of the IOF), the antlers of which spread out into branches and foliage that covered the curved lower surface.

The construction of the Temple Building was one of

*Because the basement was only partly below street level, the Temple Building was sometimes described as eleven storeys high.

the first steps in the development of the Bay Street office area. Below King, the street was lined with large warehouses; but when, in 1888, it was decided to locate the third City Hall at the corner of Queen and Bay, most of the upper part of the street was still lined with small commercial buildings—as in plate 74, on the right—and small frame and stucco cottages, like those in the extreme left and right of plate 75. The immediate success of the Temple Building marked the beginning of Bay Street as an office area. (So successful was it, in fact, that a tenth floor was added in 1901; the two photographs, taken in 1899 and 1902 respectively, offer a comparison.) Other new businesses were attracted to the area, including the romantically Flemish-styled restaurant to the north, designed by Gouinlock in 1898.

In 1970, the year the Temple Building was demolished, it was little changed, except for minor alterations done in 1931 by the Toronto firm of Shepard & Calvin.[119] Replaced by the large complex of rather boring office buildings at 390 Bay Street, it could have been saved as part of a new development had there been enough incentive and concern expressed at the time.

74 BAY STREET, LOOKING NORTH,
WITH THE TEMPLE BUILDING ON THE LEFT, 1899

75

76

JOHN BISHOP'S BLOCK
Adelaide Street West at Simcoe (NE), c.1885
1833

Although Toronto was not densely populated west of Yonge Street before the 1850s, many of the new houses and shops gave the streetscapes a closely built character, as in crowded English cities, because they stood so often in extended rows right at the front lot line. Such row houses, which were found throughout Toronto on most streets south of Carlton and College, also gave much of Toronto a definite Georgian character, reinforcing the 'Englishness' of the city that visitors remarked on. However, the narrow width of the houses and the tightly organized plans were partly dictated by high land values—a persistent problem in Toronto.

This row was built as a speculative venture by John Bishop, one of Toronto's early butchers.[120] The five houses were intended as first-class residences and followed a traditional plan, used in Britain and the United States, that included a side stair-hall and two main rooms, front and back, on each floor. Since side windows interfered with the planning of the rooms in houses like these, it is likely that most or all of the shutters in the end façade of the corner house were included to ornament and relieve the otherwise blank wall.

There is very little decorative detail on the exterior of these houses because they were built for rental or later sale rather than as an expression of the owner's taste. Typical of the decade are the stone lintels over each of the windows and doors that are incised with a simple pattern (derived from Greek Revival practice). Shortly after the houses were completed, an attic storey in wood was added, with a shallow pediment over each window that broke up the horizontal line of the roof.

By the late 1850s the houses had ceased to be fashionable as newer residential areas were developed north of Queen Street and the city's commercial district expanded to the west. Even so, some of them remained residential as boarding houses and as shops with apartments above. Others were turned into private schools and offices, and the two houses at the corner were remodelled as a hotel with a rebuilt corner entrance. The four nearest units in the row still stand today: the corner pair, much extended, are a tavern, and the other two have been altered into shops. Like the Bank of Upper Canada (plate 52), however, the row has been so denatured by these alterations, and so badly neglected, that it is almost unrecognizable and in need of immediate attention if it is not finally to disappear.

77

ST PATRICK'S MARKET
234-40 Queen Street West (N), east of John, 1893
1854 by Thomas Young

St Patrick's Market was opened in 1836 as Toronto's second public market—after the earlier market on King Street East at Jarvis—and was intended to serve the community that was then known as West Toronto.[121] It was built on land given by D'Arcy Boulton Jr—part of Park Lot 13, which the family had acquired as a suburban estate and where, in 1817, Boulton had built The Grange as his principal residence. As the only resident landowner in the area, Boulton exercised immense influence on the development of the community by giving to the city first the market property and, in 1844, just before he died, a site on John Street for the Church of St George the Martyr. He thus transformed the jumbled collection of houses in Toronto's west end into a true community with a commercial, religious, and social focus. These donations—which followed a long-established paternalistic tradition among British country landowners—were made at a time when the southern portion of the family estate was being subdivided for commercial and residential building; they helped to increase the value of these lots when the property was offered for sale.

The first market building, erected shortly after the gift of the land, was of frame construction, with a two-storey pedimented centre block and lower flanking wings (not unlike the design of the first St Lawrence Market). In addition to housing the market, it also served as the first firehall in the west end from 1842 to 1854, when it was replaced by the building shown here. The new building, like the old, served primarily as a dignified screen along the street front for the jumble of market stalls behind. More like a European city gateway than a standard public building in design, it did not require interior space, except perhaps for a caretaker's apartment and a manager's office. It fulfilled its requirement admirably in a block of brick and stucco that was only one shallow room deep and that spread a balanced façade, with a central entrance and flanking windows, along the street front. Vaguely Italianate—with its strong corner piers, round-arched windows, and ground floor ornamented by horizontally channelled rustication—the façade had the dignity of a public building but at relatively small cost. Above rose a tall belvedere with broad eaves, which identified the market in the streetscape—just as the taller Gothic spire of St George's Church nearby identified the spiritual centre of the community.

The 1854 building stood until 1912, when it was replaced by the present market building, designed by the City Architect, G.F.W. Price. Now a poultry shop, it is a minor public building with classic piers and a pediment—simplified versions of those that ornamented the more elaborate buildings of Edwardian Toronto.

78

THE MECHANICS' INSTITUTE
75 Church Street at Adelaide (NE), 1868
1854-61 by F.W. Cumberland & G.W. Storm

The Mechanics' Institute was the fifth major public building in Toronto to be designed by F.W. Cumberland's firm within a five-year period.* Founded in 1830 on the model of similar organizations in Edinburgh (1821) and London (1824), the Mechanics' Institute was dedicated to the concept of the education and basic dignity of the workingman.[122] Cumberland's problem was the creation of an architectural image for the Institute that would commemorate its successful growth and the place it had gained as one of the city's public institutions. However, there were few accepted architectural precedents to which Cumberland could turn. For earlier buildings such as St James', the Court House, or the Seventh Post Office there had been established precedents. The Mechanics' Institute not only lacked the traditional religious and aristocratic associations of most other public buildings; it was also already best known as a semi-public lending library, and the new building was to include a music hall as a source of income. Cumberland chose not to emphasize any specific function in style or detail but to stress the more general public character of the organization—opting, in the words of G.P. Ure (1859), for 'a combination of the florid, or decorative, with the substantial', to give the building 'an impressive and stately appearance.'[123]

This photograph, taken in 1868, shows the main entrance facing Church Street on the left, and on the right the Adelaide Street façade (actually the side façade), with the entrance to the music hall. The basic form of the building has a Neo-Classical squareness and solidity. The central three bays on the Church Street façade step forward to frame and emphasize the main entrance, but the projection is slight: the arched entrance, and the Corinthian pilasters it supports, are actually decorative surface patterns without the severity or structural meaning found in the design of the Post Office at 10 Toronto Street (plate 59). Other details were designed both to catch and please the eye with variety: the cornice and the parapet—raised in the centre with a broken silhouette against the sky; the variety of windows; the paired pilasters that frame one of the large music-hall windows and ornament the Adelaide Street façade; and the broken pattern of the cornice along this front. The decorative character of the Mechanics' Institute shows the trend in the firm's work away from the relative purity of the Post Office and the Court House to the

opulence and complexity, both in planning and detail, of the central portion of Osgoode Hall, which was designed almost immediately after this, in 1857.

The interior arrangements of the building were more complicated than the regularity of the exterior would seem to indicate. Included were a semi-circular lecture hall that rose in tiers, like an amphitheatre, from the basement level to an entrance on the ground floor; a library with a separate reading room; and on the second floor, served by two grand stairways, the music hall (plate 79, a photograph taken about 1900). It was 76-1/2 feet by 56 feet, with a coved ceiling 35 feet high ornamented by a central dome, and was lit on the Adelaide Street façade by three tall windows. At one end (shown in plate 79) there was a curved musician's gallery supported on twisted columns of cast iron, and at the other a stage framed with columns, like a triumphal arch. In the 1860s the walls of the music room were painted with large panels in the fashionable Neo-Rococo style. The dome was also painted and the entire ceiling, with its framing pattern of plaster beams, must have resembled (with simpler details) the elaborate ceiling that Cumberland & Storm designed for the Osgoode Hall library. En suite with the music hall were offices, refreshment rooms, and supper rooms.

Cumberland & Storm's designs were ambitious—unfortunately too ambitious for the financial health of the Institute, because all the costs had to be raised either by public subscription or with mortgages. The cornerstone was laid on 17 April 1854; but by mid-1855, when the work was almost completed, there was no further money to pay the bills. The unfinished building was then rented to the Government of the Canadas for four years. The basic construction work was completed at public expense, and while Toronto was the provincial capital from 1855 to 1859 the post office and Crown lands departments were housed there. To this indirect government subsidy was added a $16,000 grant in 1860 that permitted the completion of the interior arrangements as Cumberland & Storm had designed them. Ultimately the cost of the building (according to the Institute's 1862 report) was $49,888.19, of which Cumberland & Storm received a token $578 in fees. However, the question of the comparatively large cost was more or less forgotten when the Institute finally moved into its new home in 1861.[124]

The variety of the interior planning of the Institute was a direct reflection of its character. Except for the music hall, the main rooms served a definite purpose in fulfilling the Institute's educational program, as stated

---

*It was preceded by St James' Cathedral, which was the first—designed in 1850—and which was followed in swift succession by the Normal and Model Schools (plate 83), the Seventh Post Office, and the York County Court House.

in its charter of 1830:

> ... the mutual improvement of mechanics and others who become members of the society in arts and sciences by the formation of a library of reference and circulation, by the delivery of lectures on scientific and mechanical subjects ... and for conversation on subjects from which all discussion on political and religious matters is to be carefully excluded.[125]

The formation of the Institute marked, in effect, the beginning of organized semi-technical education in the city, as opposed to the more traditional education in the humanities given at Trinity College and University College. It developed, as had been intended, into something like an institute of extension studies, neither so theoretical nor as distinguished socially as the Royal Canadian Institute, but fundamentally important in a period when the general level of education was still quite low.

From the beginning lectures were given in a wide range of subjects, including music, natural and experimental science, electricity, astronomy, and literature; classes were held in subjects as diverse as conversation and drawing (divided in the 1870s into mechanical and architectural drawing). A lending and reference library was part of the program from the beginning and, though it was slow in getting started, it was an important resource in a small city, especially on architectural subjects. It included three volumes of Colin Campbell's *Vitruvius Britannicus* (1715, 1717, 1731);* William Halfpenny's *Useful Architecture* (1752); two copies of Peter Nicholson's *Mechanic's Companion* (1831); Wheeler's *Rural Dwelling House* (1851); and O.S. Fowler's *A Home for All* (1848), which popularized octagonal buildings in North America. More significantly the Institute subscribed to *The Builder* (London) continuously from 1850, and to several other periodicals that were important in architectural circles, bringing illustrations and discussions of the most up-to-date design and theory directly to Toronto's architects. The drawing classes were also of great importance in the development of Toronto's architecture—especially as there were no formal schools of architecture at the time. Among those who taught or acted as examiners at the Institute were John G. Howard, Kivas Tully, James Smith and William Gemmell (of the firm of Smith & Gemmell), and Henry Langley; among the prize winners were G.M. Miller and G.A. Reid (both later teachers), David Roberts Jr, and G.W. Gouinlock.[126]

The library of the Mechanics' Institute, which very quickly became its largest single asset, included thousands of volumes. It became the principal reason that new members joined and old members stayed, with the result that many of the other educational activities became less important or ceased altogether. The situation was formally acknowledged on 1 July 1883 when, with the passage of the Free Library Bylaw, the Mechanics' Institute was taken over by the city to form the basis of the Toronto Public Library system. Part of the building was altered, the music hall becoming a reading room (as in plate 79), with large newspaper racks down the centre. The library opened on 6 March 1884 and the central and reference libraries remained there until 1906, when the new Carnegie Library was opened at 214 College Street. Until 1927/8 the library retained a branch in the Mechanics' Institute building. In 1930 the building was re-opened as the Employment Services of Canada, set up to meet the sudden needs of the Depression years. The following year it was taken over by the city's Department of Public Welfare, which remained there until 1948/9, when it moved out and the building was demolished—to be replaced by a service station's parking lot.

An educational institution that exerted a profound influence on the people of Toronto, the Mechanics' Institute is today largely forgotten and the site of the building is unmarked.

---

*Volume I contains an illustration of the west front of Chatsworth, Derbyshire, on which William Thomas's St Lawrence Hall (1850) was based. It is entirely possible that Thomas referred to this volume while preparing his designs.

MECHANICS' INSTITUTE: THE MUSIC HALL AS CONVERTED TO A READING ROOM, 1900

RICHMOND STREET METHODIST CHURCH
Richmond Street West (S), between Bay and Yonge, 1868
1844 by Richard Woodsworth, master builder

The Richmond Street Methodist Church was the fount of Methodism in Toronto, the mother-church of most of the later congregations established in the city.[127] Methodist circuit riders first visited York in 1796, and the first church, of simple frame construction, was built by Robert Petch in 1818 on the southwest corner of King and Jordan Streets. A second church was built by Petch in 1832, on the southeast corner of Toronto and Adelaide.[128] It was not until 1844, however, when the Richmond Street church was built, that the Methodists had a building whose architectural nobility reflected their own importance in the province and matched the quality of design of the Anglican and Presbyterian churches erected a decade and a half before.

In some early buildings in Canada the Methodists had adopted the sharply defined and geometrical forms of Neo-Classicism. Their sources were such American pattern books as those by Asher Benjamin that popularized Neo-Classical and Greek Revival styles, and specific British churches. Richard Woodsworth, a Yorkshire-trained builder, took the latter course for Richmond Street Methodist. He modelled the most important element in his design, the portico—with its pediment capped by an attic parapet to conceal the wider gable of the auditorium roof—on the pediment that had been added in 1813 to John Wesley's City Road Chapel in London.[129] The religious symbolism of the four fluted Roman Doric columns was long established: since the Italian Renaissance the order had been used in Christian buildings that honoured religious figures whose doctrines were masculine and severe in character—like those of Wesley. The reference to Wesley's own chapel was not only important in itself, but would have satisfied those in the congregation who considered the American character and 'pagan' origin of Greek Revival objectionable; nevertheless the overall effect of the design—with its crispness of detail and the large scale of the portico, which dominates the entire building—clearly shows American influence.

The grandeur of the portico did not impress later commentators, who were accustomed to the colourful elaboration of the Gothic Revival. To John Ross Robertson, writing in 1886, the church was 'a plain common-looking brick structure with not a single exterior ornamentation to relieve the painful severity of its plainness.' And yet he was enthralled by the contrast between its simplicity—for example, its bare, square auditorium, with galleries on three sides and yellow pine pews upholstered in red—and the more elaborate Methodist churches that were built later:

> One mission after another was born in Richmond Street and has grown into a large successful church, disdaining the simple, old-fashioned, decrepit building of its birth, and beginning a career more in harmony with the rapid developments of later civilization. . . . But while all this meagreness of furniture and severe simplicity is something unrecognized in modern churches, it is really [more] in accordance with the self-sacrificing and self-denying principles of early Methodism than that wealth of appointment and luxury of worship noticeable elsewhere. There is something attractive almost to fascination in these old, worn-out rooms, when thinking of the hundreds who have worshipped there and have now gone never to return.[130]

The end came in 1888. The church was demolished, except for a small part that was rebuilt as the Methodist Book Room. True to an established pattern, the congregation moved north to a new church on McCaul Street, south of Dundas, built in 1888-9 in the fashionable Romanesque Revival style, without any reference to its predecessor (and also demolished).[131]

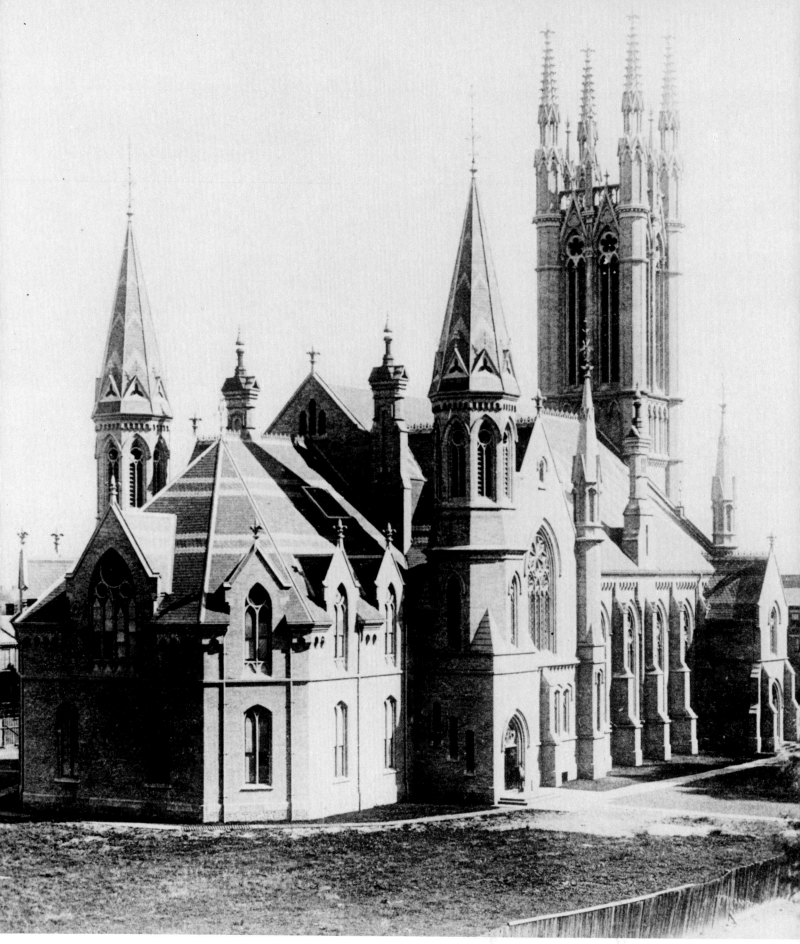

81

114

METROPOLITAN METHODIST CHURCH
Queen Street East, between Bond and Church (N), c.1873
1870-3 by Henry Langley

Toronto in the 1870s, 80s, and 90s was almost indecently proud to call itself a 'city of churches'. The anonymous author of *Toronto, the Queen City of Canada, Illustrated* (1891) counted 114 churches, including 27 Episcopal (Anglican), 18 Presbyterian, 28 Methodist, but only 9 Roman Catholic, and 8 described as 'miscellaneous'—more churches for the population than in any other city in the world, and ample evidence of the 'religious fervour' and the 'absolute surrounding of sincerity which pervades the whole city.'[132] The multitude of churches was in large part the result of the frequent schisms in congregations over differences in doctrine and allegiances to different preachers. But the church, or at least church-going, was an essential element in Toronto society and business. C.S. Clark, in *Of Toronto the Good* (1898), wrote:

> Any young man commencing life in the city, and seeking advancement socially, financially or otherwise, will find no habit that will produce such advantageous results as to become a constant attendant at some church. It carries with it a respectability that no other course of action does, while to abstain from church going is almost enough to make him a social outlaw.[133]

The religious beliefs, often fundamentalist, of Toronto's middle and upper classes affected most elements of Toronto life, forbidding band music in Queen's Park and the running of streetcars on Sundays until the mid-1890s. But regardless of the heavy piety that Methodism occasionally laid on Toronto, it also spurred the Victorians to build larger and larger churches that were impressive not just for their size, but also for the richness of craftsmanship and design that ornamented them. Their splendour, which seems so out of keeping with the stern religious doctrines that were preached on Sundays, was visible evidence of the commercial prosperity and increasing social and political importance of certain Toronto Methodists.

Metropolitan was the largest and most lavish church erected in Toronto by the Methodists.[134] The congregation had previously been established in an 1832 church, at Toronto and Adelaide Streets, but in 1870, prodded by the increasingly commercial character of Toronto Street and supported by the wealth of its congregation, it decided to move north, closer to the upper Jarvis Street area, where many of the members lived. The new site—bounded by Queen, Bond, Shuter, and Church Streets—was then known as McGill Square. It was part of the land grant, running north to Bloor Street, of Captain John McGill (1752-1834). The part of the estate

south of Carlton was subdivided about 1840 and the area around McGill's large cottage was tentatively reserved as a public square.[135] (As such it would have complemented St James Square, formed in 1850 as the site for the Normal and Model Schools (plate 83).)

Earlier and later Methodist churches were easily distinguished from the buildings of the Roman Catholics and Anglicans—which were usually Gothic Revival by the mid-century—by their Classical or Romanesque Revival architecture. But the Methodist churches built in the late 1860s and 1870s were frequently also Gothic in style. This was perhaps a sign that the increasingly powerful Methodist groups were adopting the more traditional usages of the establishment. The new Metropolitan Methodist was to be the greatest of these churches—sumptuous, noble, and stately; it was the third greatest of such churches in Toronto, and aimed to surpass both St James' Anglican and St Michael's Roman Catholic. With Henry Langley as architect the congregation could look to his additions to St Michael's (executed in 1865-9 with his late partner Thomas Gundry) and his several Anglican churches—all Gothic Revival in style—for assurance that their new church would be all that they hoped for.

Langley's initial design resembled a fully articulated Gothic cathedral from the outside, with a pinnacled tower over the main entrance at the south end, a long nave, and a large chancel at the north end.[136] Inside, however, it was very different—because whatever their architectural ambitions, the Methodists still had no use for the liturgical forms and services of the Anglicans or Roman Catholics. What appeared from the outside to be a nave with side aisles was actually a rectangular auditorium with galleries around three sides. Part of the fourth was dedicated to a pulpit and choir, with no trace of an altar. The chancel-like extension at the north end was actually a separate Sunday School wing, with its own small auditorium surrounded by classrooms. This basic plan remained constant, but in the later stages of the design Langley was asked to make it more elaborately and picturesquely Gothic. To this end he redesigned the tower so that the upper levels of the solid piers became successively more open, ending in elongated and sculpted pinnacles that gave it a spiky silhouette against the sky. Beside the smaller towers over the side entrances, which led to the Sunday School, Langley added tall gables in imitation of cathedral transepts. These extensions actually had little effect on the interior space of the auditorium.

82 METROPOLITAN METHODIST CHURCH: INTERIOR, 1873

Langley enriched the basic details of his original design, adding multiple mouldings around the windows and doors, abundant cut-stone trim, patterns of coloured slate on the roofs, and more elaborate patterns of window tracery. Nowhere was this elaboration more apparent than in the main auditorium. In the first design the roof beams had been exposed and supported on cast-iron columns. The columns remained in the completed church, but the ceiling was reworked as a tent-like canopy of Gothic vaults executed, complete with ribs and bosses, in plaster that was brightly painted with stylized foliage patterns. The focus of the space was really the great organ, mounted above the pulpit and replacing the altar of the Anglican and Roman Catholic churches; containing 3,315 pipes, it was said to be the best in Canada. (With a fine choir under the direction of organist F.H. Torrington, Metropolitan became one of the most important centres for music in Toronto.) Langley prepared at least three designs for the organ case. The first was relatively simple, but the second was a dazzling confection of weblike iron work, carved wood, and painted and gilt pipes. The final scheme was almost as elaborate, but more solid in character, with the pipes organized between carved pinnacles that were the interior equivalent of the cresting of the tower.

Metropolitan Methodist was finished in 1872/3. A short time after these photographs were taken, the two acres of grounds were landscaped as a semi-public park, with flower beds and ornamental trees. The setting was completed by a cast-iron fence in a simple Gothic Revival pattern, designed by Langley to establish visually the limits of the churchyard without seeming to intimidate visitors. The removal of the fence in 1961 was an unfortunate loss. *

Twelve hours after the evening service of 30 January 1928—at which a sermon was preached on the text '. . . the God that answereth by fire, let him be God' (1 Kings 18:24)—the church caught fire and was almost completely gutted.[137] There were initial proposals that the city should acquire the grounds as a park, but the congregation decided instead to rebuild. The new church, designed by J. Gibb Morton, retained the image of the old by preserving the front wall and tower of Langley's church (all the other walls had been weakened or destroyed, together with the interior, by the fire); but behind this façade Morton laid out a more cathedral-like plan with nave, side aisles, transepts, no galleries, and a full chancel with altar table. There were immediate and vociferous objections from some that the new plan was a denial of the nonconformist ideology of Methodism in favour of something perilously close to Anglican forms.[138] But it reflected the changes that Methodism had undergone, the most notable of which was the union with a substantial portion of Presbyterians and Congregationalists in 1925, to form the United Church of Canada.

---

*A section survives in front of the Heliconian Club at 35 Hazelton Avenue.

THE NORMAL AND MODEL SCHOOLS
St James Square, 1868
1851-2 by Cumberland & Ridout

The block bounded by Gould, Victoria, Gerrard, and Church Streets—now the site of Ryerson Polytechnical Institute—was once St James Square, a seven-and-a-half-acre park, in the centre of which stood the imposing building that housed the Normal and Model Schools. The land was originally part of Colonel John McGill's park lot and had been tentatively subdivided by 1842. Little, however, had actually been developed when, in August 1850, the province bought the block for £4500 as a site for the schools, which had been established in 1847 in Elmsley House and moved in 1849 to the Temperance Hall on Temperance Street.[139]

The Normal School, for teacher training, and the Model School, a private boys' school sometimes used for practice teaching, were both founded by Egerton Ryerson as the cornerstone of the Ontario public school system. The building itself was meant to lend dignity to the system and be an ornament to the city. As completed by F.W. Cumberland & Thomas Ridout,* it had a central block with an applied portico of Roman Doric piers, and flanking wings. The arrangement of the front was Palladian and eighteenth-century in inspiration, but the detail was influenced by the crisper, more massive and decorative forms of the Renaissance Revival. Above the portico a tall open cupola brought the building to a height of 96 feet. Though rather squat in proportion, the façade effectively terminated the vista as one looked north up Bond Street. The front entrance led to a central hall and beyond to the school's auditorium or theatre. It was apsidal and galleried, and the windows, columns, and arches were Gothic in style, with many of the details executed in cast iron.[140] The use of two dissimilar styles in conjunction was uncommon earlier but accepted in the second half of the nineteenth century when integrated in truly eclectic fashion. Cumberland, like most architects of the period, was practised in a wide range of styles.

St James Square was one of downtown Toronto's few planned open spaces. It became the focus of a residential neighbourhood almost as fashionable as Jarvis Street, with St James Square Presbyterian Church and the College of Pharmacy on Gerrard Street, and several large houses—all overlooking the park.[141] The later history of the building was unfortunate. In 1896 a third floor was added to Cumberland's building, destroying its proportions, and the cupola was raised and rebuilt as

'a fearsome thing', in Eric Arthur's words, 'half classic, half Gothic'.[142] The building and the square disappeared almost totally, replaced in 1962-3 by new buildings designed for the Ryerson Institute of Technology (founded in 1948) in an abysmally ersatz 'modern Georgian' style. The ruin was completed, literally, when a mere fragment of the front façade of Cumberland's central pavilion was retained—the epitome of token preservation, lost and largely forgotten in the Ryerson quadrangle that is all that remains of St James Square.

---

*Thomas Ridout, a member of a prominent Toronto family, was Cumberland's partner for two years; but here, as in most of the designs executed by Cumberland & Ridout, and until 1865 by Cumberland & Storm, it appears that Cumberland was in charge.

THE HOUSE OF PROVIDENCE
Power Street, south of Queen Street East; lithograph of 1855
1855-8 by William Hay

The House of Providence stood on spacious grounds south of St Paul's Roman Catholic Church, with which it was associated, on the east side of Power Street. Without distinction of religion, it served the aged and orphans, the poor and the sick, and destitute immigrants newly arrived in Toronto.[143] To give the building the dignity appropriate to its function, and a fanciful air that would blunt the hard edge of charity, Hay chose a style loosely based on French architecture of the sixteenth century and influenced by the steep-roofed forms of the Second Empire. With a broken roof line of gables, dormers, and towers, ornamented by lacey wrought-iron cresting and gilded vanes, it was designed to look more like a palatial country house in a nobleman's park than a refuge.

The building was H-shaped in plan, with wards and private rooms for each of the various uses on separate floors. On the second floor of the central block was the chapel, three storeys high, with an open-beamed roof and an apsidal sanctuary lit by Gothic windows. The west end of the chapel was open to the corridors of each of the three upper floors to provide galleries from which the residents could observe the service.

The House of Providence was an important agency of social welfare in the city. In the 1890s part of its functions were taken over by St Michael's Hospital. It continued its services until the building was demolished, along with a large part of the residential district that surrounded it, to make way for the Richmond Street exit ramp from the Don Valley Parkway. Today nothing but an open lawn marks the site.

85 THE HOUSE OF PROVIDENCE, c.1875

TRINITY COLLEGE
Queen Street West (N), opposite Strachan Avenue, c.1870
1851-2 by Kivas Tully; with later additions by Frank Darling

Trinity College was founded in 1851 by John Strachan (1778-1867), the first Anglican Bishop of Toronto, after the reorganization and secularization of King's College (plate 94) had been decreed by the provincial parliament in 1850. Strachan had supported King's since its inception, but in his opinion it had been made 'godless', and was effectively destroyed, when control of the government-endowed university had been taken from the Church of England. He immediately began a campaign to found a new college which, like the colleges of Oxford and Cambridge, would be open in its allegience to the Church of England. Strachan himself went to Britain to raise support. With donations from the Society for the Propagation of the Gospel in Foreign Parts and from eminent figures such as the first Duke of Wellington, a staunch supporter of social and political conservatism, and with some £2500 contributed by Torontonians, Trinity was established and confirmed in 1852 by a Royal Charter from Queen Victoria.

For his new college Strachan had been offered sites in Hamilton, Cobourg, and Niagara-on-the-Lake. However, he preferred to have Trinity accessible to the capital city and his own headquarters. In 1850—two years before the charter was granted—Strachan bought twenty acres of land on the north side of Queen Street (at the top of the present Strachan Avenue) from Miss

Cameron of Gore Vale. The property was added to, by purchase and gift, up to 1882.[144]

Strachan was undoubtedly acquainted with the traditions of British collegiate architecture, but for the guidance of the as-yet unchosen architect who would build Trinity, he brought back from London the first plans for St Aidan's Theological College in Cheshire (1850 by Wyatt and Brandon). These plans for a symmetrical Tudor Gothic building around a court formed the basis for discussions of the new Trinity in early 1851. Cumberland & Ridout, then building St James' Cathedral for Strachan, and Kivas Tully, architect of the new Bank of Montreal, were invited to submit proposals. Tully's were chosen.[145]

Tully's designs for the new college were organized around a quadrangle, 120 feet by 170 feet, ornamented with grass, walks, and a fountain that would have been the main source of water for the residents.[146] The complex was to include a chapel, library, refectory, museum, classrooms, professors' rooms, two private residences for professors, rooms for eighty students, and a Provost's Lodge. Tully designed the college in what was described at the time as 'the style of the third period of pointed English architecture [the style now called Perpendicular]'. Gothic was, in fact, the only possible style in the mid-nineteenth century for a building that was religious, collegiate, and Anglican. Though the initial inspiration may have come from the design of St Aidan's, the overwhelming influences were Tom Tower at Christ Church, Oxford (as completed in 1681-2 by Christopher Wren) and New Court, St John's College, Cambridge (1825-31) by Rickman and Hutchinson, the most important of the early Gothic Revival buildings in Oxford and Cambridge. As a result, Trinity was romantically picturesque rather than religious in character. Designed to be seen, as it is in plate 86, slightly elevated on a grassy terrace, surrounded by mature trees and approached by a broad avenue from Queen Street, the building rhetorically proclaimed the lineage and importance of the new college. From a distance the central bell tower, and the flanking turrets, chimneys, and pinnacles shining white against the clear blue sky, caught the eye and the imagination. The viewer could forget the North American location, and the simple Gothic details in white brick and Ohio cut stone, and think of the new Trinity as a college transplanted from Oxford or Cambridge.

Only the front block of Tully's design for Trinity was actually completed when the college officially opened in January 1852. Even that much had cost £8000, which taxed the available resources. Among the elements left unbuilt for reasons of economy was the chapel, symbolically and functionally one of the most important parts of a college such as Trinity. As it grew in wealth and numbers, additional buildings were planned. In 1858 William Hay presented a design for a chapel that was much more 'serious' and archaeological in character than Tully's work, without the lightly picturesque touch.[147] However, Hay's chapel was not built. It was not until 1873, when Frank Darling became adviser to the college (and in 1878 its official architect),[148] that new plans for the expansion of Tully's original building were made. William Hay had long since returned to Britain and Tully was preoccupied with his work as architect to the Province of Ontario; so Darling, just back from training in Britain and connected through his family to Toronto's Anglican establishment, was a logical choice as architect.

Darling's first design for Trinity was Convocation Hall, seen here in a photo of about 1900 (plate 87), which was built in 1877 in memory of both James Henderson of Yorkville and Bishop Strachan as a dignified setting for college ceremonies, examinations, and social events.[149] Located behind the Tully block (and connected to it), it was a simple box-like building with an open timber roof, modelled on medieval English baronial halls; it was lit from three sides, with a dais at the north end and a gallery at the south. As in later work for the college, the buff brick of the 1851 building was used for the exterior, and in designing the windows Darling used the same wide proportions of the Late

Gothic style that Tully had chosen. Only the use of red brick inside, horizontally striped with white stone, indicates the later date and the influence of still-fashionable English Victorian polychromy on Darling's style. The sharp colour contrasts, which were introduced as permanent decoration, gave the hall a feeling of breadth, where it otherwise might have seemed narrow and cramped.

The college chapel (plate 88) was not begun until 1883; it was made possible by a gift from the Henderson family in memory of Millicent Henderson.[150] Standing apart from the east end of Tully's block, it was connected to it by a low corridor. Such a separation was influenced by contemporary work in England and proclaimed visually the special character of the chapel. But it also freed Darling from the need to continue Tully's Late Gothic forms, by now unfashionable, to build in the Early English style—with its relatively narrow lancet windows between tall, massive buttresses—which was considered more 'correct' by the architectural and ecclesiastical establishments. Finally, the separation respected the value of Tully's skyline as a symbol of the college, particularly as Darling did not include a towering spire for the chapel.

The immediate impression of the design, both inside and out, was of its simplicity and solidity compared with Tully's work. In plan it was, like many collegiate chapels, a long rectangle, with an apsidal sanctuary at the east end and a south transept for the vestry and organ loft. As the visitor entered through a low vestibule at the west end under the gallery and passed through a carved wooden screen into the chapel proper, the space rose around him. His eyes were directed toward the apse by the long parallel rows of pews and stalls down the sides and by the horizontal bands of white stone laid into the red brick walls. Above, the hammer-beam roof seemed to stretch over the main space like a canopy, while the coved ceiling above the apse, supporting a semi-dome, billowed like a tent to contain the space. All of the interior details were of the simplest character to avoid a stacatto accent that would break the unity of the space or focus it more precisely on one feature. The window reveals were shallow; the organ was completely recessed behind the line of the south wall; and the strong forms of the window arches were paired or grouped, like the seven windows of the apse. On the exterior the heavy, solid buttresses were probably unnecessary in structural terms, but they created deep sheltering bays around the windows and rose above the eaves as if to hold in, and contain, the interior space.

After the completion of Darling's chapel in 1884, the room in Tully's block that had served as a chapel since 1852 became—as Tully had originally intended—the college library (plate 89). Located on the second floor

87 TRINITY COLLEGE: CONVOCATION HALL, C.1900

88 TRINITY COLLEGE: THE CHAPEL, *c.*1900

89 TRINITY COLLEGE: THE LIBRARY, C.1900

immediately over the main entrance, it was lit from each end by bay windows, and from above by an octagonal skylight (below the central bell turret). The book stacks—lined up in ranges at right angles to the length of the room and forming bays between, in the traditional collegiate pattern—could not have been in place when the room was a chapel and were probably designed by Darling. Certainly the flattened arches that span the bays are found in his early churches; so is the pattern of the lower panelling—small squares centred on bull's-eye ornaments, a motif of the Queen Anne style that was popular in the 1870s and early 1880s). This photograph does not really do the room justice; it tends to minimize the sense of the library as a long gallery, defined by the regular rhythm of the book stacks and flooded with light from the two bay windows and the skylight. The photograph does show, however, the fanciful Gothic character of Tully's interior detail overhead, with its elaborately moulded wooden ribs and turned bosses, imitating the forms of rib vaulting and the intimate, almost domestic (rather than monumental) character of the room as a whole, which typified the best features of his building.

Darling's later work for Trinity included a new west wing (1889-90) and the east wing (1894), both in a very restrained 'Modern Gothic' style that did not conflict with the older parts of the college and was at the same time appropriately and comfortably residential in character.[151] The west wing (on the left in plate 90), in addition to residence space, included both physics and chemistry laboratories for the new science subjects that Trinity planned to add to its curriculum. The need for still more facilities, and the great cost of supplying them, were among the main reasons that drew Trinity into federation with the provincially funded University of Toronto. The federation became a fact on 18 November 1903. It became inevitable that Trinity would move to the main campus in order to make the facilities of the university as a whole readily available to Trinity's students, although no date was set at that point.

As part of the arrangements for the move, in 1912 the City of Toronto paid $225,000 for the 31 acres of the Queen Street grounds (now called Trinity-Bellwoods Park) and all the buildings except the chapel, with the college to have free occupancy for five years.[152] In the end, because of the Great War and construction delays, Trinity did not finally move to Hoskin Avenue until 1 August 1925. Even before the move, City Council voted to sell eight acres close to the centre of the Queen Street site for a baseball stadium—a project that required the immediate demolition of the college buildings. Under

90 TRINITY COLLEGE, WITH THE WEST WING, c.1898

strong public pressure Council reversed itself, but refused to act on proposals that Trinity be renovated as a museum or a soldiers' convalescent home. (The specious arguments against re-use and renovation, all made before Trinity had moved out—that the buildings needed new roofs, new heating and electricity, and that it was useless to attempt preservation—have a strangely contemporary ring.[153] They have been heard since in the discussions about Old City Hall, St Lawrence Hall, the Asylum at 999 Queen Street, Laughlin Lodge, and the Don Jail; and they will continue to be used whenever an owner or public body wishes to ignore the possibilities of preservation.) Finally, the main building became the 'K' Athletic Club, sponsored by the Central Kiwanis Club. The attempt at re-use was noble, but casual neglect was the basic order of the day. (It was confirmed by the destruction of the chapel by fire on 4 March 1929.)[154] The buildings slipped gradually into decay until 1955-6, when the site was cleared. Today in Trinity-Bellwoods Park only the gate piers survive, along with a short section of railings, both designed by Frank Darling and erected in 1904-5. In the mournful tale of the destruction it is not really possible to fault Trinity, which moved for very good reasons. Perhaps the Diocese of Toronto could have done more. But the fault must rest squarely with the city council of the day for lack of foresight and a crushingly narrow sense of history and civic pride.

91

THE PROVINCIAL LUNATIC ASYLUM
999 Queen Street West (S), opposite Ossington, 1868
1846-58 by John G. Howard

Prior to 1839 the treatment of the mentally ill in Ontario was primitive in the extreme, as it was elsewhere in North America and most of Europe. They were mainly cared for by their families, without any real treatment, and only those who were dangerously violent or destitute were considered the government's responsibility: they were confined in the common jails. But in 1839 the government of Upper Canada authorized the establishment of a proper mental asylum, and primitive (but at least specialized) facilities were established in 1840 in the vacated 1824 jail on King Street East, at Toronto Street. This was followed in 1844 by a design competition for a new facility in which John G. Howard won the first 'premium' of £50. The fifty-acre site on Queen Street West, then well outside the city, was given by the government from the original military reserve; the cornerstone was laid on 22 August 1846 and the first section was completed in 1850.[155]

'The instructions I received from the Building Committee,' Howard wrote, 'were to design a Building for the care (not incarceration) of about 500 of the Insane of Upper Canada, and I made a tour of the United States in serch [sic] of the best information upon that subject.'[156] The new asylum was conceived as both a medical and a public building. The principal problem the architect faced—the organization of large ward spaces in a building that had to be for the most part naturally lit and ventilated, and could not be more than four or five storeys high because there were no elevators—was one never before encountered in Canada on such a scale. In fact, no building as large, except for major fortifications, had ever been built in Canada. Probably only Howard had the knowledge and experience to organize such a space efficiently. He chose as his particular model for the exterior William Wilkins' National Gallery on Trafalgar Square in London, completed shortly before Howard immigrated to Canada in 1832. The main façade of the asylum was 584 feet long—huge even today, but stupendous in its own time. The design was arranged around a pedimented central block nine bays wide. Howard broke the great length of the side wings into two pavilions each—one large, with its own pediment, and one only three windows wide—to ease the monotony of an extended façade. He then drew the composition together, as Wilkins had done in the National Gallery, with a small, rather too-delicate dome above the central pediment. The Gallery is only two storeys high, but to provide the space he needed in the asylum, Howard doubled the height, with the two lower storeys designed as a massive base for the third and fourth floors. The effect of solidity was emphasized by the severely flat cut-stone mouldings around the windows and the use of unadorned buff-coloured brick for the walls. The whole composition would have been considerably less forbidding and more decorative had the central feature been completed before money ran out: a raised portico of six fluted Ionic columns in stone, its pediment ornamented with the Royal Arms.

The entire main block facing Queen Street (the only section completed by Howard) cost £56,500. Howard's budget permitted little in the way of architectural pyrotechnics; more importance was placed on efficient planning. The central block was devoted to administrative space, with receiving rooms for patients, visiting rooms, and staff offices on the first and second floors. On the third floor, behind the long windows shown in plate 92, was a ballroom, 55 feet by 25 feet, and two infirmaries, while the fourth floor housed three chapels: Protestant, Roman Catholic, and non-denominational. The attic—actually a full storey high—contained rooms for twenty-four male and female patients who worked with the staff, and the dome housed an 11,000-gallon iron tank, which was pumped up daily by a steam engine to provide running water and water closets throughout the building—luxuries that were uncommon in all but the most expensive houses of the period. There was also a steam-heating system for the entire building and a ventilation system that, until the turn of the century, was one of the finest in North America.

More important than the purely technical arrangement of the central block was the arrangement of the side wings according to the most advanced theories of mental-health care. The patients were divided, with men in the west wing and women in the east, and housed on each of the three upper floors according to the severity of their condition, those on the second floor requiring constant attendance. Each floor was a self-contained unit—much like the pavilions of the present hospital—with its own dining room (serviced from the first-floor kitchens by dumb waiters), two large dormitories, twelve smaller bedrooms, and two day or sitting rooms, all opening into a wide corridor lit from the south, which served as an indoor exercise and social area. At the end of each corridor there was a partially enclosed veranda sunroom that overlooked the landscaped grounds and gardens—with a wall and farm buildings by William Thomas—that were intended to provide outdoor exercise, till then virtually unknown in mental-health care. The whole complex was, in the rather sanctimonious opinion of *The Globe*, a building 'exceedingly handsome, commodious, healthful and safe . . . a monument to the Christian liberality of the people'; a true asylum 'where disturbing influences are absent—not a mere hospital or prison—where every good part of human nature is brought into play.'[157]

Unfortunately the ideals and advanced theory that went into Howard's design were in large part nullified by the government's decision, first to build only the front block of the design, omitting the two lateral wings extending south that Howard had included in the original project; and then, after these wings had been built by Kivas Tully to a more cramped design, by the tendency to consider the asylum the only facility necessary to serve a growing population. The main block was designed for 264 patients, but 308 were registered by the end of 1850 (the year it opened) and the numbers continued to grow. Gross overcrowding and understaffing made the progressive treatment envisioned in 1846 quite impossible. The public saw only the outside of the building, with its ornamental fountain and wandering paths, and were happy to remain cheerfully ignorant of the problems within.

During 1912 definite plans were made for moving the asylum to a suburban site, but as with other projects, the turmoil of the Great War resulted in the cancellation of the plans. With the low priority given to mental-health care until after the Second World War, and with the reduced maintenance in anticipation of a complete move, the interior of the building deteriorated badly. The fine classicism and the intelligence of the plan were obscured in a cloud of horror stories and frightened imaginings. Outside, the buff brick darkened to a muddy grey in the Toronto smog, the fountain disappeared, the garden went uncared for, with large parts paved for parking. This writer worked there as a volunteer while at university and can testify to the atmosphere of defeatism that dominated the hospital, lightened only by the devotion of the staff. It clung, like the rancid smell of the place, to every visitor, worker, and patient. Inevitably the building itself became a symbol of all the errors and horrors of mental-health care.

In 1968 the total demolition of the old hospital was thought necessary if the image of mental-health care in Toronto was to be changed. But during the controversy surrounding attempts to preserve Howard's building, the general feeling was that its design was somehow the villain of the piece. Many of the hospital administrators and politicians involved encouraged this impression, which safely obscured the inadequacies of the system, with its long record of poor financial support and poor maintenance. When it had been colourfully embroidered by the Toronto press, it assumed the force of gospel.[158]

The Queen Street Mental Health Centre—the name finally chosen in the 1950s to conceal partially the function and conditions of the hospital—was to be rebuilt in stages. The new complex began with the demolition of Kivas Tully's east and west wings. In their place rose multi-storey pavilions, like collegiate residences, and an elaborate community centre—features not unlike those Howard had included in his design and that had been wiped out by overcrowding. It was not until December 1974 that the Ministry of Government Services applied for demolition permits for the Howard block, with plans to replace it with a parking lot and to spend several million dollars on the renovation and extension of the administration building that had been added in front of Howard's block in 1956. Under the terms of the Ontario Heritage Act of 1974, the City of Toronto attempted to delay the demolition permits. Then, in June 1975, the Toronto Historical Board, with support from the Ontario Heritage Foundation, commissioned A.J. Diamond—one of Toronto's leading architects, with a personal and professional commitment to preservation—to study the possibilities for renovation of the old building. The Ministry of Government Services had earlier requested such a study from its own staff, and had issued a report in April 1975 estimating the renovation costs at $34.5 million, or the incredibly high sum of $178 per square foot of floor space. With the support of Toronto's leading cost analyst, Diamond concluded that only $18 million would be necessary for renovation of a building that was fundamentally sound. The Ministry, while questioning the figures, revised its own estimate (which by October 1975 had risen to $39.5 million) downward to $30 million, without comment or explanation.

Having failed by its own logic and figures to disarm opposition, the Ministry planned a pre-emptive stroke, and on 3 December 1975 it announced that demolition would begin immediately. There was a brief occupation and vigil at the Howard block in an effort to prevent this. The minister responsible, Mrs Margaret Scrivner, represented the government's determination to demolish as if it were a personal crusade, and all appeals against the decision were futile.

The asylum deserved to be saved by all objective criteria. It was without doubt John G. Howard's most important work and the one that most completely showed his remarkable talents as an architect. (So few of his buildings survive in anything approaching their original condition.) More important, the Asylum summed up the concern of Toronto in the 1840s and 50s for the health and welfare of its citizens, expressed in monumental yet thoroughly functional architecture. Even in its deteriorated state it remained as much a symbol of that concern as E.J. Lennox's City Hall was a symbol of Toronto's civic pride and confidence in the 1890s. Just as the rich detail and fine masonry of Old

92 THE PROVINCIAL LUNATIC ASYLUM: REAR VIEW, 1868

City Hall has reappeared from under a thick coat of grime, so the Howard block, when cleaned and rebuilt inside, as proposed by Jack Diamond—and supplemented by the new facilities that replaced Tully's wing—would have been returned to efficient use and revealed as one of the outstanding monuments of Neo-Classicism in Canada. The site is now another parking lot.

93

THE BROADWAY TABERNACLE
College Street at Spadina (NE), c.1891
1887-9 by E.J. Lennox

Broadway Tabernacle took its name from 'The Broadway', the unofficial name for the section of Spadina Avenue that extended north from College Street around Spadina Crescent to Bloor. The street had been laid out in the 1830s by Dr W.W. Baldwin as part of the speculative development of his family estates, but it was not until the 1880s that it seemed likely to develop into a prosperous neighbourhood of comfortable middle- and professional-class houses, like the Annex to the north (see plate 119). The congregation itself was of fairly recent date, having been founded in 1870 as a mission of the New Connection Methodists on Temperance Street, where it remained until 1875, when a temporary church was built on the Broadway site.[159]

The commission to design the new church came to E.J. Lennox not only because of his work on Toronto's third City Hall (1889-99), but also because of the success of the Bond Street Congregational Church at 76 Dundas Street West, which he had built in 1879. On 29 July 1887 the Broadway congregation specifically resolved to build 'an entirely new church after the general plan of the Bond Street Congregational Church'.*

Following their wishes, Lennox repeated the basic plan of the Bond Street church on a larger scale, creating an auditorium that seated 2,000 people. The exterior design was without doubt one of his best in the Romanesque Revival style. Each of the main façades was centred on a tall gable with a triple-arched window that marked the cross-axis of the auditorium. There was also a short tower at the end of each façade. But it was the third tower, at the corner of Broadway and College, that lifted the entire design. Rising from a solid square

base, with a shaft lightened by pairs of blind arches on each side, to an arcaded bell stage and pyramidal roof covered with tiles, the tower was both the symbolic feature of the church and a key element in the open, mostly residential, streetscape of the area. Broadway Tabernacle was built in red brick with a sparing use of light-coloured rock-faced stone—in massive courses for the foundations and in narrow horizontal bands above that linked windows and arches. At the base of the main tower the foundation course rose well above the height of a man passing by on the sidewalk to give an impressive sense of the building's solidity; the same rock-faced stone was used in the wide arches of the two main entrances, giving them emphatic presence in the design. However, it was the brickwork of the building— as in the Armouries on University Avenue (plate 96)— that attracted attention by the confident manner in which it was handled to create both the heavy squared base of the tower and the smoothly rounded forms of the turrets. On the main tower and elsewhere the wheeling arches, with their outline mouldings, and the bands of basketweave detail, were also of brick and contributed richly patterned areas of light and shadow. The sure composition of the tower and gables, and this careful use of brick and stone masonry, made the Broadway Tabernacle the equal of the third City Hall as an indication of Lennox's flair for the Romanesque Revival style.

The Tabernacle prospered with the great expansion of the suburbs west of the university in the 1890s. But by the 1920s most of the congregation had moved north to newer suburbs, like many of the churches in the city's core, and Broadway closed in 1926/7. Late in 1930 the church had been demolished and the present commercial building erected on the site, to take advantage of the new character of Spadina.

---

*The Bond Street Congregational Church, with its superb interior, still stands, and is now known as Evangel Temple. It is threatened by redevelopment.

KING'S COLLEGE
Queen's Park, 1886
1842-5 by Thomas Young

King's College was chartered in 1827 as an arts college for Upper Canada. The first act of the council of the new college was to purchase, in 1829, the University Park, a large area of previously undeveloped land that included the present Queen's Park and much of what now forms the University of Toronto campus. The first building erected, the gate-house at Queen Street by John G. Howard, had little to do with the educational functions of the college, but it was Howard who submitted a scheme for the main college buildings about 1835.[160] His perspective drawing of the proposal survives in the collection of the Toronto Historical Board and shows a grandiose complex modelled on the great English Palladian country houses of the mid-eighteenth century (it most closely resembles Stowe in Buckinghamshire): a spreading central block, with portico and cupola, extended by one-storey quadrant colonnades that curve forward to define a huge forecourt.

Howard's design was probably submitted without a commission from the college, for in 1837, when active planning was begun, it was Thomas Young who was engaged to design and supervise the building of the new college, at a salary of £200 per annum. Young is best known today as a topographical artist, some of whose work was reproduced by Currier & Ives, and as the designer of the Huron County Jail (preserved in nearly pristine condition as a museum) at Goderich. He was a capable architect who probably trained in England. A wooden model of his design, made in London, has been lost;[161] but many of his drawings for this project are preserved in the Archives of the University of Toronto. The design called for not fewer than three separate buildings of cut stone connected by one-storey covered walkways, and a large forecourt about 450 feet wide. The main block—with a façade about 200 feet wide, two storeys high, and dominated by a full Greek Doric portico with six columns and a pediment—was to house the library, museum, and convocation hall, each with finely detailed monumental interiors. The southeast block, the only section actually built, was intended as a students' residence. (It is illustrated here in a photograph taken in 1886, when it was being demolished.) The southwest block was to contain classrooms, lecture halls, and laboratories. Both were simpler in form than the central block, with porticos of half columns. Contemporary descriptions indicate that Young proposed adding buildings for the college hall and chapel, although these are not shown in the drawings.[162]

If Young's college had been completed it would have been among the most elaborate in North America,

rivalling in architectural grandeur University College as it was eventually built, Trinity College (plate 86), and even the final stage of Osgoode Hall. His designs were probably influenced by William Wilkins' Downing College, Cambridge, which had introduced the Greek Revival style for academic buildings in 1806. The one block that was erected—crisply detailed, with emphatic corner detailing, simplified mouldings, and the baseless Greek Doric columns of the Parthenon—had a formal severity that also suggests strong American influence.

The full scheme was far beyond the means of King's College. Nevertheless, encouraged by the Lieutenant-Governor, Sir Francis Bond Head, and in spite of the disorders surrounding the Rebellion of 1837, tenders were called for. The eagerness to proceed likely had to do with a desire to spend King's endowment before the Assembly could divide it among the other religious groups in the province that wished to found universities.* Politics were a continuing factor. When Sir George Arthur replaced Head in 1838, he was dismayed by the college's record of expenditures—most of them incurred to support the elaborate projects for Upper Canada College—and ordered work suspended. Young was discharged, and it was not until 23 February 1842, after Sir Charles Bagot replaced Arthur, that work was resumed. Bagot himself laid the cornerstone of the southwest wing in a colourful ceremony on 23 April 1842, and it was completed in 1845 at a cost of £13,895—appreciably higher than the original estimates. It opened as a residence.[163]

During construction the college had used the Parliament Buildings on Front Street (plate 25), since they had been vacated when the government moved temporarily to Kingston in 1841. Just when it seemed as though it could move into its own building, political controversy again intervened. This culminated in the Baldwin Bill of 1849 that secularized the college and effectively stopped all new construction. That same year the government moved to Toronto, and the

---

*As established in 1827, King's was directly affiliated with the Church of England and endowed with 225,000 acres of Crown land. John Strachan, as Archdeacon of York, was its President ex officio. To the other religious groups in the province—particularly the Methodists and the Presbyterians, and their representatives in the Assembly—the idea of government support for a self-governing Anglican university was unacceptable, and the college became the target of bitter political attack. The other groups established their own denominational colleges and received public moneys, but because there was never as much support available for them as King's received from its endowment, the controversy refused to die away. It came to a head once King's opened for teaching.

college, now the University of Toronto, was evicted from the Parliament Buildings. It had to cram itself into the residence block, which was supplemented by a brick building—in similar Greek Revival style—called Moss Hall, which was completed in 1850 on the site of the present Medical Sciences Building. Official harassment culminated in a bill passed in 1853 by Sir Francis Hincks to expropriate an unspecified portion of the University Park as a site for new Parliament Buildings. Under this provision the existing buildings were taken over. The university had to return to Front Street, only to move back the next year to its now-gutted building when Parliament returned hurriedly to Toronto after a sojourn in Quebec. The ultimate insult came in 1856

when Young's building was once again appropriated by the government, this time to be re-established as the University Lunatic Asylum, leaving only Moss Hall to house what had now become University College. This was the situation when, in 1856, work began on the present University College building.[164]

The University Asylum was closed in the 1860s when the final wings of the Asylum at 999 Queen Street West (plate 91) were completed. After this, the King's College building seems to have remained largely empty and neglected until it was demolished in 1886 to make way for the east wing of R.A. Waite's Parliament Buildings (1886-92). Today a plaque commemorates what was one of Toronto's most splendid lost architectural causes.

UNIVERSITY AVENUE
Looking south from Queen's Park, c. 1890

University Avenue—along with the section of College Street running west from Yonge to what is now Queen's Park—was laid out in 1829 by the Trustees of King's College (plate 94), to designs by John Wedd, as the stately entrance to University Park, which had been purchased as a campus for the new college. College Avenue, as University was originally called (College Street was Yonge Street Avenue), served a very necessary function, since there were no proper roads leading to the campus. Like Thomas Young's plans for King's College, it was laid out for the grandest possible effect: a width of 120 feet was made into a central carriageway with boulevards and walkways on either side, shaded by double rows of pink flowering chestnuts.* Never planned as an urban street lined with major buildings, it was thought of from the beginning as

a processional approach inspired by famous English counterparts: the long drives that lead down tree-lined vistas to great country houses, or (perhaps a more direct inspiration) the avenues that cut across the gardens of Oxford and Cambridge—especially Queen's Road and the drives along the Cam in Cambridge, which would have been well known to the many Cambridge graduates involved with the founding of King's.

From the beginning a sense of the avenue's isolation from the growing city was carefully maintained—both in the interests of a secluded collegiate life and to preserve the tranquillity of the grounds. There were gates and lodges flanking both the Queen and Yonge entrances to the campus, and the gatekeepers were instructed to deny access to commercial traffic. Originally no streets were permitted to cross College Avenue. However, pedestrians could use both the park and the avenue, which together became a popular promenade and rendezvous, described in 1868 in

*The chestnuts were specially imported from the United States and were used here for the first time in Toronto.

Toronto in the Camera as 'one of the great lungs of the city'.

In a growing city that was dedicated to the free development of commerce and accustomed to the predictable regularity of a grid system of streets, the avenue eventually came to be seen as a barrier to both commerce and development. In particular it offended the laissez-faire liberalism of George Brown, and in September 1855 he editorialized in the *Globe*:

> It is also noticeable how comparatively few houses are going up north of Queen Street—a fact difficult of satisfactory explanation. It may however, be in a great measure owing to the circumstances that the College Avenue, being surrounded by fences, imposes a positive barrier to the locomotion of the residents in that vicinity, and they find themselves called on every occasion when journeying in a westerly or easterly direction, to make a considerable *detour* to arrive at their destination. This is an inconvenience which, in the interest of land owners and residents, should at once be remedied. It is no argument to contend that the beauty of the Avenue would thus be destroyed, and its privacy as a park intruded on. In reply to the first objection we have the examples of the Parks in London and the Champs Elysees in Paris, all intersected by public ways and affording short communicating roads from one part to the other of the respective cities in which they are situated, while by making the Avenue a place of greater public resort a positive advantage would ensue. . . .[165]

Brown's criticisms were not without justice, and it was to solve just such problems that Frederick Law Olmstead was at this time inventing the sunken roads that allowed traffic to cross New York's Central Park without interfering with the use of the park itself. Unfortunately no similarly inventive solution was developed to preserve the secluded character of College Avenue. In 1859, when the City of Toronto took a 999-year lease on both the avenue and the present area of Queen's Park, College Avenue was simply opened to general city traffic. Not surprisingly, it became one of the principal north-south arteries in the city.

This photograph, taken about 1890, looks south from Queen's Park, down the rows of chestnuts that C.P. Mulvaney enthusiastically described in 1884 as a 'glorious propylaeum of trees'. The cast-iron fountain stands on a site (now occupied by Hamilton McCarthy's statue of Sir John A. Macdonald) that had been loyally reserved for a statue of Queen Victoria. A statue of the Queen by Marshall Wood was unveiled on 1 July 1871, much to the pleasure of City Council. Unfortunately it later turned out that Mr Wood meant to sell, not donate, the statue to the city. The misunderstanding had not been settled by mid-1874; when notified that the price had risen from $3,000 to $7,500, Council declined the honour and asked Mr Wood to remove the statue. In the summer of 1875 it installed on the site a far less

expensive ($559.50) fountain. C.P. Mulvaney was not pleased with the fountain and its landscaping, noting that it stood on

> a mound like what boys construct when they play at taking a fort, . . . surrounded by an unspeakably mean little fence. . . . At the side of the mound are piled a few bits of stone to give the effect of a rockery, and the city fathers expend a sum apparently not exceeding fifteen cents in sowing larkspur and other cheap annuals, every spring . . .[166]

Mulvaney's criticisms aside, College Avenue—especially when the vista was climaxed by the new Parliament Buildings in 1892—remained a beautiful enclave well into the twentieth century. It inspired the first important schemes for replanning the downtown area (plates 98 to 100) and was one of their central features.

The avenue's transformation began in the last decade of the nineteenth century, not long after this photograph was taken. The Parliament Buildings gave it a new role in the city as a public, as opposed to a university-oriented, street. Other buildings followed: the additions to Osgoode Hall in the 1890s; the Armouries in 1893 (plate 96); the Toronto General Hospital, on the southeast corner of College and University,* in 1913. The avenue was redesigned, with a wide boulevard dividing north- and southbound roadways.

For a short time, especially when the trend to larger buildings was confirmed by the erection of the Canada Life Building in 1929-31, it seemed that the new University Avenue would be a worthy successor to the old College Avenue—though imperial and elegantly formal rather than pastoral and quiet. Unfortunately the years that followed, especially the 1950s and 1960s, saw the construction of blocks of faceless institutional buildings that typified the worst clichés of mid-twentieth-century architecture. During the same period traffic problems, caused by an ever-increasing number of automobiles, completed the transformation, eating up what remained of the chestnut trees and producing instead a narrow median—one of the truly frightening places to walk in Toronto—lined with skimpy boxes filled with forlorn trees, bushes, and flowers. The University Avenue of today is a heartbreaking contrast to the tree-lined promenade it supplanted.

---

*On the left of the avenue in the photograph.

96

THE ARMOURIES
University Avenue at Armoury Street (SE)
1891-3 by Thomas Fuller

In the 1880s and 1890s the federal Department of Public Works, under Thomas Fuller, created a series of towered and castellated buildings to house local militia regiments. Rising like medieval castles in towns and cities across Canada, these armouries amply expressed their military function in massive and round-arched forms influenced by the Romanesque Revival.

Fuller's Armouries in Toronto—which were the ultimate, though hardly the last, expression of this building type—stood on one of the most prominent sites in the city, facing University Avenue, immediately north of Osgoode Hall.[165] With a drill hall measuring 280 feet by 125 feet, and 72 feet high from the floor to the inside ridge of the roof, they were the largest in Canada and for a while the largest in North America. There was also additional space in the basement for bowling allies, rifle ranges, and other rooms around the perimeter of the hall and in the towers. Fuller, and most designers of similar buildings, used the bulky castellated towers that gave the Armouries their military character to break the long horizontal lines and in part conceal the immense roof, which was framed in metal. However, to the modern observer the aesthetic problem of the roof and its solution are of far less interest than the superb craftsmanship with which the brick and stone of the building were manipulated. The walls were of thick load-bearing masonry and the solidity of the brick and stone was made an essential element in the overall scheme. The brick was an even red in colour and was finely bonded with coloured mortar to create a smooth surface, even in beautifully rounded corners, as if the walls were a single mass rather than a unity of small parts. Against this surface, rock-faced grey Kingston limestone was used to accentuate the foundations, the window-sills and lintels, and the tower crenellations as strong horizontal lines, so that the building impressed the viewer with its earth-hugging, impregnable solidity. The same stone also articulated the great wheeling arches of the windows that lit the hall and dominated the end façades. Because of the immense size of the building, the Armouries were an ideal structure with which to express the power and strength that resided in materials—a basic tenet of the Romanesque Revival.

The Armouries served through the Boer War and two world wars; but with the appearance of high-rise buildings on University Avenue in the 1950s and early 1960s, they were thought to be out of place, while their actual size became less necessary. Finally, in 1963, when more land was needed for the expansion of the provincial courts at Osgoode Hall, they were demolished. They are commemorated both by the name of Armoury Street, running east from University Avenue, and by a memorial plaque erected on the site.

BETHANY CHAPEL
University Avenue at Christopher Street (NE), c.1900
1893 by Henry Simpson

Bethany Chapel was founded in 1890 as a non-denominational church, with definite Congregational leanings, that was just one of several experimental and inquiring sects to establish themselves in Toronto in the late 1880s and 1890s. Though it was not a separate denomination, it represented a fundamentalist and evangelical doctrine that was centred on a belief in 'Divine Healing' and in the pre-millenial coming of Christ to rule the world for a thousand years of peace before the Last Judgement.[166]

For both client and architect it was difficult to conceive such a doctrine in architectural terms. Henry Simpson had recently completed Cook's Presbyterian Church (1891), at 88 Queen Street East, with stylized Gothic and Romanesque details. But for Bethany these traditional forms would not have been thought suitable. Choosing instead to house the galleried auditorium of the chapel in a cubic brick box, Simpson created mural or wall architecture that managed to convey an impression of simplicity and security, of primitive and near-eastern roots. (In point of fact, in its strong horizontal surface pattern and small window openings, Bethany Chapel was related to the 'tomb' built for the secret Scroll and Key Society at Yale University, by the well-known American architect R.M. Hunt, in 1869-70; Simpson's design, however, was simpler in material and detail.) The walls were divided into tiers that corresponded approximately to the interior levels of the auditorium. The corner entrance was simply carved out of the mass, and 'port hole' windows were punched through the horizontally channelled rustication of the middle level, leaving the purity of the shape and the impression of thick walls to give the building its striking character. The multi-cusped arches of the other openings and the grouping of most of the windows at the top of the building gave it a strongly Venetian look, both Gothic and Mediterranean, that underscored in a vague way the religious use of the building and the exotic nature of the sect.

The Bethany Chapel was built for a congregation of 300, but as early as 1901 the group had dwindled to only 80 members. In 1908 the chapel was closed. The land was bought by the trustees of the Toronto General Hospital and in 1910 the chapel was demolished. Christopher Street itself was closed, to make way for the first buildings of the hospital.

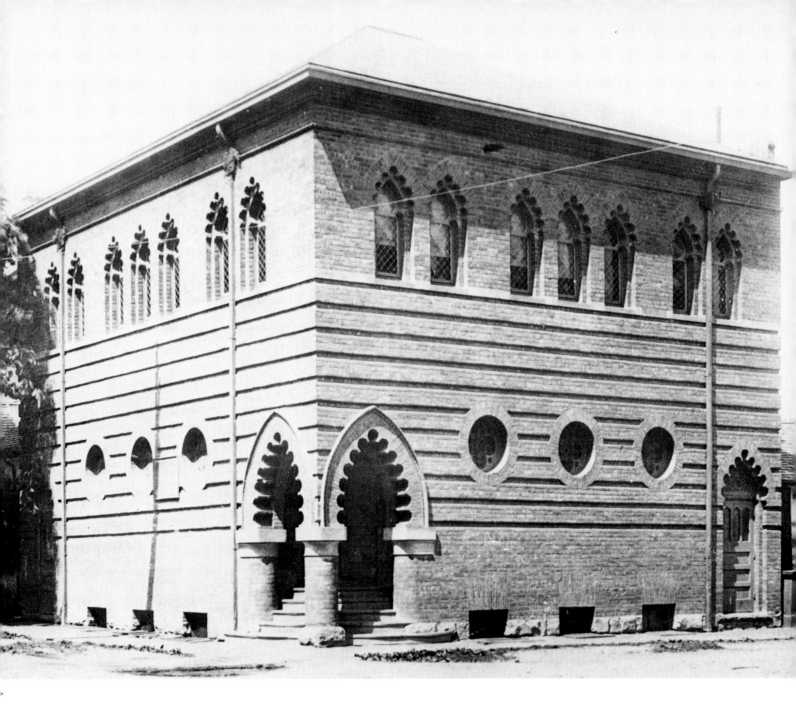

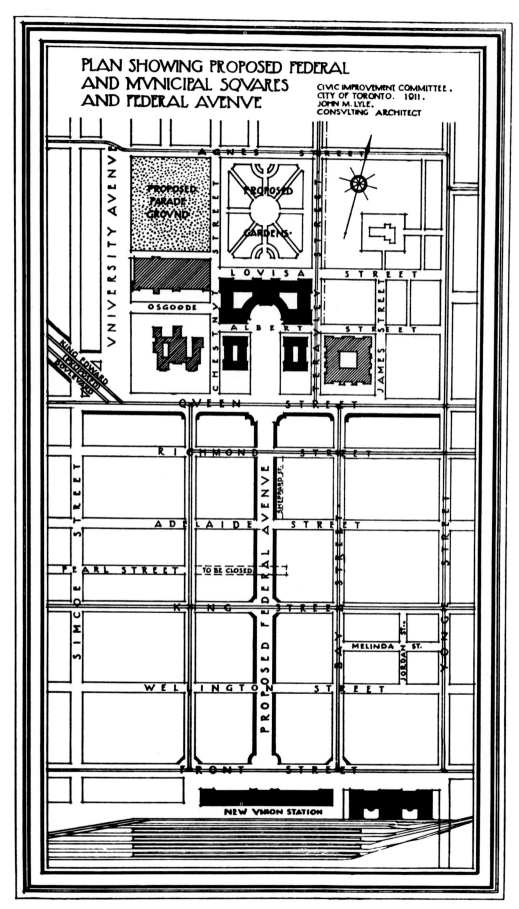

PLAN SHOWING PROPOSED FEDERAL
AND MVNICIPAL SQVARES
AND FEDERAL AVENVE

CIVIC IMPROVEMENT COMMITTEE.
CITY OF TORONTO. 1911.
JOHN M. LYLE.
CONSVLTING ARCHITECT

98

MAP OF THE PROPOSED FEDERAL AVENUE
1911 by John M. Lyle

York was laid out on a grid of streets meeting at right angles, which in its geometrical rationale appealed to the eighteenth-century, and military, mind. Apart from a few localized schemes attempted by large landowners during the nineteenth century (Spadina Avenue, Moss Park), Toronto, as it grew away from the harbour front, expanded along streets that were simply extensions of those of York—despite serious problems caused by the many ravines that crossed the city. By the early 1890s the city had become a manufacturing and shipping centre, with factories located in the downtown area. At the same time new suburbs had spread north and west of the commercial core, effectively separating the workers from their businesses, and enormous volumes of wheeled traffic had to travel over narrow old streets, generally by circuitous routes, to get out of the city. Only two streets had a useful width, University and Spadina Avenues, and neither one connected directly with the other, with the downtown, or with the countryside.

In this period Torontonians—especially the city's architects and its increasingly wealthy commercial aristocracy—were comparing Toronto with New York, Boston, Philadelphia, and Chicago, and finding it not properly up to date. American cities in this period were experimenting with planning and enjoying the first successes of the City Beautiful Movement—the democratic and essentially bourgeois emulation of the royal and imperially sponsored schemes of city beautification in European cities.[169] It had grown out of movements for better parks and sanitation; then, encouraged by the Exhibitions in Philadelphia in 1876 and Chicago in 1893, public and private patronage dotted American cities with parks, galleries, university buildings, theatres, monuments, and experimental housing. Most dramatically, there was a spate of major urban replanning schemes that increased transportation efficiency while providing aesthetic improvements such as spacious boulevards and parkways radiating from great squares and public monuments.

Most early interest in revamping Toronto's plan was concentrated on improving the waterfront, especially the relationship of the Esplanade and the railways. But as early as 1891 proposals were made to enlarge the intersection of King and Yonge and direct traffic in a circle around a fountain.[170] Organized interest in the City Beautiful Movement seems to have begun with the formation of the 'Adornment League' at the 1895 convention of the Ontario Association of Architects, but little came of it. It was effectively replaced by the Guild of Civic Art, founded in late 1897.[171]

In 1905 the Guild raised the necessary funding for a comprehensive planning study organized by the OAA, with the assistance of the Architectural Eighteen Club and the Engineers' Club. The plan, which was to be co-ordinated by an architect trained at the Ecole des Beaux Arts in Paris—probably John M. Lyle—consisted of three sections: (1) the creation of a series of commercial and park areas on landfill along the waterfront; (2) a system of parks and driveways encircling the city; and (3) a series of diagonal avenues connecting the core area with the suburbs and cross-country roads. The immediate occasion for the plan was undoubtedly the fire of 1904 that levelled much of the waterfront and sections of Bay Street. As it cleared the south side of Front, between Bay and York, this area was bought by the city and reserved as the site for a new Union Station. (Plans for the station were drawn by Darling & Pearson, E.J. Lennox, Alfred Chapman, and also by Carrere & Hastings of New York. Though it was not begun for several years, it was and remained the focus of this and later planning schemes.) The plan was presented for discussion in 1906 and received strong support from Toronto's business community. This was summed up by Sir Edmund Walker, president of the Canadian Bank of Commerce:

> To me, it is not a question of the city beautiful; it is just a question of practical common sense. Do we really believe in the city of Toronto?[172]

Unfortunately nothing was accomplished beyond the plan. However, the idea and the Edwardian optimism that had encouraged and supported it remained alive. In February 1909 the city council formally established a City Improvement Committee and the 1906 plan seems to have been brought out again, with the addition of a system of playgrounds (another interest of the City Beautiful Movement). The committee, chaired by Sir William Meredith, did not report until 28 December 1911, presenting a plan that aimed at a tentative solution to the city's traffic problems. There were many recommendations: two, the building of the Bloor Street viaduct and the northwest extension of Church Street to Davenport Road, were eventually completed. But the heart of the plan was Federal Avenue, shown here in a drawing by John M. Lyle.

The Avenue was designed to break up the long block between Bay and York, leading north from the Union Station site (to the left of the Dominion Public Building as it was projected at the time), across King and Queen to a monumental civic plaza. Terminating the vista was to be a new public building flanked by separate blocks, set as the focus to the grouping of Osgoode Hall, the Armouries (plate 96), and the City Hall. Conceived as a processional way from the 'Open Gate' of Union Station, Federal Avenue was to be another element in the re-creation of Toronto as the confident, wealthy, and imperial focus of Canada—like the new banks on King Street, the new buildings on the university campus, and the new Government House at Chorley Park (plate 122).[173]

Federal Avenue must be regarded as one of the grand lost causes in Toronto's architecture. In 1929, on the eve of the Depression, it was revived as Cambrai Avenue (plate 99), the last of Toronto's Beaux Arts City Beautiful schemes, but nothing came of that either. In 1929 there was even a feeling that the chance for it had already passed. But even today signs of it can still be seen. The grandly columned Sheppard Street façade of the Graphic Arts Building (1913 by F.S. Baker) on Richmond Street was to have fronted proudly on the new avenue. The Toronto Star Building (1928 by Chapman & Oxley, now demolished) was to have formed the northeast corner of the avenue's intersection with King Street; and the main block of the Royal York Hotel (1929 by Ross & Macdonald) was designed to fill exactly the block between Federal Avenue and York Street along Front. However, the building of the east wing of the Royal York effectively rendered impossible Toronto's most important town-planning scheme—one that, had it been completed, would have given the city's downtown the focus and grandeur it sadly lacks.

CAMBRAI AVENUE
Looking north across King Street West, as projected in 1929

The Federal Avenue project (plate 98) was revived in 1929 as the centrepiece of a new report of the Advisory City Planning Commission. Much of the plan was conceived as a public memorial to Canadians who had fought in the Great War, and the avenue was renamed Cambrai Avenue after the town in northern France that was liberated by Canadian troops on 9 October 1918. As before, the street was to be 110 feet wide, but at the north end it was replanned because the Federal Building on Richmond Street (1922) and the Concourse Building on Adelaide (1928 by Baldwin & Greene) now blocked the original line of the avenue. In the revised plan it split at Pearl Street, encircling a large island to be fronted by a monumental public building, before continuing at Richmond into the public square, now to be called St Julien Place (commemorating the Battle of Ypres).[174] The solution as a whole is reminiscent of the path of Park Avenue around Grand Central Station in New York. On the right in this perspective drawing by Earle C. Sheppard is the Toronto Star building, one of the major skyscrapers of the 1920s, which was planned to fit the eventual development of Federal Avenue.

· CAMBRAI AVENUE · LOOKING NORTH FROM KING ST ·

99

·LOOKING SOUTH ACROSS VIMY CIRCLE·

100

VIMY CIRCLE
Looking north and south from Vimy Circle (at Richmond Street) as it was projected in 1929

The major goal of the 1929 commission that recommended Cambrai Avenue was to find the best solutions to Toronto's traffic problem, and particularly to the question of how University Avenue (plate 95) should be extended south from Queen to Front, through the built-up area between York and Simcoe. By 1928 there were about 70,000 cars in the city requiring direct roads to and from the suburbs, and there had been no decision about where to put the roads and how to finance them. Problems of finance had killed the earlier plans, and supporters of the new improvements offered possible solutions. In 1929 S.G. Curry suggested that all motorists in the city be taxed $10 to $50 each. But even Curry realized that such a tax was unlikely, complaining that 'in this age the majority of people show a very great interest in dodging taxation, and loading it upon others who are less able to pay, and who do not receive any direct benefit.'[175]

Interest in the extension of University Avenue had been aroused in July 1918 when W.J. Gage proposed it as a fitting memorial, or 'Hero Avenue', honouring those who fought in the Great War.[176] It remained in the air until 1927, when it was actively taken up by the provincial government, which passed the University Avenue Extension Act on 3 April 1928.[177] This froze property values along the line of a straight extension of the avenue to Front Street and gave the city expropriation power. The commission appointed by the city recommended the building of a circular plaza at the intersection of Richmond Street and the extended avenue (to be called Queen's Park Avenue) to unify the intersection of several other new streets that were to connect the core of the city to the suburbs. To be called Vimy Circle after the Battle of Vimy Ridge, it was inspired both by the circuses of Regent Street in London, particularly as they were being rebuilt at this time, and by the grander *places* of Paris, with their radiating boulevards. In the centre was to be the provincial war memorial. The commission rejected a southward extension of University Avenue to Front Street for

economic reasons and proposed instead the building of Queen's Park Avenue, with a width of 100 feet, from Vimy Circle southeast to meet York Street at Front. This scheme—which, without Vimy Circle, was basically what was built—seems to have been first proposed by Watson Griffin in late 1928, in an article in *The Globe*. Today the angled street looks haphazard and incomplete, but in its original suggested form it began at Front Street in an open space called Britannia Square and ran north to Vimy Circle at Richmond. It would therefore have had visual identity, with a definite beginning and end.[178]

The perspective illustrated here, drawn by Earle C. Sheppard for the 1929 report, shows the grandly proportioned Beaux Art buildings that were projected to line the streets. With such buildings in mind, the commission urged the city council to require a uniform cornice line for the façades of 100 feet and that any buildings taller than this should rise in free-standing towers, with zoning and density bonuses given to encourage high-quality design. For once City Council followed advice and in July 1931, when demolition was nearly complete—the street opened formally on October 1931—it established a review committee to judge designs. The new buildings were to be non-residential and strictly regulated; cornice height and exterior colours and materials were also to be controlled; while overhead wires, billboards, and illuminated signs were forbidden. Every effort was made to produce a grandly urbane streetscape. But in a city and economy crippled by the Depression, and burdened with an excess of office space, major buildings of the type conceived in the halcyon days of the late twenties were out of the question. In the end only the small Parker Pen Company building at 154-6 University (1933, now the Reynolds Building) approached the quality projected for the extension, and only the Canada Life Building at 330—in the original section north of Queen (1929-31 by Sproatt & Rolph)—really indicates the monumental effect that the commissioners sought in 1929.

ALBERT STREET (N)
Between Chestnut and Elizabeth, 1912

The area bounded by University Avenue, College, Yonge, and Queen was one of early Toronto's largest working-class residential districts. The section east of Chestnut Street originally belonged to Dr James Macaulay, army surgeon first to the 33rd Regiment and then to the Queen's Rangers. Before his death in 1822 he began to subdivide the land into small lots along streets named for members of his family and friends. His sons continued the development after his death and by the 1840s a new suburb had grown up. The area east of Bay, centred on Trinity Square, was known as Macaulay Town. The land west of the Macaulay holdings was bought in 1826 by Sir John Beverley Robinson. He first sold a strip on the west side for the building of University Avenue, and then the ten acres fronting on Queen as a site for Osgoode Hall. In the 1830s and early 1840s he followed the Macaulays' example and laid out the rest of the area, making Chestnut (originally Sayre Street, named for his wife) and other streets a continuation of the Macaulay Town development.[179]

Both the Macaulay and the Robinson estates were divided into lots with narrow street frontages that were intended from the beginning for working- and middle-class houses. The growth of the area was slow; but during the second quarter of the century—as the city's population snowballed from about 7,500 in 1834, to 18,000 in 1844 and 30,000 in 1852 (largely because of immigration from Britain and Ireland)—the district became one of the most populous in the city. It was scattered with public institutions, like the House of Industry on Elm Street (1848 by William Thomas and now threatened with demolition), a few churches, and small or medium-sized factories. Most of the streets were lined with small two-storey houses, one-storey cottages, and the occasional shop.

Plate 101 shows the northeast corner of Albert and Chestnut—an area now covered by City Hall and Nathan Phillips Square—as it was on 15 May 1912. The two-storey house in the centre of the photograph—built about 1850, with most of its ground floor occupied by a shop—is typical of the kind of working-class house that was once very common in this area and in Yorkville (where indiscriminate speculative development has largely replaced them with parking lots or commercial buildings of the worst kind). Built of wood frame covered with wooden sheathing and finished in stucco (before the fire regulations were strengthened in the area), it follows the same pattern that inspired the design of Bishop's Block (plate 76) and the houses that later formed Sword's Hotel (plate 9). Countless similar examples, executed in brick or stone, can still be found in the provincial towns and villages of Britain and in towns of the Maritimes and eastern Ontario. Grouped, as this house was, with similar or smaller buildings, they give the streetscape a romantically and quietly small-town character. Whether built of brick or clapboard—or, as here, of stucco and frame—such houses were part of a strong vernacular or folk tradition

102 94-8 ALBERT STREET, 1912

in architecture that was brought to Canada by immigrant British and American craftsmen. Under the influence of more cosmopolitan and consciously artistic traditions in architecture a basic, simplified, and serenely pleasing pattern had evolved that in Canada is known as Late Georgian or, less accurately, as Regency. There was a basic symmetry to the building—three windows on the main façade, above the shop front, and three on the side, more widely spread and centred on the side door. Proportion, whether understood consciously or simply accepted as the way things were done, was an important element, relating the height and width of the doors and windows, the area of each window to the area of the wall between windows, and the height of the wall to the slope of the roof.

This tradition and formula gave even the smallest cottage something of the graceful character of larger, more expensive houses. Craftsmanship in carpentry, stone, and brickwork was the basis for the tradition, and almost all the houses had decorative details that distinguished them from their neighbours. In the house-shop on the corner of Albert and Chestnut in plate 101, the piers in the Greek Revival style and the projecting cornice of the side door case, as well as the mouldings that decorate the eaves, are quite simple but still creditable examples of craftsmanship in the fashion of the period. The cut-stone window lintels of the two-storey brick house at 98 Albert (on the left in plate 102) are characteristic of an earlier period. They indicate that

this house is more likely of the 1840s than the 1850s. With its raised ornament of keystones and incised lines, it is a particularly good example of the careful craftsmanship that could be found in small as well as large houses. In many cases such detail is an indication of the principal trade of the man who built the house: a carpenter was more likely to include elaborate woodwork in his building and a mason elaborate stonework in his. In the house at 96 Albert, to the right of the taller house, the construction was very likely supervised by a bricklayer who ornamented the front windows with alternating sections of red and 'white' brick, forming flat arches, instead of with decorative stone work.

Though they were small, these houses provided accommodation that was up to the standards of the period. The lots were narrow, but most of the early houses, like Mackenzie's house on York Street (plate 67), had gardens behind that provided food and the breathing space necessary for healthy living. In later years many of the houses were substantially altered. The dormered mansard roof of 98 Albert is a good example—it was probably added in the 1870s to provide more useable space. Also, as the area changed in character, several of the houses were partially converted to commercial uses. The shops that fill the ground floors of the three small houses at 90-4 Albert (on the right in plate 101) and the corner house in plate 102 were probably installed in the 1870s. However, by the turn of

103 THE REGISTRY OFFICE, C.1917

the century the comfortable character of these houses, suggested by the photographs, largely belied the actual conditions inside. Though they were nowhere nearly so badly maintained as the houses of the same age in Cabbagetown, most of them had been subdivided into tenements and crowded by later commercial development along the narrow streets and in former backyards.

However, it was not the slow deterioration of the houses that led to the transformation of the neighbourhood. More important was the proximity of the area to the growing commercial and government centres of the city that were developing in the 1890s and later. East of Bay, the expansion of the T. Eaton Company before the Great War changed the entire face of Macaulay Town, surrounding Trinity Church with six- and twelve-storey factories and transforming Trinity Square into an enormous loading dock.[180] West of Bay the changing character of University Avenue immediately affected the residential streets. The expansion of Osgoode Hall, and the building of the Armouries and the Toronto General Hospital complex, took great bites out of the area and led to the closing of streets and the demolition of houses and other buildings. But this

development was piecemeal and without a co-ordinated plan until the presentation of such schemes as Federal Avenue (plate 98), by John M. Lyle.

To terminate the northward vista of Federal Avenue, Lyle proposed a palatial civic government centre that would have occupied the two city blocks bounded by Chestnut, Louisa, Bay, and Queen and bisected by Albert. Unfortunately the elevation sketches do not seem to have survived, but the scale and character of the new buildings, and the huge square they were to frame, are clear from the plan of Federal Avenue. Behind, a formal public garden was to stretch back to Dundas (then known as Agnes Street); to the west, north of the Armouries and opening onto University Avenue, was to be a great public parade square. Such was the confident prosperity of Toronto at the time, and the ambitious vision of its commercial and civic leaders, that the project seemed practical and an immediate possibility. Accordingly in 1912 Council began to plan the new complex. They were encouraged, as they had been in the preparations for the building of the new Union Station at the south end of Federal Avenue, by the knowledge that new accommodation for certain civic departments and services was necessary in any case.

Without great difficulty the new civic buildings could be designed to fit the larger scheme: by stages, and without enormous expense, the city would obtain the monumental grouping that Lyle was planning.

The first of the new buildings was to be the Registry Office, on the north side of Albert, between Chestnut and Elizabeth, where it would replace the block of houses illustrated in plates 101 and 102 and stand as the separate block defining the western side of the new civic square. As was normal in the period, City Council sponsored a competition to obtain the designs.[181] In their presentations the competitors were limited by the role that the new building had to play in Lyle's plans and the definitely Beaux Arts and classical character that he had already established for the complex. At the same time the functional needs of the Registry Office were made very clear. It was to be organized into two wings—one for the east and one for the west end of the city—connected by an entrance hall and stair hall, with each wing having its own public reading room and work areas. In each of the three prize-winning designs the building was a simple block with the south façade dominated by a majestic portico of eight stone columns two storeys high. Though each of the designs also included a domed entrance foyer, they were markedly different in character and represented—as had the designs submitted for the 1909-10 competition for a new Government House (plate 122)—a compendium or summing-up of current taste and fashion in monumental public architecture. Charles S. Cobb's winning design was very much influenced by the Roman classicism made popular by C.F. McKim of the New York firm of McKim, Mead & White.[182] His smooth unfluted columns supported a heavy but finely detailed entablature, above which rose a plain attic storey. This, and the detailing of the corners where the walls were faced with large blocks of smooth masonry, gave the building an air of substantial solidity that was rather aloof and severe in its sophistication.

In the final decision the commission was given to Cobb for the facility with which he planned the working spaces and impressive interior public spaces. His central domed hall was more dramatically conceived than the others as a separate space, detailed and lit from the crown by a skylight, in emulation of the Pantheon in Rome. Behind and separate from it was a wide staircase rising to the upper floor, and to either side there were public reading rooms—lower than the foyer but lit by great skylights that filled the entire ceilings.

In the execution of Cobb's design no expense was spared to create a building that would be worthy of later inclusion in the proposed civic centre. The interior walls were faced with Champville marble imported from France, with baseboards of Botticino marble, and the floors were laid in patterns of pink and grey Tennessee marble. For the window sills and counter tops Cobb chose a newly available marble from Regina.* The work began in 1914 and the building opened in 1917. However, by the time the Registry Office was completed the same problems that had grounded the Federal Avenue scheme had also made any continuation of the civic-centre program unlikely. The schemes presented in 1929 (plate 99) included the Registry Office in the design of St Julien Place, the re-worked version of Lyle's civic square at the top of Cambrai Avenue, but again there was no further construction. After the failure of this project, Cobb's building languished on its side street, hidden from view behind the increasingly slummy section of Queen, between Bay and Osgoode Hall. It was not until 1958 that the concept of Lyle's civic square was again revived.[183] But by then the International Style and the Modern Movement were the order of the day and there was no place made for the Registry Office. The terms of the competition for the new City Hall—eventually won by Viljo Revell—made no mention of Cobb's building.

Construction work, which was completed in 1965, briefly gave the Registry Office a measure of the prominence for which it had been designed when all the buildings along the Queen Street edge of the site were demolished. But then it too was demolished, to make way for the western side of the podium that is partly enclosed by the towers of City Hall.

---

*At this time there was a concerted attempt to find Canadian equivalents to the expensive foreign marbles, stones, and granites that were so important in Beaux Arts architecture. The only lasting result of this search was the development of the Tyndall limestone quarries in Manitoba.

28-32 CAER HOWELL STREET
West of Murray (N), c.1871
1871/2 by William Forbes and John Ford

The land between University Avenue and McCaul Street, originally granted to Chief Justice William Dummer Powell, was long known as the Caer Howell reserve, after the Powell family seat in Wales.[184] (Caer, or Castle Howell, was the stronghold of the mythical Welsh hero Hoel, from whom the ap-Hoels, or Powells, claimed descent.) In the 1830s William Street (now an extension of Simcoe) was laid out to run north from Queen, through the estate, to end at the Powell family graveyard. This land became more valuable as the city expanded and in 1868 and 1869 the graveyard was closed, the tombs were moved to St James Cemetery, and a new east-west street—Caer Howell—was laid out from University Avenue to McCaul, in front of the former burial ground. The site of the graveyard was later occupied by Erskine Presbyterian Church (1878-9 by E.J. Lennox), but the rest of the street was laid out in small lots suitable for working-class houses.

The three cottages illustrated here were built in 1871 or 1872 by two small Toronto builders, William Forbes and John Ford, working in partnership. (Like many of the small builders of the day, they lived briefly in the houses before they were sold.) A comparison with the houses and cottages on Albert Street (plates 101-2) will indicate basic similarities. Like the earlier dwellings, these were built of frame and stucco; the stucco of number 30, in the middle, was lined in imitation of ashlar masonry—a technique more characteristic of the thirties and forties than the 1870s. The use of these materials, like the symmetry of the individual houses and the grouping of the three in a row, continued the earlier traditions of vernacular design. But the Gothic Revival details of number 28 (on the right) and 32—drip mouldings in wood nailed to the wall surface over the first-floor windows and doors; scroll-sawn bargeboards that decorate the pointed front gable, breaking the regularity of the roof-line; and the pointed window in the gable of number 28—all indicate different, more consciously picturesque, stylistic influences. Such decorative details were often copied from the pattern books that were popular in the last half of the century, or were directly borrowed—usually in a simplified form—from the designs of more important buildings in the city. This was certainly true of the dormered mansard roof of the middle house. The Second Empire style appeared in Toronto first in the late 1860s, in such important buildings as Government House (plate 29) and also in popular pattern books imported from the United States and Great Britain. After a short interval simple versions of the details, like those seen here, had become part of the stock in trade of small builders: they freely introduced them into their work to give houses and cottages an up-to-date and fashionable character.

These houses stood until about 1925/6, when they were demolished to make way for a Toronto Hydro cable yard. Today the site is occupied by a nurses' residence.

THE TORONTO ARCADE
131-9 Yonge Street (E), between Adelaide and Richmond, 1888
1883-4 by C.A. Walton

The Toronto Arcade was born from the desire to provide commercial space on several levels that would attract both shopkeepers and customers to an indoor 'street' and be comfortable and protected from the winter weather. The pedigree of such buildings goes back to diverse sources, like the deep arcades of medieval Italian towns and the enclosed bazaars of the Middle East. But the first glass-covered shopping streets appeared in England and France at the end of the eighteenth and the beginning of the nineteenth centuries—the Passage Feydeau in Paris (1790) and the Burlington Arcade in London (1818-19)—culminating in the greatest of all arcades, the Galeria Vittorio Emmanuelle II in Milan (1865-7). The European elegance and aristocratic 'chic' associated with such arcades, as well as the more intensive and profitable use

106 THE TORONTO ARCADE: INTERIOR, 1888

of core-area land that they represented, made them attractive models for North American commercial design.[185]

In Toronto, as in most North American cities, the fashionable commercial district was quite small. Unless a shop could be built on Yonge Street between King and Queen, or on short sections of King on either side of Yonge, a landlord had little hope of setting a high rent and the proprietor would be even less hopeful of attracting the 'carriage trade'. The Arcade created, in a street frontage of five standard-size shops, accommodation for twenty or more that all had an address on Yonge; and there was the added advantage of protection from the weather. This grouping of individual shops enabled the small proprietor to meet the challenge from the new department stores in the city,

such as Eaton's and Simpson's, which offered a variety of goods under one roof. Finally, the Arcade connected Yonge Street with Victoria, thus giving the city a much-needed new 'street' and the shopkeepers a steadily passing stream of potential customers, many of whom worked on Toronto Street and King Street East.

The Toronto Arcade—the first such building in Canada—represented an important change in the city's commercial scale, comparable to the development of suburban shopping centres in the 1950s and 1960s. This change was made possible by the frank exploitation of cast iron and glass, used with relatively little ornament to create a tall space bathed in bright natural light. (Such an impressive interior space had previously been found only in a few of the city's churches and public buildings.) The arrangement of the building was quite simple. There were four-storey blocks at each end, on Yonge and Victoria. Between ran the actual arcade, three and a half storeys high, with a peaked glass roof 130 feet long and 35 feet wide, 24 shops on the ground floor, offices on the second—connected by a balcony that ran round the open area and was reached by stairs in the front and rear blocks—and on the third floor a mixture of offices and artists' studios. For the ground-floor shops the passage was an indoor street. For all the shops, offices, and studios the arcade was a spacious light well. To allow maximum light to enter the interiors, the central roof was entirely of iron-framed glass, and the inner walls were the lightest possible frame of cast iron, filled with wide sheets of plate glass. It was a type of construction that the architect, C.A. Walton, knew well from ten years' practice in Detroit (1866-76), and later used in the first Mutual Street Arena.[186] Like the designers of buildings with cast-iron fronts in the 1870s, Walton did not skimp on the decorative detail needed to make the Arcade attractive. There were Corinthian capitals on the piers of the shopfronts and a pierced balustrade with gaslights mounted on tall, slender standards—all in cast iron.

The Yonge Street façade was intentionally the most impressive feature of the building. Four storeys high—five, if the central pedimented arch is counted—and constructed in red brick and contrasting Ohio sandstone, with carving by Holbrook & Mollington, it was meant to attract attention away from its smaller and more conventional neighbours, as well as to meet the architectural challenge of Eaton's and Simpson's stores a little further to the north on the opposite side of Yonge.

All the shops were drawn together into one unit dominated by the two-storey arch in the centre, whose curve suggested the glass-vaulted passage down the centre of the building; without doors, it beckoned to passers-by. The emphasis of the central pediment was balanced on either side by lower pediments that were in fact false fronts with no space behind them. Essentially the façade of the Arcade was conceived more to be noticed than as a consistent exercise in any style, although it was described as 'Neo-Grec' or freely classical in composition and details, designed in a 'bold free manner, not too much loaded with elaborate detail'.[187] (The piers flanking the entrance arch were described as 'Egyptian' for no apparent reason.)[188] Like many commercial buildings in Toronto, the detail was richly eclectic and was appreciated as such.

By the early 1950s the development of Yonge Street south of Queen as a street of offices had undermined the attractiveness of the Arcade. It stood until 1955 when, after being vacant for two years, it was demolished. The name and something of the basic interior form—though nothing of the rich detail and play of light—are commemorated in the present Arcade Building, built in 1958-60. What is much more striking is the fact that the arcade principle currently enjoys an immense vogue once again and was a motivating factor in the design of both the Eaton Centre and the Royal Bank Plaza. Had the Toronto Arcade survived into the 1970s, a coat of paint and a sympathetic owner could have made it a unique centre of commercial activity on lower Yonge Street, with an atmosphere that cannot now be recreated.

107

THE PROJECT FOR EATON'S COLLEGE STREET
412-48 Yonge Street at College (SW)
1928-30 by Ross & Macdonald; Sproatt & Rolph, associate architects

Eaton's established its commercial success on Timothy Eaton's policies: 'One price and cash only' and 'Satisfaction or money refunded'. With the issuing of the first mail-order catalogue in 1884, the beginning of the company-owned factory system in 1886, and the opening of the huge Winnipeg store in 1906, it came to dominate the middle- and working-class markets in Canadian retailing. But after Timothy Eaton's death in 1907, the new management began to change its merchandising policies. First in Toronto, and then elsewhere, it started to challenge the smaller specialty shops with new services and lines of merchandise that would attract the wealthier 'carriage trade', who were as interested in fashion as in cost. The new policies were formed by John Craig Eaton (knighted in 1915), who succeeded his father in the presidency, and they were decisively influenced by his acquaintance—and that of his wife, Flora McCrea Eaton—with London stores such as Harrod's, Selfridge's, and Debenham's, and their American counterparts like Altman's in New York.[189] Some of the changes must have seemed daring at the time, especially bringing Paul Poiret, one of Paris's leading couturiers, to Toronto in 1913 to show his collection and give three lectures.[190] Other changes were long overdue, including the development of the store's restaurant from a simple buffet counter, established in the 1890s to give tired shoppers a cup of tea or a glass of milk, into the Georgian Room, which opened in 1923 and provided Toronto with a much-needed luncheon place in elegant surroundings.[191]

Architecture played an essential part in the transformation of the store's image. Timothy Eaton had been thoroughly pragmatic about the store's premises, adding new space when necessary and ending up with a confused collection of buildings of varying dates that had little real presence in the streetscape and no corporate image. In 1907 the extension of the store north, along Yonge to Albert Street, marked the beginning of a rebuilding program under the supervision of Sproatt & Rolph. It continued for more than twenty years and was influenced by René Cera, a French architect who joined the store's full-time staff in the early 1920s and designed the palatially columned eighteenth-century setting of the Georgian Room for Lady Eaton.[192]

The culmination of this period of expansion was not the remodelled Queen Street store, however, but an immense new store-and-office complex planned for the corner of Yonge and College Streets, and shown here in an architect's drawing. The chosen site was a block of about ten acres, bounded by Hayter, Yonge, College, and Bay Streets. (Here stood Wykeham Lodge, a villa built in 1841 that was the home of Bishop Strachan School from 1869 to 1915.) The choice of the site was based on the assumption that College would replace Queen as Toronto's major east-west shopping street, and that a new store at Yonge and College would be in an ideal location to serve Toronto's western and northern suburbs.

Planning for Eaton's College Street, as the store was called, began about 1916, but work did not begin until 1928.[193] The entire site was to be covered with a seven-storey podium that would house the store. Each of the façades was dominated by rows of four-storey piers that separated tall panels of windows. The piers were to stand on a strongly horizontal base of framed display windows, and support an entablature with carved aluminum cresting (stained to look like bronze). At the centre of each façade was to be a tall portal—like a triumphal arch—to mark the main entrance for that face. Above the podium was to rise a skyscraper of offices, topped 670 feet above the street by a tall beacon silhouetted against the sky. The simplified classicism of the detailing, the successive set-backs, and the long rows of piers on the street façades were undoubtedly influenced by contemporary American and British work. But the immense scale of the project (with a total floor area of almost 4,200,000 square feet, which would have made it one of the largest complexes in the world) was completely unprecedented in Canada.

Construction of the new building was planned in stages, beginning in 1928-30 with the seven-storey block at the corner of Yonge and College and extensions of the main floor south to Hayter and west to Bay (outlined in white on the drawing of the entire scheme). This first stage was opened in 1930, with great fanfare, as Eaton's Home Furnishings Building (only later were other departments opened at College Street). But by this time construction difficulties and the Depression had made the completion of the building highly unlikely. In the end, nothing more was built and the project became one of Toronto's most celebrated, indeed legendary, architectural misadventures.

Eaton's College Street was conceived primarily as a corporate landmark, but its monumental elegance and fine materials reflected a concern that the company should be seen to be doing its share for the good of the city. Even though the complex was still-born, the fine finish of the existing building made it a credit to the company and an ornament to the city, just as the elaborate warehouses and banks of the nineteenth century had been. (Here Tyndall limestone was used for most of the exterior stonework, with detailing in cast

108 EATON'S COLLEGE STREET: LAMP DEPARTMENT, MAIN FLOOR, 1930

and carved aluminum and brass and polished brown Gananoque granite.) But the first phase of the development made a more direct contribution: Eaton's donated strips of land along College and Yonge to permit these streets to be widened, and paid the cost of the land that was necessary to smooth into an even curve the dogleg connection, across Yonge, of Carlton and College. Both of these actions made sound commercial sense because they eased the traffic congestion around the store and gave the new building an individualized setting in the streetscape. Nevertheless they were still private gifts that made possible what general indifference and civic niggardliness had prevented for half a century.

Eaton's continued to occupy the store until 1976, when the new store in the Eaton's Centre, at Yonge and Dundas Streets, replaced both it and the Queen Street store. The older store was demolished as the first phase of the Eaton Centre was extended southward; but the College Street store and its site were sold to a consortium of developers. Fortunately they recognized both the building's aesthetic value and the commercial possibilities of its well-designed space. Their plans included renovation for commercial and office uses (almost complete at the time of writing) and the erection of apartment and office buildings to the south and west.

INTERIORS

The monumental and simplified, if rather sober, classical exterior of Eaton's College Street scarcely prepared the visitor for the streamlined and French Art Deco elegance of the interiors.[194] René Cera designed most of the fittings and detail of the main floor. Its principal feature was a long concourse that ran the length of the Yonge Street front and rose in easy steps to accommodate the change in level between Hayter and College Streets. (Originally known as the Elevator Arcade and splendidly finished in travertine and marble, it will remain in the renovated building.) The same effort and cost were lavished on the rest of the sales area. Plate 108 shows the Lamp Department at the south end of the main floor, and its mezzanine level of offices and special display areas. Here the merchandise was provided with a classically simple, but supremely elegant, background: travertine floors and stairs, warm grey marble balustrades beside the stairs, display cabinets and tables finished with walnut veneers of various tones and silvery Monel-metal fittings. The tall, elongated vases decorated with polished rings on the base and bowl were actually lighting fixtures that directed light upwards, to be reflected softly from the white plaster ceiling. The shape—derived from Egyptian forms—was very popular at this time and was used in

109 EATON'S COLLEGE STREET: ENSEMBLE SHOP, MAIN FLOOR, 1930

several ways throughout the store. Plate 109, another of the publicity photos taken in 1930, shows two models posing in front of the windows of the Ensemble Shop,* flanked by polished Monel-metal vases filled with dried and artificial flowers. This photograph perfectly illustrates how sleek architecture and detailing, rich materials, and the finest of contemporary craftsmanship were combined to create the sophisticated, chic image that the College Street Store was intended to represent.

The climax and showplace of the entire store was the suite of public rooms on the seventh floor.[195] Arranged like the reception rooms on one of the great ocean liners of the period, they included a concert hall (the Eaton Auditorium), a restaurant (the Round Room), and a long foyer between the two. The entire floor was planned by the French architect and designer, Jacques Carlu, then professor of design at the Massachusetts Institute of Technology. He had control over everything, from the furniture and architectural detail to the table linen, silver, and china—even to the uniforms of the ushers and waitresses. He designed the three areas as an ensemble that was unified by a pale monochromatic colour scheme of silvered shades of beige and grey with black.

*Located in the one-storey wing that extended west to Bay. Intended as an indoor street, it was lined with specialized shopping areas.

The largest of the rooms was the Eaton Auditorium. It was planned by the company—with the decisive influence of Lady Eaton, who was musically inclined—as a public concert and lecture hall that could easily be converted to a ballroom. Plate 110 was taken from the entrance to the Auditorium and shows the wide low space under the gallery at the back, which could be filled with chairs for important concerts. Carlu based his decorative scheme here, and in the other two areas of the floor, on abstract patterns of solid shapes, like those worked in the coloured tiling of the floor; or of thin, almost metallic, lines, like those that swept around three sides of the Auditorium to draw the eye toward the proscenium. The stage itself was framed by panels of back-lit translucent glass. (Carlu used light to animate all the seventh-floor interiors and vary the mood of each area.) There were similar back-lit fixtures of glass over the exits and marking the stairways, supplemented by the illuminated glass-and-metal ceiling set in the stepped cove of the vestibule, while light from fixtures concealed in the cornices was reflected from the ceiling. The tone, and intensity, of the light could be controlled at will.

The Foyer, shown in plate 111, was undoubtedly the most difficult of all the interiors to design. In the original scheme it was to have been U-shaped, around three sides of the Auditorium, but the third side was

10 EATON'S COLLEGE STREET: EATON AUDITORIUM, SEVENTH FLOOR, 1930

111 EATON'S COLLEGE STREET: FOYER, SEVENTH FLOOR, 1930

never built, leaving it with an L-shape. It was here that the monochromatic colour scheme and the lighting were most useful. The pale colours in shiny, matte, and leather-like surfaces seemed to make the space larger. The lighting from rounded cornice-like fixtures of frosted glass, and particularly from the exposed fluorescent tubes that ran along the centre of the ceiling, gave the Foyer a cheerful air in which the intermission crowds at a concert, or daytime patrons of the Round Room, appeared to the best advantage. But of the three areas on the seventh floor, the Foyer was inevitably the least successful: without crowds, the size and difficult proportions emphasized its emptiness and made it a rather melancholy space, where few people wished to linger—especially as it grew tattered in later years.

The Round Room (plate 112) was the finest of the College Street interiors and was entered from the Foyer through glass and Monel-metal doors (on the right in plate 111). In plan it was a circle within a square, with the corners filled by raised alcoves and the 'round' shape echoed in the pattern of circular mouldings of the coved and domed ceiling and in the circles that were worked in the tiling of the floor. As in the Auditorium and Foyer, the colour scheme was silvered tones of beige and grey with black—but Carlu's restaurant interior is more refined and radiant, as if liberated by the shape of the room, with the curve of the ceiling ringed by a wide band of polished black glass and the 'dome' enamelled a sunny lemon yellow. On the four curving walls between the alcoves, Carlu installed murals, painted by his wife Natacha, that depicted 'life in the village, the forest, the fields, and by the sea.' This characteristically French evocation of the simple pleasures of country life, in a setting of the utmost elegance, was continued with eight terra-cotta statuettes by Denis Gelin, enamelled white, that depicted elongated peasant figures and stood in narrow niches lined with polished black glass on either side of each alcove. But the focal point of the room was a circular fountain on a pedestal of circular black-and-frosted-glass plates, lit from below through the shimmering water. Placed around the fountain, like planets around the sun, were the tables, covered with white linen, and black sandlewood chairs with beige leatherette upholstery. Above the fountain a chandelier of similar design hung from the dome of the ceiling; its lowest level was an enclosed radio speaker to provide music. These two elements—the lighted fountain and the chandelier with its radio—were symbols of a modernity that united grace and technology. Together they epitomized the interior of the whole store, which combined forms borrowed from contemporary technology—like the exposed fluorescent lighting and the horizontal and vertical patterns of streamlining—with fine materials and craftsmanship, and transformed them into classic works of applied art.

During the forty-five years that Eaton's occupied the store, the main-floor interiors illustrated here were gradually made tawdry by remodelling or neglect, especially during the fifties and early sixties, when the streamlined elegance of the twenties and thirties was at the nadir of its popularity. The seventh-floor interiors were also changed by the introduction of new colour schemes, the rebuilding of the Auditorium floor on a slope, and the removal of the fountain from the Round Room. When the store finally closed in 1976 the outlines of Carlu's design could still be seen, but it was difficult to sense the brilliance and high style of the original scheme. These areas have been included here not only to give an idea of what has been lost, but to encourage both the developers and the various public agencies concerned to do everything that is necessary to restore the original distinction of these rooms and ensure their permanent preservation.

12 EATON'S COLLEGE STREET: ROUND ROOM, SEVENTH FLOOR, 1930

Front Elevation

YORKVILLE TOWN HALL
856-60 Yonge Street (W), opposite Collier Street, c.1860
1859-60 by William Hay

The village of Yorkville was laid out in the 1830s and incorporated in 1853. By 1859 it was a popular middle- and working-class suburb that was close to Toronto (which was then just beginning to spread north of Queen Street) but less expensive to live in.[196] With official status and the increase in population came the desire for a civic building whose dignity and physical importance would mark the centre of the community. (The same combination of expansion and community pride led to the rebuilding in 1858-61 of St Paul's Church—now Maurice Cody Hall—on Bloor Street East, the Anglican church that served Yorkville.)

As in Toronto's St Lawrence Hall (1850) and its second City Hall (1844, plate 40), the Yorkville Town Hall had to serve a wide variety of public functions while also including commercial space, the rentals from which would help support the mortgage of the building and its maintenance.[197] In his design (plate 113) William Hay grouped the public areas in the four-storey centre block, which rose to a wide gable and, on the left, a wooden clock tower (completed, after the photograph above was taken, in a modified version of the original design). On the ground of this block the arch on the right led to Yorkville's police station; that on the left to the council offices on the second floor and a galleried public hall on the third; while the centre arch was wide enough to permit the Yonge Street horse cars to pass through to stables and barns in the rear yard. Hay placed the shops on either side of the main block, extending the façade, but the much greater height of the centre clearly indicated the greater importance of the public functions. He had prepared two designs for the public portion of the building, the other being only three storeys high, and the Council chose the larger and more expensive version—although the $12,000 it cost must have severely taxed their resources. There can be no doubt that the expense was justified because the greater height successfully proclaimed the existence of Yorkville in the mostly two-storey streetscape of upper Yonge Street.

Hay designed the Yorkville Town Hall in an up-to-date High Victorian style that was an amalgam of traditional English Gothic elements and newly appreciated Continental features. The style had definite religious overtones that were especially apparent when Hay included a large rose window filled with stained glass as the central feature of the façade. (There were three more such windows on the rear façade; all four lighted the public hall.) But this religious character was one of the reasons for the popularity of the style in public buildings, especially in Britain: it implied the earnest and serious attitude to responsibilities, and to life in general, that was considered appropriate in municipal affairs. By far the most striking element was the use of vibrant colour contrasts. Red bricks were used to decorate and enliven the buff or 'white' brick of the façade in red-and-'white' or solid red bands around the arches, and in combination with bricks that were blackened (by dipping them in creosote) to pick out the

rows of arched corbels that decorated the gable, the tower, the eaves of the shop fronts, and that ran across the façade on either side of the rose window. This richness and visual interest, belying the simple materials used in construction, were the ideal complement to the tall, picturesque massing of the building in the streetscape. Henry Scadding in *Toronto of Old* compared it to a Flemish 'hôtel de ville'—suggesting that it had strayed to Toronto from Ghent.[198]

The Town Hall was the home of Yorkville's council until the village was annexed by Toronto in 1883 and became part of St Paul's Ward, after which the building was called St Paul's Hall. (When the trolley cars were electrified in 1892 the Toronto Street Railway built a new set of car barns at 36 Yorkville Avenue, now altered out of recognition as the Mercedes-Benz service depot.) But the old town hall remained the heart of the area, housing the local branch of the Toronto Public Library from 1884 until 1907 (when the new building at 22 Yorkville was opened), and, for several more years, Police Station No. 5. On the night of 12 November 1941 the hall (which had been used as a servicemen's club since the beginning of the Second World War) was gutted by fire; the ruins were cleared away during the next year. In 1949 the rest of the buildings in the block were demolished to make way for Pickering Farms grocery store (later acquired by Loblaws). The site of the Town Hall became a parking lot, which still disfigures the streetscape.

Although this historic reminder of Yorkville's identity as a separate community has disappeared, the village coat of arms that once adorned the keystone over the rose window in the Yonge Street façade has recently been built into the old Yorkville Fire Hall, a building of somewhat comparable style, at 34 Yorkville

LONG GARTH
99 St George Street (E), north of Hoskin
1882, with additions in 1902 and 1905 by Darling & Pearson

Long Garth was the only house in Toronto that one would wish to have preserved as an entity—for its notable works of art, its library, and its furnishings as well as for its architecture. While not as pretentious or as elaborate as the homes of Walker's associates— Senator McMaster's Rathnelly, S.H. Janes' Benvenuto (plate 125), Sir Joseph Flavelle's Holwood, or Sir John Eaton's Ardwold (plate 128)—it was nevertheless a statement—complete, personal, and assured—of the taste and attitudes of a man who, more than any other, influenced the artistic development of early twentieth-century Toronto.

Byron Edmund Walker (1848-1924; knighted in 1910) was the prince and leader of Toronto's financial community. He began his career in Hamilton in 1861 and joined Senator McMaster's new Canadian Bank of Commerce in 1868. There he worked up through the bank's agencies in New York, London, Windsor, and Hamilton, to become general manager in Toronto in 1886. His rise was joined with that of Toronto as a commercial and banking centre, and it was crowned by the presidency of the bank in 1907, a post he held until his death.[199] But he did not regard this career, or the self-centred accumulation of money, as the only proper goal of a business man. His views were summed up in his 1910 Dominion Day address as president of the bank:

> When we find a man who has devoted his life only to making money, and who has not created anything worthwhile in doing so, who cannot read books, enjoy beautiful things, or indulge in sport, we know that he has thrown his precious life away.[200]

For Walker the success of his career in banking provided the opportunity for the creation of an important art collection. It included major oil paintings by Homer Watson, Paul Peel, Charles-François Daubigny, and works representing the French Barbizon and nineteenth-century Dutch schools, which were popular in Toronto at the turn of the century. But his collection and his own interests were centred on engravings, etchings, and prints. His interest in engraving and etching had developed out of the need to distinguish genuine and forged banknotes, and his first purchases, bought in Hamilton, were Bartlett engravings. The years spent in New York—1873-5 and 1881-6—provided the opportunity for study and for beginning a fine collection that was added to during later trips to England—in 1902 he purchased fifty Rembrandt etchings from Colnaghi's in London—the Netherlands, and finally China and Japan in 1919.

Long Garth was the background against which the paintings and etchings were displayed, along with equally fine collections of furniture, Turkish carpets, and Oriental and European porcelain and pottery. Built in 1882 for Robert Ramsay Wright,[201] Professor of Biology at the University of Toronto, and acquired by Walker in 1889, the red brick house was Queen Anne in style. Inspired—like many fashionable houses of the period in Canada and the United States—by romantic notions of English houses of the late seventeenth century, it rose in a flurry of large and small gables and dormers, ornamented with half-timbering and decorative woodwork, to a series of picturesquely composed tall ribbed chimneys. The house was one of the first to be built on St George Street and stood in a garden that extended east to the present Devonshire Place—the long garden or 'garth' that gave the house a name and setting appropriate to its Old English country-house atmosphere and style.

Walker made relatively few changes in the house until 1902, when he commissioned Darling & Pearson to design a two-storey addition at the rear, overlooking the garden. The main room in this new wing was the library (plate 116)—a rectangular room separated from the front of the house by a wide, panelled sliding door and lined by two tiers of bookcases with leaded glass doors. Much the most dramatic part of the library was the vaulted ceiling, designed by Gustav Hahn and decorated with trees, stylized in the manner of the English Art Nouveau, and with rib-like borders with meander patterns.* To complete the room, Walker commissioned G.A. Reid to paint an allegorical cycle depicting the seasons, in the manner of Puvis de Chavannes. (The section of the mural above the bookcases depicted Spring.) The library was also designed to house the collection of etchings. Next to the doorway, where he could see it from his desk, Walker had installed a special cabinet with plate-glass doors in which he displayed a changing selection of his favourite works against fabric-covered panels.

The library was Walker's inner sanctum and he lavished most of his attention on it. The other main rooms in the house—far less dramatic and pretentious in their decoration—were settings for his collections of eighteenth- and early-nineteenth-century furniture and his Oriental carpets. The dining room (plate 117) and the drawing room (plate 118) were both located in the original part of the house. The dining room, like most of the other main rooms, was finished in dark wood, with a panelled wainscot that rose almost to the ceiling. (It was thought at the time that wallpaper, or fabric hangings, would retain the smells and smoke of cooking.) Into the panelling was built a commodious buffet and china cabinet, trimmed—as were many Queen Anne interiors of the 1880s and 1890s—with half-columns, arches, and mouldings derived from the late eighteenth century. The result was unlike anything Sheraton or Hepplewhite might have designed, but it completely satisfied Late Victorian notions of efficiency in dinner service and storage. In the centre of the side wall was a hanging curio cabinet—glazed in small panes like a miniature bay window. At first this may have provided sufficient space for Walker's collection of European and Oriental pottery and porcelain, but by about 1912, when these interior photographs were taken, the collection had overflowed onto the plate rail above the wainscot, which was crowded with rows of plates, jars, and other objects. The display was as appropriate to the dining room as the Rembrandts were to the library, and it would have effectively distracted the visitor from the strange and exceedingly ugly chairs, which appear to have been influenced by Continental art nouveau. (A table cloth patterned with art-nouveau foliage covers the dining-room table—seen here without its extension leaves.) The drawing room—one end of which can be seen in plate 118—was located at the front of the house, opening off the main hall. It was not very different in character from the dining room and provided an unassuming background for the various

---

*The ceiling closely resembles that of the entrance hall of Sir Joseph Flavelle's Holwood (1901-2), which was also designed by Darling & Pearson and contained Hahn's decorative work. The subacqueous greens and blues, highlighted with gold and red, of the Holwood ceiling were probably used in the Long Garth library.

6 LONG GARTH: THE LIBRARY, C.1917

117 LONG GARTH: THE DINING ROOM, C.1912

collections, with Chinese stoneware displayed on the cabinets, Oriental rugs on the floor, numerous small paintings—including a Tom Thomson oil sketch on the mantel—and a few pieces of fine furniture.

In 1905 Walker added a second wing (the one on the right in plate 115), again designed by Darling & Pearson. It included a sky-lit billiard room and an arcaded entrance hall, approached from the street under a glass-and-iron canopy. Like the library, these new areas were designed around the collection; the hall, for example, was carefully finished—in a manner quite unusual for the period—with a black and white marble floor and walls covered with grey burlap as a neutral background for prints by Whistler, Dürer, and Millet.

Although Walker devoted much of his time to his collection, he was a thoroughly committed champion of humanist values in private and civic life over the Spartan and utilitarian materialism so often associated with Victorian and Edwardian capitalists. As general manager, and later president, of the Canadian Bank of Commerce he commissioned a magnificent series of banking buildings—most of them designed by Darling & Pearson—that were conceived as both an enhancement of the bank's image and an ornament to large and small communities across the country. At the same time he founded, or played a central role in, numerous cultural institutions: the Champlain Society, the Mendelssohn Choir, Appleby College in Oakville, the Royal Ontario Museum, the National Gallery of Canada,[202] the Art Gallery of Toronto (now the Art Gallery of Ontario), the Toronto Guild of Civic Art, and the University of Toronto. To Sir Edmund Walker,

118 LONG GARTH: THE DRAWING ROOM, *c.*1912

more than to any other man, Toronto owes the quality of its cultural institutions.

Walker died at Long Garth in 1924. The following year the house was sold to Trinity College, which used it as the women's residence for St Hilda's College. (The college later built a new St Hilda's at the east end of the garden, facing Devonshire Place.) In 1969 Long Garth was destroyed to provide a parking lot for the new Robarts Library of the University of Toronto. This demolition—sponsored, as it was, by the university—was more than an act of vandalism. It must be considered a classic example of the philistinism that Walker had hoped to eradicate by supporting and encouraging that same university and its sister institutions.

THE TIMOTHY EATON HOUSE
182 Lowther Avenue at Spadina Road, c.1965
1888-9

The most important factor in the development of Toronto at the end of the nineteenth century was the opening of the area north of Bloor Street, on either side of St George, to residential development. In 1873 two new streets were laid out: Walmer Road, curving north from Bloor to Lowther; and Spadina Road, running straight north to Davenport.[203] By about 1887 the area between Walmer and Bedford was completely established—in large part by S.H. Janes of Benvenuto (plate 125). Although most of it was designed to attract well-to-do middle-class families, much larger lots were intended for wealthier buyers along Walmer and Spadina Roads and the extension of St George north of Bloor. In the late 1880s and early 1890s the Annex—as the district became known after it was annexed to the city in 1883—became one of Toronto's most fashionable residential areas, and it was to the Annex that Timothy Eaton moved in 1889 from his first large house on Orde Street, just west of University Avenue.

In 1919 Timothy Eaton was described as a man who

> never had a desire for a big house, just because it was big, or for mere style in decoration and furniture. He wanted the best, but he believed that elegance should be tempered by great simplicity and a maximum of real comfort. He loved the long crowded tables, the chattering rooms, the festive times when he could feel the great joy of being not only a great merchant and a powerful citizen, but the father of a family and the head of a clan that reached out and out to the people.[204]

Though a description like this contains a certain amount of pure flattery, it was not inappropriate for the house that Eaton built at Lowther and Spadina. This was not the largest or the most elaborate residence in the Annex; that honour went at the time (as it goes today) to the house at 135 St George Street that David Roberts Jr designed in 1891 for George Gooderham. But the Eaton house (which may also have been designed by Roberts) was obviously the home of a man of wealth and prominence. In design it was entirely typical of the large, and many of the smaller, houses of the Romanesque Revival in the use of a tall corner tower to mark the building in the streetscape, in the tile-hung gables and tall chimneys to break up the prominent roof, and especially in the richly textured surfaces of red brick, terra cotta, and Credit Valley stone. Together these elements formed a calculated composition that was picturesque and individualized, yet fitted well into the closely built streetscape of the Annex. This photograph, taken about 1965, shows the house as it was after extensive additions were made in 1904-5, adding short wings to the right and left and, in front, a columned porch with a sunroom above.[205] The additions were uninteresting in themselves, and unfortunately their heavy, spreading horizontality negated the important vertical accents of the original design.

The focus of the house was its central hall, where guests were received and from which the main stair rose in several flights to the upper floors. In larger houses of the period, like Benvenuto, such halls were thought of as useable living spaces—rather like medieval great halls—that were warmed by their own fireplaces, comfortably furnished for informal lounging, and spacious enough for large-scale entertainments. The other rooms of the main floor opened freely into the hall—though often screened by curtains, like those seen on the right and left—and there were often bays and inglenooks arranged for secluded, comfortable seating. Even the multiple landings on the stairway became room-like spaces. But clearly in Timothy Eaton's house, the hall—probably because it was small in proportion to the adjoining rooms—became a cluttered gallery of the family's most prized possessions and souvenirs, hung with art wallpaper and scattered with sentimental statuary, bits of interesting pottery and glass, and ferociously uncomfortable furniture, like the unyielding chair in the centre. Through it all the visitor passed quickly to more comfortable and less showy family living rooms beyond.

However, the house did have a fine example of one of the small seating nooks that were popular at the time: a low-ceilinged room under the stairway, in the background of plate 121. Entered under a wide cusped or scalloped arch supported on columns decorated in gold, it was furnished as a miniature seraglio, following the same fashion of the 1890s for things Moorish that influenced the interiors of Massey Hall and Euclid Hall, the Hart Massey house at 515 Jarvis Street. A row of narrower cusped arches on columns stood around the space, which was lit by two small windows at the far end and was infinitely expanded by mirrors on the side walls. Lining the walls were heavily padded divans scattered with cushions and bolsters, and tables of painted wood and polished brass supported statues, art pottery, and various plants. The atmosphere was exotic, but thoroughly Late Victorian and middle class in its cluttered comfort—with, needless to say, none of the erotic and risqué overtones of the harems that had inspired its design.

Several members of the Eaton family built or bought houses in the Annex, and Timothy Eaton's house on

Lowther was the centre of the family universe. Eaton
died there in early 1907, but his wife continued to use it
until 1928/9. It then passed to Timothy's daughter,
Josephine Burnside, who in 1934 gave it to the Imperial
Order of the Daughters of the Empire for its national
headquarters. In 1965 the house was vacated and
demolished and the present apartment building was
constructed on the site.

120 TIMOTHY EATON HOUSE: THE HALL, *c*.1900

121 TIMOTHY EATON HOUSE: THE SITTING NOOK OFF THE HALL, *c.*1900

122

CHORLEY PARK
Roxborough Drive, c.1916
1911-15 by F.R. Heakes

When the provincial government decided to build a new Government House in 1909, they purchased a large site on the north side of Bloor Street East, now occupied by the Manufacturers' Life building. The Ministry of Public Works held a design competition and twelve architects submitted projects. The winning entry was by G.W. King in the French Renaissance style; but the finest one was by John Lyle, in a simple Anglo-French classicism inspired by the late eighteenth century.[206] However, the Provincial Architect, F.R. Heakes, advised the minister that none of the entries was suitable for the purpose and that all were too expensive.[207] As a result, Heakes was instructed to prepare a new design.

By early 1911 the conditions under which the competition had been held were completely changed by the government's decision to find a new site. The pre-war period was one of great change in the physical character of the city, and it was soon realized that the Bloor Street property would inevitably be surrounded by commercial development. Accordingly it was sold (at an immense profit) and the proceeds were used to acquire a new site. The government settled on Chorley Park—a broad, fairly level area of 14 acres in northern Rosedale, looking southeast across the still-rural Don Valley. Outside official circles the choice was greeted with howls of derision. It was thought too far from the Parliament Buildings and too secluded for a public building. In those days Government House was an ornament to the city, one that had to be easily accessible to school children for their education and to visitors for their enjoyment. The controversy came to a head in the spring of 1911 when W.J. Gage offered his estate at Bathurst and Davenport Road as a new site. The price was $120,000, the same as for Chorley Park, but Gage offered to use the money to buy a further ten acres on the south side of Davenport, which he would give to the city as a botanical garden. This proposal was then unofficially supported by City Council with an offer to purchase the Chorley Park site from the province for use as a park. There was considerable public support for the idea because it would have given the city two parks for the price of one and, interestingly, because it was seen as a way to preserve the natural character of the escarpment from haphazard subdivision; indeed, it would have encouraged a more open and carefully planned development of the area south of Davenport. However, in a manner that seems all too predictable in retrospect, the government refused to discuss any change and pushed ahead with the planning for Chorley Park.[208]

The house was modelled by Heakes on the French Renaissance châteaux of the Loire Valley, as interpreted by such American architects as Richard Morris Hunt. The exterior design was largely copied from G.W. King's rejected project for the Bloor Street site, while the plan was directly copied from Lyle's designs. Although the style was scarcely as fashionable as Lyle's Anglo-French classicism, the house as built was peppered with romantic details in grey Credit Valley stone under a red tile roof (though the corner turrets were too small). Seen from the Don Valley, isolated and framed by trees, it was wonderfully picturesque—far more so than Lyle's more restrained and formal design would have been. Chorley Park was also very much within the sphere of the Château Style, which had by this time been adopted by the railways and the federal government as Canada's 'national style', both for its picturesque character and for its reference to the early French history of the country.

The gardens surrounding the house were planned by C.W. Leavitt of New York.[209] They combined a formal entrance—across a rusticated concrete bridge to the square forecourt—with a more informal series of terraces that raised the house on fortification-like walls above the slope of the site; the formality of the house was thus complemented without breaking the natural character of the view from the valley. Unfortunately Leavitt's role in the project roused the anger of Toronto's emerging group of landscape architects, and political pressure led to his replacement by H.B. & L.A. Dunnington-Grubb, who completed the work with few changes.[210]

The house was conceived on a scale that far outshone even the Governor General's residence at Rideau Hall in Ottawa. The changes Heakes made to Lyle's plan were slight, except for redesigning the hall (plate 123) as a sky-lit three-storey space, surrounded by galleries—like the interior of the provincial legislature itself. Decorated in marble and Caen limestone and vaguely described as 'Louis XVI', the hall was undoubtedly pretentious. Yet it was one of the most impressive ceremonial interiors in the city, designed not for day-to-day living but as the backdrop for somewhat theatrical government ceremonies and entertainments. Off the hall, screened by open colonnades, was the main stair and a corridor that led to the ballroom, with its gilt chandeliers and domed glass ceiling. To the right was the Jacobean State Dining Room panelled in fumed oak, with a Caen limestone fireplace carved with the Arms of Ontario. On the right was the main suite of reception rooms, which with the conservatory looked out across the Don Valley. Here the interiors were again Louis XVI, with off-white walls and rosewood furniture. (The scheme was designed by the T. Eaton Company, which at this time commanded the finest interior-design talent in the country—competent, if not inspired, in almost any historical style.)[211]

The magnificence of Chorley Park took four years, and over a million dollars, to bring to completion.[212] This was a staggering sum for the period, all the more so as only $215,000 had been budgeted. But it was generally agreed that the time and money were well spent for a building that was certain to last for generations. Unfortunately the expense of maintaining the house and its staff became a political thorn in the flesh of the Conservative government. The complaints began to be heard in 1920. With the coming of the Depression, the maintenance costs assumed exaggerated importance. The United Farmers of Ontario made no secret of their disapproval, and in 1937 their strength in the legislature encouraged the Liberal premier, Mitchell Hepburn, to close Chorley Park. There were loud protests, but most of the preservationists who might have fought for it were engaged in the fight to save Cawthra House at Bay and King (plate 66). In the end there was a week-long sale of the contents at Ryan's Art Galleries.[213] The empty house became a military hospital, and so it remained until 1956.

The grounds were gradually overrun by a maze of temporary buildings, some of which were used to receive refugees from the collapse of the Hungarian Revolution. In 1959 the building was demolished. There had been some weak protest; but with provincial, metropolitan, and city governments that were dedicated to 'progress' and undertook to preserve the site as a park, there was little chance for successful opposition. Only the bridge to the forecourt remains. So completely were all traces of the house removed that its existence is almost forgotten.

123 CHORLEY PARK: THE HALL, *c.*1916

THE MOORE PARK STATION ON THE TORONTO BELT LINE
South of Moore Avenue
in the ravine between Hudson Drive and Brendon Road, c.1909
c.1889-90

The Belt Line railway was chartered on 23 March 1889 to provide commuter service to the developing suburbs north and west of Toronto. During the boom of the 1880s, land had been subdivided as far north as York Mills, partly as speculation but also to meet the rapid expansion of the city's population. Sir James Edgar was the guiding spirit of the railway, but Edward Osler and William Hendry of Hamilton lent $600,000 to purchase the necessary lands and to pay for construction. Even before the track was built, at a cost of $462,000, it was leased to the Grand Trunk Railway for a rental fee that paid the financing costs of the loan. Success awaited only the growth of the suburbs. In the meantime the very presence of the railway had the effect of raising both the paper value and the actual sale prices of the lands owned by the associated Belt Line Land Company.[214]

There were two routes, each with several stations. One ran west to Swansea, north along the Humber to Dundas Street, east to the GTR main line, and then back to the centre of the city. The other ran north from the Davenport GTR station at Caledonia Road, around Forest Hill and to the north of Upper Canada College (plate 130), crossing Yonge Street north of Mount Pleasant Cemetery, before heading south through the cemetery to the Moore Park Station. From there it followed the ravine out to the Don Valley below Chorley Park (plate 122), to head south and join the GTR again at the Don Station.

The stations built for the Belt Line were unpretentious and unmonumental but characteristic of most of the stations built in the late Victorian period for small communities along the Canadian Pacific and Grand Trunk Lines. (They were not unlike many that were built by railways in the northeastern United States.) The Moore Park Station, with its spreading roof that sheltered part of the platform, and with four shingled towers that made it a landmark in the natural setting of the ravine, was distantly related to fashionable American summer houses of the Shingle Style. The almost residential character of the building would be compatible with the new suburbs that were intended to develop around the stations.

The Belt Line routes were served by frequent steam trains equipped with smoking cars; the fare between any two stops was set at 25 cents. But hopes for the success of the railway were based on the assumption that the new suburbs would develop quickly and be connected to the city only by rail. However, at the same time as the economic depression of 1893 (and the subsequent economic collapse) postponed the development of the new communities, the establishment of Sir William Mackenzie's Toronto Street Railway siphoned off much of the traffic from the already established suburbs along Yonge Street. With no customers and rising debts, the Belt Line Company failed in the early 1890s. Most of the investors lost all they had put in, especially when the Land Company followed the railway into decline. The stations and the track, where not used by the Grand Trunk, were simply abandoned. Such a fate overtook the Moore Park Station—its tracks overgrown and the building slowly disintegrating, as shown here about 1909. It is not known when it was finally demolished.

124

BENVENUTO
Avenue Road at Edmund Avenue (SW), c.1914
1890 by A. Page Brown

Benvenuto, the home of Simeon Henan Janes, stood on the west side of Avenue Road, at the very crest of the escarpment south of St Clair, on land that—like the Oaklands property on the other side of Avenue Road—had been part of Senator McMaster's immense Rathnelly estate. Janes, one of Toronto's most successful real-estate developers, subdivided part of the Annex. His first home was on Jarvis Street. But the house that signalled his ultimate success to the world occupied a commanding position looking out across the new streets of Toronto, where vision and old-fashioned Victorian ingenuity had made him a millionaire.[215]

The house was begun in 1890 to designs, by the American architect A. Page Brown, that were published in the *British Architect* (6 December 1889). Brown had finished his training in the New York office of McKim, Mead & White (commencing in 1882)—the most important American firm of the period. Tradition in the

Janes family attributed the house to Stanford White, and it is plausible that Janes, in his search for the finest possible house, had requested White's services and been referred to the younger architect at a time when Brown was establishing his own practice. Before the house was completed, Brown moved his office to San Francisco and the execution of the design was supervised in part by Frank L. Ellingwood, another McKim, Mead & White alumnus.[216]

There was a family resemblance between Brown's design and Stanford White's work. As with the Osborn House at Mamaroneck, N.Y., of 1883-5, by White,[217] a pair of round corner towers with conical roofs flanked the south front of the Janes house, and the walls were of massive rough-surfaced stone (Kingston limestone at Benvenuto); both were part of the legacy of Henry Hobson Richardson, White's own teacher. However, the grey-white stone was capped with maroon 'Spanish'

126 BENVENUTO: THE HALL, C.1895

roof tiles; surrounded by the greenery of the St Clair hillside in summer, the image altogether must have been very striking. As Mercer Adam noted in *Toronto Old and New* (1891), Benvenuto was 'a splendid piece of masonry, which puts to shame the flimsy ephemeral edifices, with their stuccos and veneers, of modern house construction.'[218] Unfortunately neither Brown nor Ellingwood had complete control over the execution of the house: it is probable that Janes had his Toronto builder make several modifications. In the original design, wide banks of mullioned and transomed windows balanced the massive thickness of the walls, wrapping around the curves of the south towers, to open the interior to the spreading view across the city. But as it was completed, the windows were much smaller and in several cases round-arched—closer to the Toronto idiom of the Romanesque Revival—making the house heavier, more forbidding, and more fortress-like than Brown had intended. Plate 125 shows Benvenuto after it had been extensively altered in 1914 by Darling & Pearson and a large service wing had been added (on the right), giving the house an exaggerated length.

THE HALL

In the great houses of the 1880s and 1890s, and many that were less ambitious. the hall was the chief interior space, its focus a fireplace—usually of baronial proportions—that was the symbol of the warmth and hospitality with which guests were welcomed. Opposite the fireplace wall a spreading stair raised the mundane need for circulation to the status of an architectural event. Hearth and stair combined to suggest ampleness of means. Instead of being a cramped corridor or dark vestibule, the hall had become a generous reception area into which the major rooms opened through large archways (with draperies or sliding doors to control draughts).

The hall at Benvenuto was the largest room in the house, richly panelled and ceiled in stained wood and hung with embossed and gilded Spanish leather. To the left in this photograph (plate 126) from the Janes family album is the fireplace; in front are the twin doors to the drawing and music rooms. Behind the camera was a curtained nook with luxuriously cushioned seats for tête-à-tête conversations.

127 BENVENUTO: THE DRAWING ROOM, C.1895

Like many of Toronto's commercial élite, Janes owned a not inconsiderable collection of art, ranging in period from the Renaissance through the Victorian.[219] At Benvenuto antique furniture, statuary, and paintings were part of the decorative scheme, especially in the conservatory on the west front, which featured a collection of classical sculpture that included a Roman sarcophagus in marble. Janes acquired, specially for the house, a set of seventeenth-century French tapestries around which the dining room was designed; and he commissioned Gustav Hahn to paint murals for the second-floor billiard room.

THE DRAWING ROOM

The same search for excellence that led Janes to McKim, Mead & White in New York led him to Maple & Co., one of London's most fashionable firms of interior designers. It was they, rather than Brown or Ellingwood, who arranged the installation of the dining-room tapestries and the other interior fittings; their pièce de résistance was the suite of drawing and music rooms on the west side of the house, including the round alcove in the southwest tower. Decorated in the style of Louis XVI, the walls hung with damask and the white woodwork picked out in gold, the room must have come as a revelation to Toronto society at a time when darker, more heavily proportioned rooms were the order of the day in large houses. Although it is now impossible to say for certain, the Benvenuto drawing room was probably the first in Toronto in which an eighteenth-century atmosphere was so effectively revived. Characteristically the room, seen here (plate 127) from the round alcove in the southwest tower, was furnished with a mixture of genuine antiques and modern pastiches that filled the special functions and ideas of comfort that Victorians required in their furniture.

The 'princely magnificence' of Benvenuto remained intact only until 1897, when Janes sold the house to Sir William Mackenzie. (It was paid for, appropriately, not in cash but with shares in the Toronto Street Railway, which was the basis of Mackenzie's fortune.) It remained one of the city's major social centres; but when Mackenzie died in 1924 the expansion of the city, rising taxes and land values, and the changing life style of Toronto society effectively spelled the end of the house. In 1926 the apartment at 400 Avenue Road was built on the north part of the estate, and in 1927 another apartment (designed by Catto & Catto in the Art Deco style popular at the time) was built on the southwest corner of Edmund and Avenue Road. Benvenuto remained vacant. Lacking the sheer size and landmark value that had saved Casa Loma, it was demolished in November 1932.[220] Parts of the house were saved: the roof tiles were re-used on R.A. Laidlaw's summer house at De Grassi Point, Lake Simcoe;[221] and the gates, designed by Benedetto Zalaffi in richly Italianate wrought iron, were moved to 40-2 Burton Road in Forest Hill. Today only the massive limestone retaining wall along Avenue Road remains, although the name, unrecognized by most Torontonians, continues in the Benvenuto Place Hotel (1956) that now crowns the hill.

ARDWOLD
Walmer Road (E), south of St Clair Avenue West, c. 1920
1909-11 by Wickson & Gregg

Ardwold—which in Gaelic means 'high, green hill'—was the Toronto home of Sir John Craig Eaton and without doubt the finest of the several houses built by the family in Toronto, commanding a magnificent view from the escarpment across the city where the Eatons were of central economic importance.

When John Eaton married Flora McCrea in May 1901, the couple were given an unpretentious new house at 121 Walmer Road, not far from Timothy Eaton's house on Lowther (plate 119). In 1908, one year after he had become president of the company on his father's death, John Eaton began planning a new house that would accommodate his growing family in a style appropriate for the head of one of the world's largest retail businesses. As a site for the house, he purchased the ten-acre estate of George and Anne Austin Arthurs, called Ravenswood, which lay east of James Austin's house, Spadina, on land that had originally belonged to Dr W.W. Baldwin.[222] To the west, work had already begun on Henry Pellatt's Casa Loma; to the east were the great suburban homes of the Nordheimers (Glenedyth), the McMasters (Rathnelly), and the Macdonalds (Oaklands); while to the north there were still large open fields. The Arthurs had built a comfortable but simple house on the brow of the hill in 1868; but shortly after Eaton purchased the estate, the old house was demolished to make way for Ardwold, its outbuildings and gardens.

Ardwold was designed by A.F. Wickson, of the Toronto firm Wickson & Gregg.[223] It was built of dark red brick, with light brown stone trim and detailing. Much larger than the other Eaton houses, its façade was twelve bays wide, with the centre of the garden front (illustrated here) framed by three-bay pavilions at the ends that stepped slightly forward and rose two storeys to a high-pitched roof crowned by an octagonal lantern, or belvedere, and a balustraded walk. Wickson's design was inspired by the medium- and large-sized country houses built during the late seventeenth and early eighteenth centuries in the Eaton family's native Ireland and in Britain—notably Belton in Lincolnshire (1684-6). But like most architects of the period, Wickson borrowed from earlier styles without exactly copying the prototypes. An atmosphere of elegance and secure, long-established comfort was evoked by the generous proportions of Ardwold, the basic symmetry of the design, and a few careful details such as the roof-top lantern and the columned doorcase. But the patterns of the eighteenth century were not allowed to interfere with the necessary arrangements of the house. At each end of the façade there were two-storey porches that were specifically adapted to the needs of summer living

129   ARDWOLD: THE GREAT HALL, C.1920

in the city; while on the south or garden front a large sunroom and a semi-circular bay of mullioned casements jutted out to take advantage of the panoramic view. The gardens were more formal in character, with the various levels organized as classically balustraded terraces, and a pool and fountain aligned with the vista over the city. But they were an evocative reminiscence, not a re-creation, of the eighteenth century.[224]

Ardwold was one of the most luxurious and up-to-date houses in the city when it was completed in 1911. It had not only an indoor swimming pool, reached from the house through a tunnel, but also a private hospital, with its own operating room. At the centre of the plan was the two-storey Great Hall (plate 129), with a vaulted plaster ceiling and along one side a two-storey arcade from which the main corridors on the first and second floors opened into the room. The hall was the principal living area of the house, where Sir John had set up the Aeolian organ (its pipes filling the wall over the fireplace) that was his greatest pleasure. Unfortunately the Great Hall was far less successful than the exterior design of the house. The various historical details—especially the plaster ceiling mouldings and the carv-

ings, in the manner of Grinling Gibbons, that ornamented the walls—have a pinched and meagre character. Such poor-quality detailing was not uncommon in the houses of the period, but in the interiors of Ardwold there was also an air of empty pretentiousness that perhaps could be accounted for by the uncertain taste of the clients.

Ardwold was finished in 1911 and the family lived there until 1922. After Sir John's death, in August of that year, Lady Eaton preferred to close the house and travel. For several years she lived in Florence, and when she returned to Canada it was to the newly built Eaton Hall in King, Ont., north of the city—the estate she and Sir John had begun to plan shortly before his death. Ardwold was stripped of some of its fittings to furnish the new mansion; the rest were sold at public auction and the house was demolished in late 1936. In its place a short street, Ardwold Gate, was laid out and the property was divided into building lots. Reminders of the house exist today in the street name, the former gate lodge on Walmer Road, and a nearby section of the estate fence.

UPPER CANADA COLLEGE
Lonsdale Avenue at Avenue Road, c.1890
1889-90 by G.F. Durand

When Upper Canada College decided to move north from its buildings on King Street West (plate 32), it was seeking the semi-seclusion of a suburban site and an expansive area for the playing fields that were an essential element in the progressive educational theory of the day. But the new building was still to be public in character, and as part of the project Avenue Road was widened to 125 feet to provide a processional approach from the city, much as University Avenue had been laid out sixty years before (plate 95).*

Inevitably, given the date, the style of the new building was Romanesque Revival.[225] It was built on a foundation of roughly finished Credit Valley sandstone, with the upper walls of red brick ornamented with terra-cotta panels and string courses. The basic arrangement of the design—a projecting triple-arched entrance, a central tower, and flanking wings forming a quadrangle behind—was very common at the time, and had become firmly established in Toronto with Lennox's City Hall (1889-99) and Waite's Parliament Buildings in Queen's Park (1886-92). The location of the prayer hall, filling the centre portion of the second floor in the main block, and the tower overhead, with its stylized pediment and the college arms in carved terra cotta, also recalled similar features in the King Street buildings. In fact the new tower, rising 165 feet above the ground, like a church steeple above the surrounding trees, became the symbol of the college—an ever-present reminder to students, and to the city below the hill, of the importance of the college and the influence of the alumni that had been shaped by it.

The design of the new building was complicated. It united such widely differing elements as a basement armoury and a principal's residence, in the pavilion on the right, which was carefully designed with its own corner bay window and a side entrance. Illustrating the preoccupation of the time with sanitation and healthy living, Durand planned 300 cubic feet of air and at least 30 square feet of floor space for each student in the

classrooms. Window area was to be at least one quarter of the floor area and windows were located not more than 18 feet from any pupil, positioned so that light in most rooms fell only from the left, to reduce shadow and glare. The unusual heating system included forced-air registers under the windows and exhaust vents on the inside walls of the rooms through which the stale air was drawn to main exhaust shafts. The dormitories were carefully organized to provide 1,000 cubic feet of space for each pupil, with no more than two to a room—standards that were on the whole appreciably higher than those of any middle-class house of the period.

Durand's building was completed in 1890, but as early as 1913 UCC was making elaborate plans to move out of the city. A 524-acre site was chosen at Norval, near Georgetown, and on 30 September 1913 it was announced that the Lonsdale site had been sold for $1,100,000—a value based on its use for residential development next to the newly fashionable Forest Hill Village. Construction was to begin in 1914, with the move completed by 1916; but in the turmoil of the Great War the project was abandoned and the old site retained. In 1931 a move to Lansing, Ont., was proposed, which would have transformed the college into a completely residential school (much as St Andrews had been re-formed on its move to Aurora from Rosedale). Undoubtedly because of the deepening Depression, this project too was abandoned.[226] In 1932 the new Massey Quadrangle was added, north of the main block, in a romantically Neo-Georgian style by the Toronto firm of Mathers & Haldenby. With these additional facilities and a new gymnasium, the main block continued in use until 1956, when concern about its structural stability led to demolition and a complete rebuilding, to designs by Mathers & Haldenby. (There is some question whether demolition was justified.) The new building, of similar profile to the old one, included a new tower that rose higher above the complex than before. Though it is Neo-Georgian in inspiration, it does represent a clear descent from the old building and declares its place in the traditions of the college.

---

*Modern Toronto can therefore thank two of its often-ignored institutions for such grandly scaled city planning as exists today.

buildings is the information the view gives about the general form and character of nineteenth-century Toronto. There is more than ample proof here of the city's intimate connection with the lake and the railways. Most Torontonians of the 1970s are almost unaware of Lake Ontario: if they think of it at all they consider it a plaything for the city, a convenient recreation spot that would have to be created if it didn't exist. But the bird's-eye view emphasizes the commercial importance of the lake, and the easy transportation it permitted for the growing city, in the numerous wharves and docks that reach long, fragile fingers into the water and in the industries that—especially east of Yonge—cluster as close to the water as possible. (Without the Island, which was probably omitted for the convenience of the artist, Toronto seems even more a child of Lake Ontario.) It also shows clearly the growing strength of the railroads, which in the 1850s had begun to link Toronto to inland markets for its manufactured goods and to distant sources of raw materials. Such industries as the Gooderham and Worts distillery in the east, and in the west (south of the Provincial Lunatic Asylum) the farm-machinery factory of the Massey Manufacturing Company, can be seen in relation to the tracks that issued from the second Union Station (plate 14) and the Great Western Station (plate 3). By the 1870s the railway had taken over the waterfront and was beginning to change the outline of the harbour itself with extensive landfill. Lake shipping remained almost as busy and important as before, but the close connection between the city, the lake, and its docks was already broken by the long lines of tracks.

This bird's-eye view also shows more clearly than either maps or streetscape photographs the congestion of the downtown core and the unrelenting zeal with which the grid pattern of streets—first laid out for Simcoe in 1793—had been stretched across the landscape on either side of the arrow-straight line of Yonge. Standing out against this pattern are the few attempts to mitigate the worst aspects of the grid plan: natural changes like King Street/Kingston Road, which turns northeast on the right side of the view; the carefully planned avenues like Spadina (with its crescent at the north end) and University; and the park-like green spaces scattered throughout the city.

Perhaps the most notable feature of the nineteenth-century city is the manner in which the strict regularity of the grid was softened by trees along the streets (still very characteristic of Toronto) and by islands of greenery in public and private ownership. These green spaces formed a broken line on the west side of the city, running north from the lake through the grounds of the Parliament Buildings (with Clarence Square and its fountain, Loretto Abbey and its gardens, Trinity College, and the Asylum further west) to Government House, Upper Canada College, Osgoode Hall, University Avenue and—within sight of the wooded estates on the escarpment and the open countryside—the 186 acres of the university campus and Queen's Park. East of Yonge were the churchyards of St James', Metropolitan Methodist, and St Michael's; St James Square, with the Normal and Model Schools; and, further east, the Horticultural Gardens, with its fountain and pavilion (now Allan Gardens). Without any real planning, and almost accidentally, Toronto had a belt of open green space around its centre that as early as 1868 was valued as a great 'lung' for the congested city. It is one of the most regrettable facts in Toronto's development that much of this land has been built over or neglected.

In 1878 Toronto was not yet eighty-five years old. There were many still alive who remembered the little York of the period before the War of 1812; more who were familiar with the town of 7,500 that had proclaimed itself the City of Toronto in 1834. The city grew with a minimum of restrictions, and the result was haphazard, in places unbearably crowded. But it managed to acquire distinction—matching the self-assurance of its merchants, bankers, and politicians—with such buildings as Metropolitan Methodist Church, the General Post Office, Government House, the Union Station; with many other churches, public buildings, houses, factories, and warehouses; and with the beautiful tree-lined University Avenue. If proof were needed that the Victorians, just as much as the Georgians, were proud and capable city builders, this bird's-eye view provides it amply. A celebration of their creation, it is a lasting testimony of what had been created in Toronto.

132 BIRD'S-EYE VIEW OF TORONTO, c.1878

Notes

1 *The City of Toronto* in the series of handbooks published by Nelson and Sons (Toronto, 1860), p. 17.

2 Henry Scadding and Charles Dent, *Toronto: Past and Present* (Toronto, 1884), pp. 290-1.

3 H.F. Walling, ed., *Toronto in the Camera* (Toronto, 1868), p. 26.

4 R.C. Bebout, ed., *The Open Gate: Toronto Union Station* (Toronto, 1972), pp. 21ff.

5 John Ross Robertson, *Landmarks of Toronto* (6 vols; Toronto, 1894-1914), vol. 1 (1894), p. 306.

6 See *Monetary Times* (Toronto), vol. 7, 7 Jan. 1874, p. 680.

7 See *ibid.*, vol. 5, 12 Jan. 1872, p. 549.

8 Jesse Middleton, *The Municipality of Toronto: A History* (3 vols; Toronto, 1923), vol. 1, pp. 504-5.

9 See *American Architect and Building News* (Boston), vol. 25, 16 Feb. 1889, p. 81; vol. 28, 19 Apr. 1890, p. 39; vol. 28, 21 June 1890, p. 181; and vol. 29, 19 July 1890, p. 39.

10 Middleton, *op. cit.*, vol. 3, p. 138.

11 See A.S. Thompson, *Spadina* (Toronto, 1975), *passim*.

12 *Ibid.*, pp. 84-5.

13 The plans for the house are preserved with the Baldwin Papers in the Baldwin Room of the Metropolitan Toronto Library; one plan was published by Eric Arthur in *Toronto: No Mean City* (Toronto, 1964), p. 42.

14 L.B. Martyn, *Toronto: 100 Years of Grandeur* (Toronto, 1978), p. 77; and Robertson, *op. cit.*, vol. 1 (1894), pp. 7-9.

15 Robertson, *op. cit.*, vol. 5 (1908), pp. 514-15.

16 *Ibid.*

17 C.P. Mulvaney, *Toronto: Past and Present* (Toronto, 1884), pp. 106-8.

18 Robertson, *op. cit.*, vol. 1 (1894), pp. 28-30.

19 Thompson, *op. cit.*, p. 79.

20 Henry Scadding, *Toronto of Old*. Abridged and edited by F.H. Armstrong (Toronto, 1966), p. 27.

21 Robertson, *op. cit.*, vol. 1 (1894), pp. 326-8; and Bebout, *op. cit.*, pp. 21-4.

22 See the *Canadian Illustrated News* (Montreal), vol. 8, 2 Aug. 1873, pp. 72-3; and H. Kalman and D.S. Richardson, 'Building for Transportation in the Nineteenth Century', in the *Journal of Canadian Art History* (Montreal), vol. 3 (Fall 1976), pp. 1-2.

23 C.S. Clark, *Of Toronto the Good* (Montreal, 1898), p. 5.

24 See Robertson, *op. cit.*, vol. 2 (1896), pp. 960-71.

25 'Scrapbooks containing newspaper clippings, photographs, etc., relating to the City of Toronto' (hereinafter cited as 'The City of Toronto Scrapbook'; 12 vols, kept on microfilm in the Metropolitan Toronto Library), vol. 6, p. 231—an article published in 1921 in the *Telegram*. See also *Canadian Architect and Builder* (Toronto), vol. 9, 8 Aug. 1896, supplement.

26 C.H.J. Snider comp., *Annals of the Royal Canadian Yacht Club, 1852-1937* (Toronto, 1937), p. 138.

27 'The City of Toronto Scrapbook', vol. 4, p. 340—an article published on 10 May 1918 in the *Mail*.

28 Mulvaney, *op. cit.*, pp. 263-76.

29 The Students of the Toronto Island School, *A History of the Toronto Islands* (Toronto, 1972), pp. 8-9.

30 Middleton, *op. cit.*, vol. 2, p. 781.

31 *Ibid.*, vol. 1, p. 312.

32 Mulvaney, *op. cit.*, pp. 264-6.

33 Robertson, *op. cit.*, vol. 5 (1908), p. 355.

34 *Ibid.*, vol. 4 (1904), pp. 51-5.

35 Quoted in Mulvaney, *op. cit.*, p. 267.

36 R. Poulton, *The Paper Tyrant* (Toronto, 1971), p. 162.

37 *Ibid.*, p. 162.

38 *Ibid.*, p. 170.

39 See Robertson, *op. cit.*, vol. 1 (1894), pp. 351-9.

40 The lithograph by Thomas Young of Chewett's design was published by Eric Arthur in *Toronto: No Mean City* (Toronto, 1964), p. 49.

41 G.P. Ure, *A Handbook of Toronto* (Toronto, 1858), pp. 267-9.

42 Robertson, *op. cit.*, vol. 5 (1908), pp. 566-75.

43 *Final Report of the Commissioners of Inquiry into the Affairs of King's College University and Upper Canada College* (Quebec, 1852), p. 35; and Robertson, *op. cit.*, vol. 5 (1908), p. 567.

44 See Ure, *op. cit.,*; Alfred Sylvester, *Sketches of Toronto* (Toronto, 1858), pp. 21-3; and the *Builder* (London), vol. 13, 3 Nov. 1855, pp. 530-1.

45 Robertson, *op. cit.*, vol. 5 (1908), pp. 569-74.

46 W.S. Wallace, *A History of the University of Toronto* (Toronto, 1926), pp. 70-1.

47 Henry Langley, 'Description of the Lieutenant-Governor's Residence', in the *Report of the Commissioner of Public Works, 1869* (Toronto, 1870); see also William Dendy, 'Government House, Toronto, 1866-70' in the *Canadian Collector* (Toronto), vol. 12, no. 5 (Sept.-Oct. 1977), pp. 21-5.

48 *Report of the Commissioner of Public Works, 1872* (Toronto, 1873), p. 60.

49 Mulvaney, *op. cit.*, p. 52.

50 Edith Firth, *The Town of York: 1815-34* (Toronto, 1966), p. 161.

51 See Robertson, *op. cit.*, vol. 1 (1894), pp. 144-55; Alfred Sylvester, *Sketches of Toronto* (Toronto, 1858), p. 72; and Ure, *op. cit.*, pp. 107-9.

52 Robertson, *op. cit.*, vol. 1 (1894), pp. 151-2. See also Scadding and Dent, *op. cit.*, p. 284.

53 Mulvaney, *op. cit.*, p.90.

54 Clark, *op. cit.*, p.78.

55 Robertson, *op. cit.*, vol. 2 (1896), pp. 1087-95.

56 Ure, *op. cit.*, pp. 189-204.

57 Robertson, *op. cit.*, vol. 2 (1896), pp. 1093-5.

58 *Monetary Times* (Toronto), vol. 12, 20 Sept. 1878, pp. 369-70, with an illustration facing p. 380. See also James Lorimer, *The Ex* (Toronto, 1973), pp. 1-15.

59 Middleton, *op. cit.*, vol. 1, pp. 306-7.

60 James Lorimer, *The Ex* (Toronto, 1973), p. 17.

61 *Ibid.*, pp. 17-43.

62 Minutes of City Council, 6 Nov. 1843; typescript in the City of Toronto Archives.

63 'Report of the committee appointed to advertise for and receive Plans, and specifications for the New Market Building proposed to be erected on the Farmers' Store House lot', 4 March 1844; original in the City of Toronto Archives, Council Papers.

64 Ure, *op. cit.*, pp. 225-6; and Robertson, *op. cit.*, vol. 1 (1894), pp. 290-2.

65 W.H. Smith, *Canada: Past, Present and Future* (Toronto, 1852), vol. 2, p. 5.

66 Original in the City of Toronto Archives, Council Papers.

67 The Symon proposal was published by City Council as a pamphlet; copy in the City of Toronto Archives.

68 Robertson, *op. cit.*, vol. 1 (1894), pp. 221-3, 380-4; and vol. 3 (1898), pp. 45-8.

69 City of Toronto Building Permit no. 445, 1 Aug. 1891, in the City of Toronto Archives.

70 W.R. Blackwell, 'Bank Architecture and the Bank of Toronto', in the *Canadian Banker* (Toronto), vol. 45 (1937-8), pp. 62-4;

and an untitled article by R.J. Gould in the former in-house magazine of the bank, the *Bantor News* (Toronto), June 1946, pp. 5-6.

71 Information from the file on the Kauffman building in the Premises Department of the Toronto-Dominion Bank, Toronto.

72 Ure, *op. cit.*, pp. 249-51.

73 Some of James Grand's drawings are preserved in the Langley Collection in the Baldwin Room of the Metropolitan Toronto Library. Eric Arthur published the plans in *Toronto: No Mean City* (Toronto, 1964), p. 115.

74 Robertson, *op. cit.*, vol. 3 (1898), pp. 290-2; and *Canadian Architect and Builder* (Toronto), vol. 8 (January 1895), pp. 8-11.

75 Walling, *op. cit.*, p. 10. I am indebted to Marion MacRae for information about William Irving's career.

76 Thompson, *op. cit.*, pp. 129-30.

77 See *Monetary Times* (Toronto), vol. 5, 7 July 1871, p. 8; and vol. 6, 5 July 1872, pp. 8-9.

78 Mulvaney, *op. cit.*, pp. 230-4.

79 City of Toronto Building Permit no. 179, 14 Nov. 1882, in the City of Toronto Archives.

80 *Building News* (London), vol. 4, 20 Aug. 1858, p. 846; see also Walling, *op. cit.*, p. 23.

81 City of Toronto Building Permit, no. 28, 28 Apr. 1899, in the City of Toronto Archives.

82 Robertson, *op. cit.*, vol. 1 (1894), pp. 15-16, 268-70.

83 *The City of Toronto*, Nelson and Sons Handbooks (Toronto, 1860), p. 17; and Ure, *op. cit.*, p. 237.

84 Edith Firth, *The Town of York: 1793-1815* (Toronto, 1962), p. 124; and Robertson, *op. cit.*, vol. 1 (1894), pp. 17-19.

85 Alfred Sylvester, *Sketches of Toronto* (Toronto, 1858), p. 11.

86 Mulvaney, *op. cit.*, p. 41.

87 Walling, *op. cit.*, p. 42; and Robertson, *op. cit.*, vol. 5 (1908), p. 12.

88 James Sutherland, ed., *The City of Toronto Directory for 1867-8* (Toronto, 1867), p. 328.

89 J. Russell Harper and Stanley Triggs, *Portrait of a Period: A Collection of Notman Photographs* (Montreal, 1967), pp. 58, 113, 122, 128; and the City of Toronto Assessment Rolls for 1872-4 in the City of Toronto Archives.

90 Robertson, *op. cit.*, vol. 1 (1894), pp. 81-3.

91 *Ibid.*, vol. 5 (1908), pp. 361-3; and the *Monetary Times* (Toronto), vol. 31, 13 Aug. 1897, supplement following p. 204.

92 Arthur R.M. Lower, *Canadians in the Making: A Social History of Canada* (Toronto, 1958), p. 424.

93 *Building News* (London), vol. 3, 4 Sept. 1857, p. 938; and Ure, *op. cit.*, pp. 245-8.

94 *The City of Toronto*, Nelson and Sons Handbooks (Toronto, 1860), pp. 45-6.

95 Ure, *op. cit.*, p. 246.

96 *Monetary Times* (Toronto), vol. 13, 26 Mar. 1880, p. 1145 and illustration facing p. 1153.

97 Scadding and Dent, *op. cit.*, pp. 191-2.

98 Thompson, *op. cit.*, p. 147.

99 Eric Arthur, *Toronto: No Mean City* (Toronto, 1964), p. 172.

100 See *Monetary Times* (Toronto), vol. 7, 7 Jan. 1874, facing p. 652. Several of Langley's drawings for the General Post Office are preserved in the Baldwin Room of the Metropolitan Toronto Library.

101 See *Canadian Architect* (Toronto), vol. 1 (January-February 1956), p. 15.

102 Edith Firth, *The Town of York: 1815-34* (Toronto, 1966), p. 44, fn.

103 'William Cawthra' by G. de T. Glazebrook in *The Dictionary of Canadian Biography*, vol. 10 (Toronto, 1972), p. 155.

104 'The City of Toronto Scrapbook', vol. 10, pp. 94-5.

105 I am indebted to Marion MacRae for this information and for information about efforts to save the Cawthra house.

106 'The City of Toronto Scrapbook', vol. 9, pp. 158, 377; vol. 10, pp. 94-5; and vol. 12, p. 6.

107 See Robertson, *op. cit.*, vol. 1 (1894), pp. 6-7, 196-9.

108 See The United Empire Club, *Rules, Regulations and List of Members* (Toronto, 1875). (There is a copy in the University of Toronto Library.) See also the City of Toronto Assessment Rolls, 1873-6; and Mulvaney *op. cit.*, pp. 119-20.

109 See *Monetary Times* (Toronto), vol. 23, 24 Jan. 1890, p. 903; and 6 June 1890, illustration facing p. 1502. See also James Nicoll, 'Buildings of the Canadian Bank of Commerce' in the *Canadian Banker* (Toronto), vol. 45 (1937-8), pp. 204-14.

110 City of Toronto Building Permit, no. 314, 2 Sept. 1902, in the City of Toronto Archives.

111 See Andrew Saint, *Richard Norman Shaw* (New Haven, 1976), Chapters 8 and 9.

112 City of Toronto Building Permit, no. 11,016, 13 May 1908, in the City of Toronto Archives.

113 See 'Carrere & Hastings' in *Architectural Record* (New York), vol. 27 (January 1910), pp. 1-120.

114 Nikolaus Pevsner, *A History of Building Types* (Princeton, 1976), p. 205.

115 Robertson, *op. cit.*, vol. 1 (1894), pp. 478-91; *Canadian Illustrated News* (Montreal), vol. 10, 29 Aug. 1874, pp. 129, 134; Nathan Silver, *Lost New York* (New York, 1967), pp. 78-9; and J. Timperlake, *Illustrated Toronto: Past and Present* (Toronto, 1877), pp. 240-1.

116 Mulvaney, *op. cit.*, pp. 117-18. For the later history of the theatre, see Raymond Massey, *When I Was Young* (Toronto, 1976), pp. 85-7.

117 Douglas Richardson, ed., *Romanesque Toronto* (Toronto, 1971), pp. 14-15.

118 City of Toronto Building Permit, no. 1886, 27 Mar. 1895, in the City of Toronto Archives.

119 See *Construction* (Toronto), vol. 15 (January 1922), pp. 12-16.

120 See Robertson, *op. cit.*, vol. 1 (1894), pp. 529-30; and Edith Firth, *The Town of York: 1815-34* (Toronto, 1966), plate between pp. lxiv and lxv.

121 Robertson, *op. cit.*, vol. 1 (1894), pp. 293-5; and J. Armstrong, ed., *Rowsell's City of Toronto and County of York Directory for 1850-51* (Toronto, 1850), p. lxxxi.

122 Robertson, *op. cit.*, vol. 1 (1894), pp. 398-9; vol. 2 (1896), pp. 756-60.

123 Ure, *op. cit.*, pp. 242-3.

124 *Builder* (London), vol. 13, 3 Nov. 1855, p. 531; Robertson, *op. cit.*, vol. 2 (1896), p. 758; and *Report of the Toronto Mechanics' Institute* (Toronto, 1862), p. 15.

125 Robertson, *op. cit.*, vol. 1 (1894), p. 398.

126 Information drawn from *Reports of the Toronto Mechanics' Institute*, library catalogues, and other records of the Mechanics' Institute in the Baldwin Room of the Metropolitan Toronto Library.

127 Robertson, *op. cit.*, vol. 4 (1904), pp. 342-8.

128 Marion MacRae and Anthony Adamson, *Hallowed Walls* (Toronto, 1975), p. 210.

129 *Ibid.*, p. 211.

130 Robertson, *op. cit.*, vol. 4 (1904), p. 343.

131 *Ibid.*, pp. 406-7.

132 *Illustrated Toronto: The Queen City of Canada* (Toronto, 1890), p. 49.

133 Clark, *op. cit.*, p. 148.

134 Robertson, *op. cit.*, vol. 4 (1904), pp. 348-50; and Scadding and Dent, *op. cit.*, pp. 277-8.

135 Robertson, *op. cit.*, vol. 1 (1894), pp. 223-5.

136 Several of Langley's drawings for Metropolitan Methodist Church are preserved in the Metropolitan Toronto Library.

[137] The *Star*, 30 Jan. 1928.

[138] 'The City of Toronto Scrapbook', vol. 8, p. 239—an article published in the *Mail*, 9 Oct. 1928.

[139] Ure, *op. cit.*, pp. 259-63; and Robertson, *op. cit.*, vol. 3 (1898), pp. 35-9.

[140] Illustrated in Eric Arthur, *Toronto: No Mean City* (Toronto, 1964), p. 108.

[141] Mulvaney, *op. cit.*, pp. 101-2.

[142] The rebuilt Normal and Model Schools are illustrated in Arthur, *op. cit.*, p. 108.

[143] Ure, *op. cit.*, pp. 234-7.

[144] T.A. Reid, *A History of Trinity College* (Toronto, 1952), pp. 37-40.

[145] *Ibid.*, p. 42.

[146] *The City of Toronto*, Nelson and Sons Handbooks (Toronto, 1860), pp. 58-9; and Sylvester, *op. cit.*, pp. 78-9.

[147] *Building News* (London), vol. 4, 20 Aug. 1858; illustrated in Arthur, *op. cit.*, p. 124.

[148] Reid, *op. cit.*, p. 80.

[149] *Ibid.*, p. 79.

[150] *Ibid.*, p. 89.

[151] *Ibid.*, p. 103.

[152] *Ibid.*, p. 141.

[153] 'The City of Toronto Scrapbook' vol. 6, pp. 27-9.

[154] *Ibid.*, vol. 9, p. 122.

[155] Robertson, *op. cit.*, vol. 3 (1898), pp. 28-31; and Edward Jackson, *Demolish: The Politics of Architectural Conservation*, an as-yet unpublished manuscript prepared for Heritage Canada and the Ontario Institute for Studies in Education in 1977-8, pp. 39-59.

[156] John G. Howard Papers, Section III, 1368 (Metropolitan Toronto Library).

[157] Quoted in Jackson, *op. cit.*, p. 40.

[158] For a detailing of the various studies of the building and the controversy surrounding its demolition, see Jackson, *op. cit.*, and also *City Magazine* (Toronto), vol. 2, nos 3-4 (Summer 1976), pp. 34-59.

[159] Robertson, *op. cit.*, vol. 4 (1904), pp. 384-7.

[160] *Ibid.*, vol. 1 (1894), pp. 27-8.

[161] *Final Report of the Commissioners of Inquiry into the Affairs of King's College University and Upper Canada College* (Quebec, 1852), pp. 24, 34.

[162] J. Armstrong, ed., *Rowsell's City of Toronto and County of York Directory for 1850-51* (Toronto, 1850), p. lxxv.

[163] Wallace, *op. cit.*, p. 33; and the *Final Report of the Commissioners of Inquiry into the Affairs of King's College University and Upper Canada College*, pp. 35, 222, 241, 243.

[164] Wallace, *op. cit.*, pp. 70-1.

[165] Quoted by W.R. Browne in *Browne's Toronto General Directory* (Toronto, 1856), p. xii.

[166] Mulvaney, *op. cit.*, pp. 98-101. The story of the fountain and the statue of Queen Victoria can be traced in the minutes of the City Parks and Gardens Committee, kept in the City of Toronto Archives.

[167] *American Architect and Building News*, vol. 42, 23 Dec. 1893, p. 145.

[168] Robertson, *op. cit.*, vol. 4. (1904), pp. 495-7.

[169] For the American work that particularly influenced Canada, see T.S. Hines, *Burnham of Chicago* (New York, 1974).

[170] *Canadian Architect and Builder* (Toronto), vol. 4 (April 1891), p. 43; and vol. 5 (August 1892), pp. 75-6.

[171] *American Architect and Building News* (Boston), vol. 59, 12 Mar. 1898, p. 85.

[172] *Architectural Record* (New York), vol. 20 (November 1906), p. 437.

[173] *Ibid.*, vol. 18 (November 1905), p. 397; vol. 20 (November 1906), p. 438; vol. 27 (March 1910), p. 278. See also John M.

Lyle, 'Proposed Federal and Municipal Scheme for Toronto' in *Construction* (Toronto), vol. 4 (July 1911), pp. 51-3; and the *Report of the Advisory City Planning Commission* (Toronto, 1929), pp. 16, 19, 21, 24.

[174] *Report of the Advisory City Planning Commission* (Toronto, 1929), pp. 38, 42, 45.

[175] S.G. Curry, 'Toronto's Traffic Problem' in *Construction* (Toronto), vol. 21 (May 1928), pp. 156-8.

[176] 'The City of Toronto Scrapbook', vol. 4, p. 255.

[177] S.G. Curry, 'University Avenue Extension, Toronto' in *Construction* (Toronto), vol. 21 (December 1928), pp. 420, 428; and the *Report of the Advisory City Planning Commission*, pp. 23-5, 29-31.

[178] S.G. Curry, 'Suggested Improvements for Toronto's Downtown Section' in *Construction* (Toronto), vol. 22 (February 1929), pp. 62-8; *Report of the Advisory City Planning Commission*, pp. 25-9; and *Construction* (Toronto), vol. 24 (July 1931), p. 214.

[179] Robertson, *op. cit.*, vol. 1 (1894), pp. 393-7; and Arthur, *op. cit.*, p. 265.

[180] For the development of the T. Eaton Co. Ltd, see 'The Scribe' (Edith Nielson Macdonald), *The Golden Jubilee 1869-1919* (Toronto, 1919).

[181] See *Construction* (Toronto), vol. 6 (December 1913), pp. 467-76.

[182] See *ibid.*, vol. 10 (October 1917), pp. 334-44; also S.G. Curry, 'A Further Study of Toronto's Traffic Problems' in *Construction* (Toronto), vol. 21 (September 1928), pp. 304-6.

[183] See *Canadian Architect* (Toronto), vol. 4 (April 1959), pp. 44-65.

[184] Robertson, *op. cit.*, vol. 1 (1894), pp. 193-4.

[185] See *The Arcade Guide and Record* (Toronto, n.d.). A copy is in the Baldwin Room of the Metropolitan Toronto Library.

[186] *Industries of Canada: Historical and Commercial Sketches of Toronto* (Toronto, 1886), p. 121.

[187] *The Arcade Guide and Record*, p. 9.

[188] C.C. Taylor, *Toronto Called Back* (Toronto, 1887), p. 331.

[189] Flora McCrae Eaton, *Memory's Wall* (Toronto, 1956), p. 145.

[190] Margaret Etta Macpherson, *Storekeeper to the Nation: The Eatons* (Toronto, 1963), p. 54.

[191] 'The Scribe' (Edith Nielson Macdonald), *The Golden Jubilee 1869-1919* (Toronto, 1919), pp. 149ff.; and Eaton, *op. cit.*, pp. 144-8.

[192] Eaton, *op. cit.*, p. 147.

[193] *Journal of the Royal Architectural Institute of Canada*, vol. 12 (December 1928), pp. 431, 451.

[194] *Construction* (Toronto), vol. 23 (November 1930), pp. 350-69.

[195] J. Carlu, 'The T. Eaton & Co. Department Stores in Toronto and Montreal', in *Architectural Record* (New York), vol. 69 (June 1931), pp. 446-56.

[196] Mulvaney, *op. cit.*, pp. 260-1.

[197] Robertson, *op. cit.*, vol. 5 (1908), pp. 516-17. Several of Hay's drawings are preserved in the Langley Collection of the Baldwin Room, Metropolitan Toronto Library.

[198] Scadding, *op. cit.*, pp. 299-300.

[199] Middleton, *op. cit.*, vol. 2, p. 12.

[200] K.A. Jordan, *Sir Edmund Walker, Print Collector* (Toronto, 1974), p. 14. This catalogue for an exhibition at the Art Gallery of Ontario is the best recent study of Walker's art collection.

[201] Martyn, *op. cit.*, pp. 221-4.

[202] Jean Sutherland Boggs, *The National Gallery of Canada* (Toronto, 1971), pp. 6-17.

[203] Thompson, *op. cit.*, pp. 80-1.

[204] 'The Scribe', *op. cit.*, p. 92.

[205] City of Toronto Building Permit, no. 1330, 5 Oct. 1904, in the City of Toronto Archives.

[206] See *Construction* (Toronto), vol. 4 (May 1911), pp. 49-70, 78.

[207] *Report of the Minister of Public Works, 1910* (Toronto, 1910), p. 9.

[208] 'The City of Toronto Scrapbook', vol. 1, pp. 101, 105, 144, 198.

[209] *Report of the Minister of Public Works, 1911* (Toronto, 1911), p. 10.

[210] *Report of the Minister of Public Works, 1915* (Toronto, 1915), p. 11.

[211] *Report of the Minister of Public Works, 1911*, p. 11; and *Report of the Minister of Public Works, 1915*, p. 11.

[212] *Report of the Minister of Public Works, 1915*, p. 160.

[213] 'The City of Toronto Scrapbook', vol. 5, p. 135; and vol. 11, pp. 16, 135-6.

[214] *Ibid.*, vol. 2, p. 12.

[215] Middleton, *op. cit.*, vol. 3, pp. 89-90.

[216] 'The City of Toronto Scrapbook', vol. 2, p. 5. See also Charles

[217] Moore, *The Life and Times of Charles Follen McKim* (Boston, 1929), pp. 327-8.

[217] See *A Monograph of the Work of McKim, Mead & White* (New York, 1915).

[218] G. Mercer-Adam, *Toronto: Old and New* (Toronto, 1891), pp. 144-5.

[219] Middleton, *op. cit.*, vol. 3, pp. 89-90.

[220] 'The City of Toronto Scrapbook', vol. 9, p. 96.

[221] Arthur, *op. cit.*, p. 190.

[222] Thompson, *op. cit.*, pp. 125, 199-202, 213.

[223] Eaton, *op. cit.*, pp. 100-11.

[224] Illustrated in Thompson, *op. cit.*, p. 205.

[225] Robertson, *op. cit.*, vol. 1 (1894), pp. 153-5.

[226] 'The City of Toronto Scrapbook', vol. 4, p. 125.

[227] Robertson, *op. cit.*, vol. 4 (1904), pp. 117-18.

[228] Rebecca Sisler, *The Girls* (Toronto, 1972), pp. 5-9.

Index

NUMBERS IN BOLD FACE REFER TO MAIN ENTRIES; NUMBERS IN ITALICS REFER TO PLATES.